AMERICAN LITERATURE READIN

Series Editor: Linda V

American Literature Readings in the 21st Century publishes works by established and emerging critics that help shape critical opinion regarding literature of the nineteenth and twentieth century in the United States.

Published by Palgrave Macmillan:

Freak Shows in Modern American Imagination: Constructing the Damaged Body from Willa Cather to Truman Capote
By Thomas Fahy

Women and Race in Contemporary U.S. Writing: From Faulkner to Morrison
By Kelly Lynch Reames

American Political Poetry in the 21st Century
By Michael Dowdy

Science and Technology in the Age of Hawthorne, Melville, Twain, and James: Thinking and Writing Electricity
By Sam Halliday

F. Scott Fitzgerald's Racial Angles and the Business of Literary Greatness
By Michael Nowlin

Sex, Race, and Family in Contemporary American Short Stories
By Melissa Bostrom

Democracy in Contemporary U.S. Women's Poetry
By Nicky Marsh

James Merrill and W.H. Auden: Homosexuality and Poetic Influence
By Piotr K. Gwiazda

Contemporary U.S. Latino/a Literary Criticism
Edited by Lyn Di Iorio Sandín and Richard Perez

The Hero in Contemporary American Fiction: The Works of Saul Bellow and Don DeLillo
By Stephanie S. Halldorson

Race and Identity in Hemingway's Fiction
By Amy L. Strong

Edith Wharton and the Conversations of Literary Modernism
By Jennifer Haytock

The Anti-Hero in the American Novel: From Joseph Heller to Kurt Vonnegut
By David Simmons

Indians, Environment, and Identity on the Borders of American Literature: From Faulkner and Morrison to Walker and Silko
By Lindsey Claire Smith

The American Landscape in the Poetry of Frost, Bishop, and Ashbery: The House Abandoned
By Marit J. MacArthur

Narrating Class in American Fiction
By William Dow

The Culture of Soft Work: Labor, Gender, and Race in Postmodern American Narrative
By Heather J. Hicks

Cormac McCarthy: American Canticles
By Kenneth Lincoln

Elizabeth Spencer's Complicated Cartographies: Reimagining Home, the South, and Southern Literary Production
By Catherine Seltzer

New Critical Essays on Kurt Vonnegut
Edited by David Simmons

Feminist Readings of Edith Wharton: From Silence to Speech
By Dianne L. Chambers

The Emergence of the American Frontier Hero 1682-1826: Gender, Action, and Emotion
By Denise Mary MacNeil

Norman Mailer's Later Fictions: Ancient Evenings through Castle in the Forest
Edited by John Whalen-Bridge

Fetishism and its Discontents in Post-1960 American Fiction
By Christopher Kocela

Language, Gender, and Community in Late Twentieth-Century Fiction: American Voices and American Identities
By Mary Jane Hurst

Repression and Realism in Postwar American Literature
By Erin Mercer

Writing Celebrity: Stein, Fitzgerald, and the Modern(ist) Art of Self-Fashioning
By Timothy W. Galow

Bret Easton Ellis: Underwriting the Contemporary
By Georgina Colby

FREAK SHOWS AND THE MODERN AMERICAN IMAGINATION

Constructing the Damaged Body from Willa Cather to Truman Capote

Thomas Fahy

palgrave
macmillan

First published in hardcover in 2006 by
PALGRAVE MACMILLAN®
in the United States—a division of St. Martin's Press LLC,
175 Fifth Avenue, New York, NY 10010.

Where this book is distributed in the UK, Europe and the rest of the world,
this is by Palgrave Macmillan, a division of Macmillan Publishers Limited,
registered in England, company number 785998, of Houndmills,
Basingstoke, Hampshire RG21 6XS.

PALGRAVE MACMILLAN is the global academic imprint of the above
companies and has companies and representatives throughout the world.

Palgrave® and Macmillan® are registered trademarks in the United States,
the United Kingdom, Europe and other countries.

ISBN: 978-0-230-12098-3

Library of Congress Cataloging-in-Publication Data

Fahy, Thomas Richard.
    Freak shows and the modern American imagination : constructing the
    damaged body from Willa Cather to Truman Capote / Thomas Fahy.
        p. cm.—(American literature readings in the 21st century)
    Includes bibliographical references and index.
    ISBN 1-4039-7403-9
        1. American fiction—20th century—History and criticism.
    2. Body, Human, in literature. 3. Abnormalities, Human, in literature.
    4. Abnormalities, Human, in art. 5. Freak shows-United States.
    I. Title. II. Series.

PS374.B64F34 2006
813_.5093561—dc22   2005056619

A catalogue record of the book is available from the British Library.

Design by Newgen Imaging Systems (P) Ltd., Chennai, India.

First PALGRAVE MACMILLAN paperback edition: September 2011

10 9 8 7 6 5 4 3 2 1

Printed in the United States of America.

Transferred to Digital Printing in 2011

CONTENTS

LIST OF ILLUSTRATIONS

ACKNOWLEDGMENTS

I have a number of colleagues and friends whose considerable talents, generosity, and support have helped shape this project. I couldn't have managed without them. Many thanks to Kimball King, Pamela Cooper, Townsend Ludington, John McGowan, John Kasson, Robert Spirko, Michael Everton, Sage Rountree, Lilah Morris, Fiona Mills, Jessica O'Hara, Daniel Kurtzman, and Laura Garrett.

I also want to thank the series editor, Linda Wagner-Martin, my editor at the press, Farideh Koohi-Kamali, and the talented staff at Palgrave Macmillan. Their support and hard work have made this book a reality, and I am very grateful to all of you.

Sections of this manuscript have appeared elsewhere, and I thank the following places for giving me permission to reprint them. An early version of chapter 2 appeared in *Prospects: An Annual of American Cultural Studies* 25 (Cambridge University Press, Fall 2000), and I gave a talk on this topic at the International Willa Cather Conference that year. A shorter version of chapter 3 appeared in the *Journal of American and Comparative Cultures* 26.1 (Blackwell Publishing, March 2003). Last, I have reprinted some of the material on Carson McCullers from my edited collection, *Peering Behind the Curtain: Disability, Illness, and the Extraordinary Body* (Routledge, 2002).

I am also grateful to the following places for their help with all of the visual images: the Special Collections Research Center at Syracuse University Library, the National Portrait Gallery, Smithsonian Institution, the Shelburne Museum of Art, the John and Mable Ringling Museum of Art, the National Gallery of Art, the Hoover Institution at Stanford University, and the Library of Congress.

I am also indebted to the English and Music Departments at the University of California at Davis, the University of North Carolina at Chapel Hill, California State University in San Luis Obispo, and Long Island University. They have given me incredible opportunities to grow and develop as an artist, teacher, and professional.

I am especially fortunate to have the ongoing love and support of my family: my parents, Tom and Eileen, Michael, Jen, and my niece,

Tommi Rose. You continue to keep me grounded through your laughter, compassion, and generosity.

And once again, Susann Cokal and Kirstin Ringelberg have dragged me across the finish line. They continue to be generous friends, gifted editors, and the best colleagues anyone could ask for—ever! I can't thank you enough.

Last, my heartfelt gratitude goes out to Mercedes Maruscak, who has lived with this manuscript on a daily basis for longer than she would care to remember. Her patience and support is evident on every page.

Introduction

My great-uncle once told me a story that his father told him . . .

Men with the circus never bothered much with age. If you said you were old enough, you were old enough. And I suspect most of us clowns and stagehands were thirteen or fourteen when we joined. We all had places to run from.

Too many mouths to feed, my mother always said. But God just kept giving her children. He always seemed to give more children to the Irish than anybody else. Even when there was no food.

But I ate plenty when I ran away with the circus. With strong hands and a strong back, I could dig holes, pitch tents, and move the animal cages. I even helped the snake charmer catch extra mice. For each one I bagged, he taught me to use magic cards and to make coins disappear. I was good with tricks, he said.

Soon the manager took notice. He watched me sweet-talking rubes and playing card games with a smile. That's when I started to work as a clown. He had me dress up in bright colors and wild hair to keep the customers laughing. Anything to keep them on the fairgrounds as long as possible.

In the summer of 1889, we went to England. That was the first time I saw Barnum.

People whispered his name like they were in church. That's Barnum! They cheered as he moved around the arena—staring more at him than they did at the tallest man in the world or any of the other freaks.

To me he just looked old and chubby—not the kind of man who could dig holes and pitch tents. But we had sell-out crowds every night. Every single one.

After that I came back to America, got married, and left the circus for a job with the railroads. In a few years, I became a special agent for the Harrisburg Line.

"John," my wife Margaret said, "we're going places in the world."

Many years later, after we had moved ourselves and the kids to a nice place uptown, I woke up late one night and smelled smoke. My wife wasn't in bed, but when I got to the window, I saw her in the yard outside, standing in front of the incinerator.

Then I understood. A wig slipped from her hands, and colorful shirts were being tossed into the flames. She was burning my old clown costumes.

You see, we were going places in the world.

I didn't move or say anything. I just stood by the window long enough to feel my feet get cold, watching the orange-red flames and the smoke as it spiraled up toward the face of the moon, where it hung from its chin like hair off a bearded lady.

By burning a dusty pile of artifacts that evening, my great-grandmother was trying to erase any evidence of the circus from our family's history and to claim her place in a higher social class. She and her husband had moved from poverty and transience to success and stability. They were living the American Dream. Achieving such a dream meant hiding a shameful past, and for her, carnivals and freak shows represented what she and her husband no longer were as Irish immigrants—the lowly Other.

When I first heard this story, I knew very little about freak shows and their sordid history. The circus was a marginalized form of entertainment when I was a child. Perhaps growing up in Los Angeles—a city with little need for state fairs and traveling circuses—gave me enough to look at by way of spectacle. We could always count on seeing *Star Wars* fans and Michael Jackson look-alikes on Hollywood Boulevard. But as I began my research, I was surprised to learn that the freak show had been one of the most popular forms of entertainment in the United States for almost one hundred years.

First appearing in museums and then as part of carnivals and world's fairs, hundreds of shows traveled throughout the United States between the 1840s and 1940s. For the price of admission (which usually ranged from ten cents to a dollar), one could stare at alligator men, dog-faced boys, tattooed princesses, midgets, the severely disabled, nonwhites, and anyone whose body could be presented as strange and unusual. The freak represented what the audience was not—the Other, someone excluded from mainstream society for being different. In this way, the freakish body revealed surprisingly insecure power structures and suggested underlying anxieties about the ways individuals defined and related to each other in modern America.

Novelty was essential to the appeal of freak shows. Many exhibits assumed new names and varied performances over time to keep audiences intrigued. These changes not only altered the meanings ascribed to freaks, but they also suggested that the grounds for normality were not a given but in continual negotiation with the freakish. Often surrounded by domestic furnishings, the freak enacted affection for middle- and upper-class trappings and behaviors. Bearded ladies wore elegant gowns, and armless gentlemen spent the afternoon drinking tea, holding the cups with their feet. But like an oversized winter coat, nothing about these images fit (figure I.1). The freak was not part of this community but someone who reaffirmed the cultural superiority of the onlooker. This presentation of freakishness placed conformity at the center of middle-class values, equating the deviant body with

Figure I.1 Charles Tripp with Tea Cup (1870). Photograph by Charles Eisenmann. Every detail (from the Victorian furniture and tea set to Tripp's tuxedo and neatly parted hair) accentuates his extraordinary body. Even Tripp's off-centered position in the chair suggests that he doesn't quite belong in this setting. Courtesy of the Becker Collection, Special Collections Research Center, Syracuse University Library.

extreme individualism. As Rosemarie Garland Thomson explains, "the spectator enthusiastically invested his dime in the freak show not only to confirm his own superiority, but also to safely focus an identificatory longing upon these creatures who embodied freedom's elusive and threatening promise of not being like everybody else" (*Extraordinary Bodies* 69). To some extent, this paradox between individuality and conformity in American society was mitigated by the freak, whose body made physical difference the clear basis for exclusion. Not surprisingly, the success of freak shows was contingent on their ability to maintain the distance between viewer and freak, to simultaneously challenge and reinforce binaries about gender (male and female), race (white and nonwhite), and bodies (able and disabled).[1] As soon as this distance collapsed, the freak show would be relegated to obscurity.

A Long, Curious History

Before freak shows became an organized institution with the opening of P. T. Barnum's first museum in 1841, the extraordinary body had had a long history of scrutiny as well as interpretation. The meanings attributed to these bodies changed for different cultures, eras, and individuals, but the need to interpret them, to see them as something other than a marker of individuality, persisted and still persists.

In the ancient world, monstrous bodies were considered omens of political and civil chaos. Greeks and Romans interpreted natural phenomena as the result of cosmic or divine forces: fires, epidemics, the appearance of a comet or eclipse, and the extraordinary body were believed to presage the doom of an empire and the breakdown of social order. Greek mythology is populated with Sciapodes, Satyrs, and Sirens—monstrous races that resulted from divine intervention. In both Greek and Roman societies, these types of myths and legends constructed nonwhite and disabled bodies as something to loathe and fear. By 450 BC, for example, Roman law demanded the execution of disabled children to preserve the social structure, killing them on the grounds that they could perform no meaningful function in society.

Medieval Christian writers also struggled to interpret and understand the extraordinary body. In *The City of God*, Saint Augustine views the monstrous as part of God's divine plan—evidence of both His active role in creation and His desire to rekindle man's awe in the spiritual. But very few in the Middle Ages believed that disabled bodies were merely a testament to the variety of God's creation. Instead, they were seen as divine warnings against the dangers of pride, disobedience, and waning faith. Since thinkers in the Middle Ages believed Adam to be the human who had reached closest to God, one of the consequences of the Fall was the degeneration of the species. This idea eventually linked the birth of monsters to Cain. As John Friedman argues in *The Monstrous Races in Medieval Art and Thought*, Christian treatments of Cain emphasize his "violent nature, his association with the devil, and his degradation from human status, often figured by his ugliness and physical deformity" (95). Not surprisingly, most medieval accounts of Cain during his exile accentuate his disfigurement, interpreting it as a sign of God's displeasure.[2]

In sixteenth-century Europe, imperial exploration was inspiring new commercial enterprises based on acquiring the strange and unusual. Stories of monstrous races and remote lands accompanied these rare objects, giving evidence for their existence. Shakespeare's Othello tells Desdemona about chilling lands with "Cannibals that each other eat,/ The Anthropophagi, and men whose heads/ Grew beneath their shoulders" (Act I, Scene III). Global imperialism began moving monstrosity from the realm of the imagination to the observable spectacle. This emerging role troubled Michel de Montaigne, whose essay "Of a Monstrous Child" (1578–1580) describes a family that was "leading about to get a penny or so from showing [their conjoined child], because of his strangeness." He not only questions the meanings historically imposed on these figures, but he also criticizes their exploitation:

> What we call monsters are not so to God, who sees in the immensity of his work the infinity of forms that he has comprised in it. . . . From his infinite wisdom there proceeds nothing but that [which] is good and ordinary and regular. . . . We call contrary to nature what happens contrary to custom; nothing is anything but according to nature, whatever it may be. Let this universal and natural reason drive out of us the error and astonishment that novelty brings us. (539)

Unfortunately, his warnings went unheeded. For the next 350 years, audiences throughout Europe and the United States would clamor to stare at these novel bodies.

In the seventeenth century, human curiosities as well as wild animals were commonly exhibited in the public spaces of London. Itinerant showmen set up displays at busy intersections, fairs, lecture halls, and marketplaces. One of the most popular arenas for these acts was the tavern. Already a center for entertainment, taverns had regular patrons and numerous rooms that showmen could use for charging inebriated onlookers a few shillings to see the extraordinary. Asylums participated in this pastime as well. By 1609, Bedlam charged a small fee to people who wanted to gawk at inmates. As Richard Altick explains in *The Shows of London*, "the cells were arranged in galleries, in the manner of cages in a menagerie or booths at a fair, and in each one was a chained lunatic, whose behavior, if it were not sufficiently entertaining to begin with, was made so by the spectators' prodding him or her with their sticks or encouraging further wildness by ridicule, gestures, and imitations" (45). Here the hospital staff became ad hoc showmen—making the person on display as much of a spectacle as possible. The government did not start putting limits on these exhibitions until the 1770s.

In 1757, the first public museum opened in London. Designed not to pander to the vulgar tastes of the masses, its goal was to educate people by promoting sciences and the arts. In many ways, this stated goal was a rejection of the sensational exhibits that had been capturing the public's imagination with renewed interest since the 1600s. But the rigid formalities of the British Museum did not change the popular tastes of the day. The Museum only alienated viewers, requiring those who wanted tickets to fill out formal applications that often took several months to process. Once inside, patrons could not peruse the collections freely but were required to see them in the context of a four-hour tour. Dime museums would transform this experience, incorporating live exhibits into the formalized structure of the museum.

Itinerant exhibits had been a pervasive part of early America's entertainment culture before Barnum. Fortunetellers, dwarfs, and a wide array of curiosities could be seen at most taverns, and showmen traveled throughout the country with trained animals and human curiosities, using handbills and fast-talking to attract onlookers. As early as 1729, animal shows with horses and dogs were entertaining audiences, effectively laying the groundwork for the circus. The 1809 town records of Salem, Massachusetts, list a Miss Honeywell as one of the earliest human curiosities in America: "A young woman born without hands and with only three toes on one foot [who] embroidered flowers and cut watch papers and other fancy pieces" (qtd. in Wright, *Hawkers and Walkers*, 190). Less than forty years later, a performer of this kind would have been labeled a "freak." The word itself was not used to describe the commercialization and construction of bodies for entertainment until the mid-nineteenth century. According to the *Oxford English Dictionary*, it first appears in the sixteenth century, but before the 1800s, it means a capricious or whimsical notion, a vagary. Not until the 1840s did *freak* refer to "a monstrosity, an abnormally developed individual of any species; in recent use (especially the United States) a living curiosity exhibited in a show." This distinction is important because it suggests that something about these presentations changed significantly at this time—and that change was Phineas Taylor Barnum.

P. T. Barnum's American Museum was a more dazzling version of nineteenth-century dime museums. Like their British and French forefathers, American museums were designed to educate and enlighten, allowing people to look at cabinets filled with books, paintings, and other objects of interest. Since many people earned a living in the eighteenth century by privately displaying such cabinets, public museums had to find more sensational exhibits to draw crowds. The dime museum responded by creating an environment that enabled families of diverse backgrounds to gaze at dioramas, pictures, freaks, menageries, stuffed animals, historical wax tableaux, and each other as they walked from room to room.[3] It was this element of live performance—freak acts, jugglers, dancers, singers—that distinguished dime museums from history museums, and the former reached their heyday with Barnum's American Museum. A consummate showman and entrepreneur, Barnum recognized the potential profitability of freak exhibits, advertising them through newspapers, photographs, "true life" pamphlets, transparencies, and brightly colored banners. He felt that "everything depended on getting people to think, and talk, and become curious and excited over and about the 'rare spectacles' " (76).[4] "Now and then," he wrote in his autobiography, "some one would cry out 'humbug' and 'charlatan,' but so much the better for me. It helped advertise me, and I was willing to bear the reputation—and I engaged in queer curiosities, and even monstrosities, simply to add to the notoriety of the Museum" (142).

Freaks not only occupied a prominent place in his museum, but as Robert Bogdan explains, they also fit into several distinct categories of presentation. The first category included people who displayed their disabilities and physical anomalies, such as armless and legless wonders. The second consisted of performers who made themselves into freaks through "geek acts," body piercing, and tattoos. Toward the end of the nineteenth century, for example, Captain Costentenus was the most popular and successful tattooed exhibit. He claimed that his entire body had been tattooed as a form of torture while he was imprisoned in Persia. The exotic dimensions of this story clearly borrowed from another category of freaks—the construction of non-whites as exotic savages from barbaric lands. As I will discuss later, this highly successful mode of representation appealed to racist fears during the nineteenth and twentieth centuries. Lastly, freaks who faked physical anomalies, pretending to have missing limbs or additional appendages, were known as "gaffs." Together, this ensemble was integral to the displays, performances, and modes of representation that defined freak shows.[5]

In addition to these categories, the displays themselves relied on juxtaposition and context to exaggerate differences: placing dwarfs next to giants, fabricating marriages between fat ladies and skeleton men, dressing nonwhites as exotic cannibals and wild men from Fiji, Africa, and South America, and asking audiences to guess about (and in some cases pay extra to "discover") the true sex of bearded ladies and hermaphrodites. Even contemporary novels, such as Elizabeth McCracken's *The Giant's House* (1996), Darin Strauss's *Chang and Eng* (2000), Jeffrey Eugenides's *Middlesex* (2003), and Andrew Sean Greer's *The Confessions of Max Tivoli* (2004), tap into the sexual mystery and intrigue surrounding the anomalous body. Other components of these shows further reinforced the performer's status as a freak. Dwarfs and midgets, like Charles Stratton ("General Tom Thumb") and Leopold Kahn ("Admiral Dot"), assumed elevated titles. Giants wore hats to enhance their height. Bearded ladies appeared in domestic settings with their husbands and children. And exotic exhibits wore scanty clothing, carried spears, and appeared with primitive backdrops. Freaks also participated in stage performances, acting out poorly written parodies and giving renditions of popular plays. Tom Thumb,[6] for example, sang, danced, and did numerous impersonations. Siamese twins Chang and Eng performed acrobatics, including flips and other feats of physical strength.[7] All of these characteristics ritualized the encounter with the freak, establishing what audiences expected to see and the grounds for interpreting that vision.

Freak shows challenged audiences both to question and evaluate the validity of what they were seeing. As Neil Harris explains, "the opportunity to debate the *issue* of falsity, to discover how deception had been practiced, was even more exciting than the discovery of a fraud itself. . . . Therefore, when people paid to see frauds, thinking they were true, they paid again to hear how the frauds were committed" (77). This play between humbug and truth was further promoted by supplemental materials, such as biographical pamphlets. Filled with drawings, these pamphlets often began by describing the unusual origins, upbringing, and family life of the freak. They included physical descriptions of his or her body, eyewitness accounts, and perhaps most importantly, medical evidence. Doctors and scientists were regularly cited to give credibility to an exhibit. Many such learned men gave lectures and signed documents supporting the most outlandish claims. Some even allowed public viewings of freaks' autopsies, as in the case of Joice Heth, the 161-year-old nurse of George Washington.[8] In exchange for their services, these doctors had access to an array of remarkable specimens for study. From a showman's standpoint, this type of support was necessary for an audience invested in sniffing out a possible humbug. Consider the first sentence of Barnum's 1843 advertisement for the "Fejee Mermaid"—the half-monkey, half-fish supposedly captured in the South Pacific:

> Engaged for a short time, the animal (regarding which there has been so much dispute in the *scientific* world) called the FEJEE MERMAID! positively asserted by its owner to have been taken alive in the Fejee Islands, and implicitly believed by many *scientific* persons, while it is pronounced by other *scientific* persons to be an *artificial* production, and its natural existence claimed by them to be an utter impossibility.[9]

Barnum uses the scientific debate both to entice people to judge for themselves and to suggest authenticity—if the Fejee Mermaid is a matter of such disagreement, there must be some truth to it. Right? In many respects, freak shows thrived on scientific discourse and, for a time, the medical community was happy to oblige.

The most popular artifacts from early freak shows, however, were *cartes de visite* ("visiting cards"). These photographic reproductions, which were available at exhibits and prominently featured in photographic albums of the Victorian era, sold millions of copies annually and were often taken by prominent photographers like Charles Eisenmann and Mathew Brady. These images increased profits for the performers and publicized exhibits on a national scale.

Most of these human curiosities had exhausting schedules, performing dozens of times in a day, and their living conditions were usually poor, especially when traveling museums were replaced by sideshows at the turn of the century. Though a few freaks like Charles Stratton and Chang and Eng became wealthy, most remained exploited commodities. As part of the circus, freak shows became known as "ten-in-ones" because patrons could see ten exhibits for the price of one (figure I.2). They were set apart from the featured acts of the big top, which usually included menageries, parades, music, and acrobats. This distinction began changing the atmosphere surrounding these exhibits. Within the context of a museum, freaks had more respectability; they were integrated into a whole and displayed under

Figure I.2 Ten-in-One Sideshow (1904). Photograph by Frederick Whitman Glasier. The "ten-in-one" may have seemed like a bargain for many spectators, but this presentation clearly compromises the uniqueness of each exhibit. Some of the signs beneath the performers read: Lionel: Lion Faced Boy, James Morris: Elastic Skin Man, John Hayes: Tattooed Man, and Horvath: Troupe of Midgets. Courtesy of the collection of The John and Mable Ringling Museum of Art Archives.

the guise of learning and scientific study. But on the fairgrounds, the freak show seemed dirtier. No intellectual pretexts could be given for staring. One even had to buy a separate ticket to see freaks. This is when the popularity of freak shows began to wane. By the mid-twentieth century, the ploys became less compelling, less able to mitigate the problems of viewing, and the sideshow grew increasingly distasteful—something that respectable people avoided and that parents kept from their children.

From Center Stage to Sideshow

Within the first few decades of the twentieth century, a number of changes in science and technology made it even more difficult for freak shows to entice audiences. Most notably, medical science began seeing the deviant body as pathological rather than monstrous. Thomson explains in her introduction to *Freakery: Cultural Spectacles of the Extraordinary Body* that "scientific explanation eclipsed religious mystery to become the authoritative cultural narrative of modernity. [As a result,] the exceptional body began increasingly to be represented in clinical terms as pathology; and the monstrous body moved from the freak show stage into the medical theater" (2). In fact, this shift was quite dramatic. A change in attitude toward disability—from public spectacle to a sympathetic case study—can be seen in the language used to describe it at the turn of the century. In response to a theater review by Townsend Walsh in 1898, for example, actress Minnie Maddern Fiske criticizes his use of the terms "cripple" and "crutch":

> My Dear Mr. Walsh:
>   I was much astounded, in reading the advance notice in the Springfield Republican, to see the words "cripple" and "crutch" used. The use of those words is obviously unfortunate and wholly unnecessary.
>   The heroine of the play "Love Finds a Way," is in no sense a "cripple." The word suggests something abhorrent and repellant. The woman in the play is afflicted with a slight physical infirmity. She is slightly lame. That is all. We must not give the impression of anything so utterly disagreeable as a painfully deformed person. It is true that this woman uses a crutch, but it is very advisable to make no mention of it.
>   Above all, the play is a pleasant and a wholesome one; but the impression given in this particular paper of which I speak is that the play is morbid and unpleasant.
>   At the end of the Springfield notice there appears this line: "The play is unpleasant as 'Tess' is unpleasant." I presume this impression is the result of the constant thrusting forward of the "cripple" and the "crutch."
>   Please never, so far as you are able to prevent it, permit either of these words to creep into your advance work.[10]

The emphasis on language here is particularly interesting. On one level, this letter can be read as a reflection of contemporary attitudes about disability. Since the public views disability as "abhorrent," "repellent," and "utterly disagreeable," it would avoid a play featuring such a character. Fiske even suggests that the reviewer erase any reference to Tess's crutch—another common response to disability. If the disability can't be masked, then society would rather keep it out of sight or relegate it to the sideshow. On another level, this letter is about the power of language. It implies that a different discourse has the ability to change perception. As long as "lame" can be substituted for "cripple," audiences will not consider the play unpleasant. They will not interpret Tess's disability negatively.

Within the next decade, medical science had started to provide this new language for the public. Bogdan cites an article in the 1908 edition of *Scientific American Supplement* as evidence of "the first wave of the medical profession's attack on the freak show" (64). The article, "Circus and Museum Freaks, Curiosities of Pathology," refers to human exhibits as "humble," "unfortunate," "sick," and "curiosities" to be pitied. Science also gave freak performers new labels that supposedly explained their conditions. A dog-faced boy had hypertrichosis, for example. And giants suffered from acromegaly. The language for disability began to change; as a result, so would the fate of the freak show.

In addition to science, technology also pulled audiences away from the sideshow circuit. Developments such as Henry Ford's innovations in the automobile industry transformed the workplace in the United States. The assembly line, for example, meant an increase in productivity and profit in less time. Soon laborers were getting higher wages and working fewer hours. In 1923, U.S. Steel shortened the workday from twelve to eight hours, and three years later Ford's factories reduced the workweek from six to five days.[11] More free time and more disposable income gave rise to an increasingly competitive entertainment industry.

Freak shows tried to employ new gimmicks to keep up, but they quickly lost their ability to enchant audiences. Even the owners of Coney Island's Dreamland Park, which featured sideshow performers, decided not to rebuild after it burned to the ground in 1911.[12] Technology was broadening the scope of what people could see and do, and they were turning elsewhere for amusement. As John Kasson explains in regards to the decline of Coney Island, "it was not that attendance at Coney Island declined in the 1920s—on the contrary, it increased—but the experience was less extraordinary and hence less meaningful. The extension of the subway from New York to Coney Island in the 1920s made the resort more accessible than ever before, but it also reduced the element of contrast, the distinctive sense of entering a special realm operating under its own laws" (112). The access provided by technology, in other words, made the magic of freak shows and this kind of amusement less appealing, less interesting. It made the freak show feel like a relic from the distant past.

In addition to dime museums and traveling circuses, people could now attend variety shows, dance halls, amusement parks, and world's fairs. And, perhaps most importantly, they could go to the movies. The visual magic of cinema would quickly make the legerdemain of freak shows less convincing and compelling. Even the acts performed by sideshow entertainers in Tod Browning's film *Freaks* (1932) seem awkward and artificial on the screen. In many respects, the episodic nature of *Freaks* functions more like a ten-in-one than a cohesive film. In a matter of minutes, we witness a bearded lady holding her newborn child, an armless-legless man lighting a cigarette, and the domestic squabbles of Rosco, his fiancée Daisy Hilton, and her conjoined twin, Violet. These elements don't contribute to the main story involving Cleopatra's scheme to marry and murder Hans for his inheritance; in fact, they mostly distract viewers from this rather mundane plot. As Rachel Adams convincingly argues, "the freaks, as well as many of the non-disabled performers, are introduced by a series of vignettes, which demonstrate their talents and personalities but make little effort to unify the characters through a common storyline" (*Sideshow* 65). Along with the marginal writing and poor acting in *Freaks*, these "performances" or vignettes ring false. And the disastrous reception of this film made one thing clear: freaks would never make it in Hollywood.

An Overview

Freak Shows and the Modern American Imagination examines the artistic use of freakishness between 1900 and 1950, mapping its rather sudden shift from a highly profitable form of entertainment to a reviled one. Throughout this period, the public reassessed freak shows, gradually seeing them as something shameful, and artists responded to this cultural shift by using the freakish body as a tool for exploring problematic social attitudes about race, disability, and sexual desire in American culture. Unlike other studies that tend to focus on the literary and visual uses of freak shows in the second half of the twentieth century, I am interested in the most volatile period for this entertainment—when those writing about freak shows had the opportunity to see them. These writers and artists were responding to the changing perception of freak performers at the time. They wanted to explore how profound contemporary events, such as the Great Migration, World War I, and the Great Depression, were shaping widespread interpretations of difference—of the racial and physical Other.

This focus on 1900–1950 has two broader goals as well. First, examining freak shows in art during this period can deepen our understanding of the prejudices and fears that defined—and would continue to define—the sociopolitical struggles of the twentieth century, especially the fight for civil rights among black and gay Americans. Second, these works challenge us to recognize how these problems are still with us. We tend to assume that this era is more enlightened, more tolerant, and more forgiving than previous ones. We convince ourselves that the lessons of the past have been learned. But really looking back requires an examination of ugly and difficult truths—historically as well as personally. The notion of freakishness extends far beyond the intentional presentation of bodies for money; it is also the side-effect of herding certain people together, labeling them in order to make difference less threatening. Whether it has to do with race, disability, or sexual desire, the body that doesn't fit, that violates cultural norms, is subjected to interpretation. As the literary and visual arts of the early twentieth century suggest, these problems are just as prevalent and powerful as they have ever been. This isn't to say that certain things haven't changed for the better in the last fifty years. But these works reminds us that it is not a question of figuring out how far we've come. It is a question of recognizing how far we need to go.

In Chapter 1, " 'Helpless Meanness': Constructing the Black Body as Freakish Spectacle," I examine the metaphor of freakishness in photography and fiction in the first half of the twentieth century—with a particular emphasis on the Harlem Renaissance (1917–1935).[13] With the migration of millions of African Americans from the rural South to the industrial North, the growing influx of immigrants, the rise of eugenics, and the sudden prominence of black artists in the 1920s and 1930s, white America felt increasingly threatened by ethnic and racial difference. The popularity of freak exhibits featuring non-Western cultures suggests that white audiences sought out hateful images of blackness to mitigate these fears. Such degrading images, in other words, reinforced hierarchies that kept whites on top of the social ladder. They also appealed to the notion that interracial relationships could be dangerous for the species. In the literature of F. Scott Fitzgerald, Willa Cather, William Faulkner, and Nella Larsen, freakishness reflects a society afraid of and disgusted by miscegenation. The ultimate paranoia depicted here is not simply sexual relations between black and white, but passing the ability of blacks to appear white. This practice undermined a judgment system based purely on visible difference. Through images of the freakish body, the fiction of Jean Toomer, Ralph Ellison, Richard Wright, and Eudora Welty further exposes "race" as an artificial construct. The need to label blackness—to remove any ambiguity surrounding one's ethnicity—reveals shameful hatreds and fears about the loss of cultural identity in a multiracial society.

Chapter 2, "War-Injured Bodies: Fallen Soldiers in Propaganda and the Works of John Dos Passos, Willa Cather, Ernest Hemingway,

and William Faulkner," discusses freakishness as an image for intense
social fears about U.S. involvement in World War I. Propaganda
posters often used the exotic body and freak show conventions to tap
into anxieties about ethnic difference. From monstrous apes to disfigured Huns, these images were designed to dehumanize the enemy
just as freak shows dehumanized those on display. But postwar literature by Dos Passos, Cather, Hemingway, and Faulkner presents the
damaged body as a reflection of the self. Through disfiguring injury
and allusions to freak shows, these works capture the physical and psychological horrors of war. They portray a society afraid of difference—
fears directly linked to America's increasing role as an international
empire. The dangers of extending too far beyond U.S. borders
could be seen on the damaged bodies of veterans. As a result, this new
association with physical injuries—as marked and scarred by war—
complicated the constructions of disability on the sideshow, further
marginalizing this entertainment. Ultimately, these writers use freakishness to shatter naive assumptions about war as noble and glorified,
and they suggest that true healing is hampered by social prejudices
about race and disability in America.

Chapter 3, "Worn, Damaged Bodies in the Great Depression: FSA
Photography and the Fiction of John Steinbeck, Tillie Olsen, and
Nathanael West," begins by exploring the ways that Franklin
Roosevelt challenged conventional prejudices about disability.
Though he was always forthright about his bout with polio, he
believed it was important to mask its effects in public, creating an
image of himself as someone who had overcome tremendous adversity
and could lead a crippled country out of economic depression. The
public looked up to him both as a figure who could empathize with
their struggles and as a figure of strength. As with perceptions of black
bodies during the Harlem Renaissance and injured veterans in
post–World War I America, society viewed disability differently during
and after the Depression. The physical and social costs of poverty,
unemployment, and starvation were often visible on the bodies of
working-class men and women. In the 1930s, literature by writers
such as John Steinbeck, Tillie Olsen (in her novel *Yonnondio: From the
Thirties*), and Nathanael West often invoked images of freakishness to
capture a sense of communal and personal deterioration. As their
characters begin to worry that the hardships of the Depression will
ultimately transform them into spectacles, they start seeing themselves
and others as freakish. The deteriorating body becomes a metaphor
for the broken communities and families around them. Farm Security
Administration (FSA) and other Depression photography reinforce
this type of fear about the body. On one level, Dorothea Lange's

images of fragmented bodies suggest the ways in which 1930s working conditions reduce men and women to tools for economic survival. At the same time, these body parts communicate strength, determination, and the will to work.

By the 1940s and 1950s, homosexuality was being seen as an increasing threat to heterosexual values and the nuclear family. Images of sexual ambiguity such as cross-dressing and freak exhibits displaying bearded ladies and hermaphrodites were considered dangerous in that they could seem to validate nonheterosexual desire. Few would want to change places with those onstage, but these figures often embodied freedoms that mainstream society persecuted. Like racial passing and war-injured soldiers, the queer body had become an image for something that had gone wrong in America—the breakdown of binaries held sacred by the white middle class. Chapter 4, " 'Some Unheard-of Thing': Freaks, Families, and Coming of Age in Carson McCullers and Truman Capote," examines fiction that explores the conflicted sexual desires of young adults. The protagonists of McCullers's *The Member of the Wedding* and Capote's *Other Voices, Other Rooms* have trouble reconciling their own same-sex desires with images of heterosexuality, specifically the nuclear family. Though the concept of family is idealized in these texts, the actual families in these works fail as a model for achieving happiness, and freak shows emerge as an alternative—one that recognizes and embraces behaviors that deviate from the norm.

The discussions in each of these chapters not only highlight the artistic significance of freak shows in the early twentieth century, but they also offer a new dimension to current scholarship about this entertainment—a dimension that considers the impact of immigration, a world war, and the Great Depression on the reception of the freak show. The complex ramifications of these moments in American history were often explored in sideshows and other forms of entertainment. Whether an exhibit was designed to mitigate social tensions about race or to make people forget about their own struggles with poverty, the freak show tapped into current political and social issues to entice audiences. But it did so at its own peril. As the decades of the 1920s, 1930s, and 1940s demonstrate, the artifice of freak shows started to cut too close to the bone of social turmoil in the United States. This helps explain why freak shows, which had been one of the most popular forms of entertainment in American history, became so marginalized.

With the publication of his groundbreaking study *Freaks: Myths and Images of the Secret Self* (1978), Leslie Fiedler argues that freaks are an important part of Western culture. As someone who considers himself an outsider in academia, Fiedler also identifies with their marginal status. Using elements of Freudian psychoanalysis, Fiedler reads his own psyche through freak show performers, fashioning a profoundly personal approach to this subject and his analyses of literary and popular culture. As this book demonstrates, there is something oddly intimate about freak shows. Most studies of this phenomenon, including Robert Bogdan's *Freak Show* and more recently Rachel Adams's *Sideshow U.S.A.*, turn to personal anecdotes at times. And why not? Whether one is reading about freak shows or standing in front of the "Smallest Woman in the World," the freak body challenges us to think about the culturally constructed lines between normal/abnormal, able/disabled, and ordinary/extraordinary. These exhibits invite us to imagine what constitutes "a freak" and what about ourselves is unusual, odd, and even freakish.

In this tradition, *Freak Shows and the Modern American Imagination* will turn to the personal as well. Each chapter concludes with a vignette similar to the one that began this book. These italicized sections depict aspects of my personal or familial history that reflect on some of the themes in the chapter. The body on stage invites us to think about the act of looking. The performer's gaze forces us to question why we are here in the first place. What justifications and perceptions have enabled this exchange? What social factors contribute to the construction of this person as a freak? These vignettes are my response to the personal challenges raised by some of the texts discussed here—namely the challenge to recognize my (our) own culpability and contributions to prejudice and social inequality. In the end, freak shows have the power to illuminate new dimensions of American art. They can also help us better understand the history that has shaped the racial and social climate in this country, while inviting us both to reflect on ourselves and to become more aware of how we can see the world in harmful, disabling ways.

CHAPTER 1

"Helpless Meanness": Constructing the Black Body as Freakish Spectacle

A plush photo album lay on the parlor table of every well-heeled Victorian family. Filled with *cartes de visite* ("visiting cards"), self-portraits, and postcards, these albums were a popular art form in nineteenth-century America, assembled by young wives to commemorate family and to entertain guests. Much like scrapbooks in America today, Victorian albums were designed to chronicle and celebrate special occasions. But unlike their modern-day counterparts, these ornate albums indulged in fantasy as well. They typically included images of actors, minstrel performers, freaks, military leaders, ballet dancers, athletes, and even politicians. Part of their allure, in other words, came from the novelty of the *cartes de visite* supplied by friends, which had become mass-produced consumer products by the 1860s.[1] As early as 1864, *Humphrey's Journal* reported that "everybody [in the United States] keeps a photographic album, and it is a source of pride and emulation among some people to see how many *cartes de visite* they can accumulate from their friends and acquaintances" (Welling 169–179).

As these albums became an increasingly popular and competitive form of entertainment, so did the need for acquiring new, sensational images and *cartes* from intriguing strangers. In a sense, these albums functioned as a home-constructed freak show—displaying page after page of the unusual and titillating. Some of the most remarkable examples featured tortured and exotic bodies—particularly of African Americans as lynching victims and freaks. In many ways these photographs, which continued to be sold throughout the first few decades of the twentieth century, provided a safe context for talking about race. They had the power to assuage pervasive fears about immigration and the increased freedoms of African Americans.[2] But like a dam threatening to burst, these brutal, degrading images revealed cracks in white America's ability to cope with racial difference.

The construction of African Americans as freakish and the Victorian commercialization of these images contributed to racial tensions, which reached the breaking point in the early twentieth century. During the infamous "Red Summer," for example, twenty-five race riots erupted in cities and towns across the country between April and October of 1919—including an uprising in Chicago that caused 38 deaths.[3] Not surprisingly, numerous writers in the 1920s, 1930s, and 1940s examined this racial climate through the damaged body. Willa Cather, Jean Toomer, Nella Larsen, F. Scott Fitzgerald, William Faulkner, Richard Wright, Eudora Welty, and Ralph Ellison all utilize freak show conventions to expose the hateful ways that blackness was constructed in America.

Widespread concerns about miscegenation and racial passing indicate an increasingly fluid relationship between black and white—a relationship that exacerbated white fears about America's future. As a result, many whites sought new ways to reinforce visible difference and thereby belittle and humiliate African Americans—ultimately keeping them "in their place." As these early-twentieth-century texts demonstrate, the very modes of presentation that freak shows sanctioned for racial/ethnic exhibits helped promote and justify intolerance. And the results would set the stage for the civil rights movement in 1950s and 1960s.

DISABLING VISIONS: COLLECTING HATEFUL IMAGES

In the museum exhibit and subsequent book *Without Sanctuary: Lynching Photography in America*, James Allen displays some of the visual souvenirs that were widely sold and collected at lynchings. The violence and cruelty of these images, which capture the ritualistic spectacle of lynchings from the mid-nineteenth through mid-twentieth centuries, is compounded by their commercialization and their place in many family photo albums.[4] As Allen argues on the original website for the exhibit, "the photographic art played as significant a role in the ritual as torture or souvenir grabbing—a sort of two-dimensional biblical swine, a receptacle for a collective sinful self. Lust propelled their commercial reproduction and distribution, facilitating the endless replay of anguish. Even dead, the victims were without sanctuary." The popularity of these images may also explain the success of freak photography during the same period. Appearing alongside each other in family albums,[5] both images present black and otherwise exotic or maimed bodies as spectacles for entertainment. One postcard from Allen's collection (ca. 1900) shows an unidentified victim of mob violence whose painted face transforms him into a type of minstrel figure. Unlike more explicit images of scarred, beaten, and burned black bodies, this man has been recast as something to mock; his makeup takes away his individuality and humanity, making him a symbol of grotesque blackness. This minstrel-styled blackness is aimed specifically at a white audience; minstrels entertained whites by parodying African American speech, song, clothing, and dance in theatrical performances. Eric Lott has argued that minstrelsy "[played] with collective fears of a degraded and threatening—and male—Other while at the same time maintaining some symbolic control over them" (25). This tension between fear and control is evident in Allen's postcard as well. Here, the lynched body is not enough. It must also be connected to other traditions that ridicule blacks.

Such a photograph is not surprising given that lynchings were a form of communal entertainment. As Trudier Harris explains in *Exorcising Blackness: Historical and Literary Lynching and Burning Rituals*, "mobs would frequently bring food and drink to the place of execution and would make a holiday of the occasion. To insure that an audience was available for really special lynchings, announcements of time and place were sometimes advertised in newspapers" (6). Photographs and other memorabilia, including pieces of clothing and locks of hair, were often collected after these events, reinforcing this element of celebration. One vivid example of this carnival-like atmosphere can be seen in the postcard, "The Lynching of Will James" (November 11, 1909).[6] This picture was taken on Commercial Avenue beneath Hustler's Arch in Cairo, Illinois; out of context, one could mistake the event for a circus, convention, or concert. Strings of lights illuminate the two arches overhead. Crowds pack the street. And several white men have climbed up telephone poles to get a better look. Part of the picture's power comes from its ambiguity. In fact most of the images in *Without Sanctuary* show crowds of men, women, and children, suggesting that the celebration, not merely the punishment of blacks, was being commemorated—a celebratory atmosphere that becomes bitterly ironic in the context of lynching.

These examples of lynching as entertainment also link them to the more insidious side of freak shows. Both enact distinct rituals of degradation that included photography. As evident in "The Lynching of Will James," audience participation was an integral part of lynching. It was a communal event that made people feel safe from the threat of blackness through both white solidarity and the destruction of the black body. Freak shows and freak photography, however, provided "safety" through distance. They needed to contain difference because the image didn't go away; the freak was not killed. As a result, freak shows used various methods to establish a clear, comfortable distance between audience and spectacle. The racial exhibit relied on a barker's spiel to reinforce the spectacle's freakishness and to entice customers; a stage setting supported the freak's "exotic" origins (e.g., rocks, shrubbery, sticks, scanty clothing, etc.); performances, such as crawling, growling, singing, and dancing, demonstrating his/her racial and cultural inferiority; and pamphlets and photography sold during and after viewing to advertise and commemorate the occasion.

P. T. Barnum's notorious "What Is It?" was one of the earliest exhibits to incorporate all of these ritualistic strategies. First presented in 1860, Henry Johnson, a mentally retarded African American with microcephaly, was cast as a mysterious man-animal hybrid billed with the headline "What Is It?"[7] Barnum's promotional image features Johnson standing alone (figure 1.1). His isolation here and the exotic backdrop maintain the distance between viewer and spectacle. Any possible threat that Johnson could pose to onlookers is further mitigated by Barnum's advertisement, which refers to the exhibit as a docile and harmless "man-monkey" who is "PLAYFUL AS A KITTEN".[8] While the text functions like a barker's spiel, the sketch captures his passivity in much the same way the photograph does: through the harmless twig (a dull staff in the photo) and fake rocks; the stationary pose, calm face, and averted head that invites the audience's gaze.

Johnson and other freaks were also photographed with their managers and/or other performers both to maintain the boundary between viewer and spectacle and to accentuate the singularity of an exhibit (like pairing skeleton men and fat ladies or bearded ladies with their children). In the case of "Sideshow Pit with Zip (Johnson)" (figure 1.2), the juxtaposition of several carnival entrepreneurs (wearing suits and top hats) with Zip and Johanna (who are dressed in costume) reinforce the superiority of white viewers. Even Zip and Johanna's position in the pit, standing beneath the white men, stages them as objects to be looked down on and stared at.

It is not surprising that these images remained popular through the early twentieth century, for many white Americans felt increasingly threatened by the growing presence of nonwhites in urban areas. Between 1880 and 1914, for example, over twenty-three million immigrants came to the United States, and by September of 1920 approximately five thousand new arrivals entered Ellis Island every day.[9] Even within the country, significant demographic changes were

Figure 1.1   Henry Johnson, Barnum's "What Is It?" (1872). Photograph by Mathew Brady. Barnum varied his presentation of "What Is It?" over the years. Here, the minimal outfit reinforces the stark, remote backdrop. At other times, Barnum had Johnson wear a suit of fur to support claims that this exhibit was a "man-monkey" (see figure 1.4). Courtesy of the National Portrait Gallery, Smithsonian Institution, Meserve Collection (3440: 120).

happening. In the first thirty years of the twentieth century, over 1.2 million African Americans left the South. As Ann Douglas explains in *Terrible Honesty*, "the black population in all American cities went from 22 percent in 1900 to 40 percent in 1930" (73). This new urban

Figure 1.2 Sideshow Pit with Zip, Ringling Brothers (1893). Photograph by Frederick Glasier. Like Johnson's costume, his position in the pit relative to the carnival entrepreneurs reflects social and racial hierarchies. The angle of the shot also invites viewers to look down at Johnson and Johanna. Courtesy of the Collection of The John and Mable Ringling Museum of Art Archives.

diversity—especially its inescapable visibility—fostered tremendous anger, fear, resentment, and eventually shame in those who saw non-Anglos as a threat to American society and culture. As I discuss in chapter 2, World War I intensified these prejudices and irrational fears, but it wasn't until the resurgent popularity of eugenics in the 1920s that America found the "evidence" it needed to reinforce these views.

Founded by Francis Galton in the latter half of the nineteenth century, eugenics argued that the hereditary "improvement" of humankind depended on selective breeding. By the turn of the century, eugenics provided a scientific basis—whether it was so characterized by Galton himself or came in the form of best-selling studies, pulpits, or carnivals—for the dangers of immigration in the United States.[10] As John Higham explains in *Strangers in the Land: Patterns of American Nativism 1860–1925*, "its emphasis on unalterable human inequalities confirmed the patricians' sense of superiority; its warnings over the multiplication of the unfit and the sterility of the best people synchronized with their discussion of race suicide" (150). Eugenicists, in other words, perceived immigration as a biological threat. Along with anthropologic support for racial hierarchies, this new science inspired a number of studies that helped make racism a national ideology in the United States. Eugenics was used to endorse legislation. It informed national debates over immigration. It was taught in schools. And it even permeated popular culture.[11] Best-selling books, such as Henry Goddard's *The Kallikak Family: A Study in the Heredity of Feeble-Mindedness* (1912), Madison Grant's *The Passing of the Great Race* (1916), which appeared in four revised editions within five years, and Lothrop Stoddard's *The Rising Tide of Color Against White World-Supremacy* (1920),[12] further suggest that these theories spoke to pervasive concerns about race and "mongrelization." Grant specifically argued that miscegenation weakened America's white, intellectual ruling elite by replacing it with the Other: "The cross between a white man and an Indian is an Indian; the cross between a white man and a Negro is a Negro. . . . Man has the choice of two methods of race improvement. He can breed from the best or he can eliminate the worst by segregation or sterilization" (18; 51–52).[13] In this equation, whiteness is ultimately destroyed by difference.[14]

Public entertainment also became an outlet for these racial anxieties. For example, Fitter Family Contests, which were primarily sponsored by the American Eugenics Society, first appeared at a Topeka Kansas fair in 1920 and gradually became a regular part of state fairs for the rest of the decade.[15] The ostensible goal of these highly publicized competitions was to find the best (i.e., whitest) families in America by tracing their lineage. The social message here was similar to that of the ethnological exhibits held at most international expositions and fairs—to reinforce white cultural and social hegemony in comparison with non-Anglo races. Like their freak show counterparts on the same fairgrounds, ethnological exhibits transformed human curiosities who were racially threatening (Asians, blacks, members of non-Christian tribes from Africa, and other immigrants) into representatives of remote, exotic fantasies. The "scientific" approach to exoticism thus masked the hatreds, fears, and urge for self-preservation of a new era.

In *The Adventures of Huckleberry Finn* (1884), Mark Twain explores some of the racial tensions underlying exotic freak show conventions to criticize popular fears about black freedom. The Duke's scheme to advertise Jim as a "SICK ARAB—BUT HARMLESS WHEN NOT OUT OF HIS HEAD" (152) solves his and Huck's temporary concerns about the Fugitive Slave Law by substituting one set of prejudices for another. In the style of a freak show exhibit, the Duke paints Jim's body a solid blue "like a man that's been drownded nine days" and coaches the act in a Barnumesque fashion: "If anybody ever come meddling around, he must hop out of the wigwam, and carry on a little, and fetch a howl or two like a wild beast" (152). For the time being, Jim's construction as an exotic wild man displaces his identity as a slave, preventing others from recognizing him as a fugitive. Twain thus highlights the capricious racial constructions (i.e., labels such as "slave" or "sick Arab") that white America used to maintain control over black identity and culture. The black freak doesn't threaten power, but Jim as a successful runaway slave does.[16]

Over one hundred years later, Toni Morrison would also present freakishness as socially constructed in *Beloved*, but her 1880s freak show, which is attended by an all-black audience, undermines the typical racial script of this entertainment. In this context, both white and black bodies become spectacles, highlighting the capricious nature of freak show constructions. When Paul D, Sethe, and Denver arrive at the carnival, they notice that

> [t]he barker called them and their children names ("Pickaninnies free!"). . . . Two pennies and an insult were well spent if it meant seeing the spectacle of whitefolks making a spectacle of themselves. So, although the carnival was a lot less than mediocre (which is why it agreed to a Colored Thursday), it gave the four hundred black people in its audience thrill upon thrill upon thrill.
>
> One-Ton Lady spit at them, but her bulk shortened her aim and they got a big kick out of the helpless meanness in her little eyes. (48)

In some ways, "Colored Thursday" functions like "Colored People's Day" at the White City of the 1893 Columbian Exposition,[17] with one crucial difference—in Morrison's novel black audiences are empowered through the act of looking. This freak show inadvertently fashions the derision that white performers express toward blacks (a "helpless meanness") as a spectacle. In other words, while whites see blackness as freakish (the One-Ton Lady spits and the barker shouts epithets), racism, not skin color, makes the Caucasian performers freaks. The idea of a spectacle here results from an interpretive act—some could interpret the scorn of these freaks as putting African Americans lower than the lowest of the race, but this black audience chooses not to see it that way. The gimmickry of freak shows is also undermined in this scene. When Paul D recognizes the Wild Savage, he temporarily exposes the truth behind such an exhibit: "When Wild African Savage shook his bars and said wa wa, Paul D told everybody he knew him back in Roanoke" (48–49). On one level, recognizing the identity of this man makes the exhibit laughable;[18] it exposes the humbug as well as the underlying message to white audiences that blacks are dangerous savages. On another level, however, this unmasking enables Paul and those around him to identify with the Wild Savage. They too could be constructed this way.

Both Twain's "sick Arab" and Morrison's "wild savage" place blackness into a nonthreatening context, the ethnological exhibit, but these examples also raise questions about the changing racial makeup of audiences toward the end of the century. Growing immigrant populations in urban areas not only intensified white anxieties about difference, but they also diversified audiences, creating a heightened sensitivity to the display of ethnicity in public amusements. In *Going Out: The Rise and Fall of Public Amusements*, David Nasaw explains that "amusement entrepreneurs . . . had to provide commercial amusements and amusement sites that were public in the sense that they belonged to no particular social groups, exciting enough to appeal to the millions, and respectable enough to offend no one" (5). But this attempt to appease everyone could only go so far. Even though freak shows tried to accommodate certain ethnic groups,[19] African Americans were still essential for ethnological and exotic exhibits. Of course, no one wanted to pay money to see an African American on display—that was too real, too common—so managers worked tirelessly to obfuscate their true identities. As a result, exhibits typically cast blacks and other nonwhites as fantastic Others. They incorporated strange lands and fabricated customs that were foreign to most audience members, so an American of almost any ethnic background might theoretically pay a dime to see "Congo, the Ape Man" or "The Wild Dancing South African Bushman." Yet freak shows were clearly unwilling to change for African-American audiences, consistently relying on negative images of blackness to draw white crowds. Whether those on display were from South Africa, the Congo, or New Jersey, they were presented as culturally inferior, socially barbaric, and non-American.

RINGSIDE SEATS: EXHIBITING BLACK BODIES IN THE RING AND ON THE STAGE

The popularity of African-American blues singers (Ma Rainey, Bessie Smith), musicians (Louis Armstrong, Fats Waller, Duke Ellington), performers (John Bubbles, Josephine Baker), and writers (Langston Hughes, Jean Toomer, Nella Larsen) with both black and white audiences made the Harlem Renaissance (1917–1935) an important part of 1920s America. Renaissance artists hoped to improve ties between the races and to express the distinct cultural heritage of African Americans. In many respects, however, these goals were incompatible. Uncovering past traditions meant confronting a history of prejudices about race, prejudices that were still being reinforced through degrading images of the black body.

A number of contemporary writers drew specifically on the pastime of staged fights to transform the black body into a freakish spectacle. This form of entertainment, which visibly damaged the participants' bodies, was often used by freak show managers to attract audiences. Though this sketch "Battle of the Giants" from Barnum's autobiography foregrounds the extraordinary height of these performers (figure 1.3), for example, the text makes it clear that ethnic and racial difference is central to its appeal: "One day they quarrelled [sic], and a lively interchange of compliments ensued, the Arabian calling the Frenchman a 'Shanghai,' and receiving in return the epithet of 'Nigger' " (162). Barnum doesn't intervene to prevent the fight, however. He only does so to profit from it. He must have enough time to advertise the battle and to sell tickets for it at a later date. In another promotional image, Henry Johnson stands in a mock boxing stance with Benjamin Ash, the "Spotted Boy" (figure 1.4). This photograph clearly targets white viewers interested in seeing blacks engage in physically destructive and degrading behaviors. But ethnicity is also part the appeal. Both of these performers embody the dangers of mongrelization. The "Spotted Boy" is both black and white (though he couldn't pass for white), and the costume worn by "What Is It?" (who at the time of this photograph was referred to as "Zip") implies a connection between African Americans and animals. For white audiences in particular, the underlying message of this image is about the need for racial and ethnic purity.

Figure 1.3 "Battle of the Giants" (1872). Illustration from Barnum's *Struggles and Triumphs*. Barnum inserts himself (at the left) as well as a midget (in the center) to accentuate the height of these giants. This kind of juxtaposition was a typical marketing strategy for freak shows.

Figure 1.4 Henry Johnson ("What Is It?") and Benjamin Ash ("The Spotted Boy") in a staged boxing match (1887). Photograph by Swords Brothers. On one level, both of these performers demonstrate the dangers of hybridity—black and white as well as animal and human. Courtesy of the Becker Collection, Special Collections Research Center, Syracuse University Library.

Painted in the early twentieth century, George Bellows's *Both Members of This Club* (1909) captures the performative role ascribed to blacks in fighting salons and, arguably, society as a whole. The title attempts to show an equality of sorts, which exists only within a specific context (figure 1.5). Black boxers were allowed to become members of sparring clubs—but only to keep fights between blacks and whites legal; under no other circumstance could they have entered such a place. In the painting, the ring is crowded by twisted faces and wicked smiles much like those watching the battle royal in Ralph Ellison's *Invisible Man* (1952). Inside, a bloodied white body with a distorted face recoils from the impact of a blow; a strong black body aggressively charges forward, seemingly on the verge of pushing the other boxer backward. Although both figures are indistinct, the dark one is almost completely unindividualized, suggesting white America's tendency to see all blacks as the same abstract threat. This person, in other words, becomes a nameless force (blackness/the racial Other) that needs to be stopped before it topples white America.

Figure 1.5 George Bellows *Both Members of This Club* (1909). When compared with Bellow's painting *Club Night* (1907) between two white fighters, for example, the introduction of the black body makes this later painting about race. The importance of race is also evident in Bellows's original title: *A Nigger and a White Man*. Chester Dale Collection. © Board of Trustees, National Gallery of Art, Washington.

A number of Harlem Renaissance writers also portray staged fighting as a type of freakish performance. Jean Toomer, Richard Wright, and Ralph Ellison specifically depict men disfigured by fighting as a metaphor for the degradation and coercion of blacks in America. Jean Toomer's *Cane* (1923), one of the first significant works of both the Harlem Renaissance and American modernism, was highly experimental in form and style, combining short fiction, poetry, prose vignettes, and drama in its three-part structure. Toomer examines the ways that geography, sexual relationships, racism, and class stratification prevent blacks from achieving social equality and maintaining a positive connection with their Southern folk heritage.

At the center of this text is "Box Seat," a short story that links the multiple oppressions facing African Americans with the degradation endured by freaks. The narrator and protagonist Dan Moore has followed Muriel (the woman he loves) to a comic show that features a brutal boxing match between dwarfs: "[The dwarfs] kick and spit and bite. They pound each other furiously. . . . Cut lips. Bloody noses. . . . The house roars. The dwarfs bow, are made to bow. The house wants more" (65). The real violence of this match is defused for the audience by the subsequent act the dwarfs must perform. After being made to bow, the victor, Mr. Barry, returns to the stage and sings a love song to different women in the audience. His performance, however, inverts the gaze directed at his body, for he uses a mirror to reflect each face that he sings to—essentially forcing audience members to view themselves in the act of looking. When he turns to Muriel, who is desperately trying to fit into Chicago's middle-class society, he sees her revulsion:

> Mr. Barry bows. He offers Muriel the stain upon its petals. Blood of his battered lips is a vivid stain upon its petals. Mr. Barry offers Muriel the rose. The house applauds. Muriel flinches back. The dwarf steps forward, diffident; threatening. Hate pops from his eyes and crackles like a brittle heat about the box. The thick hide of his face is drawn in tortured wrinkles. (66)

By portraying the dwarf as monstrous, the narrator captures a characteristic response to freak shows—part disgust, part derision ("the house roars"). This response to the freakish body also mirrors Dan's humiliating experiences as a black man: his rejection by Muriel, his unemployment, his fear of the police, his concern that others perceive him as dangerous, even as an animal, and his feelings of explosive rage. Ridiculed by Muriel and disconnected from both white and black middle-class society as well as his Southern African-American roots, Dan himself has become a freak. He empathizes with Mr. Barry, for Dan too feels like a spectacle—watched even by the houses on Muriel's street. Not surprisingly, he is able to read the "words from in the eyes of the dwarf" as saying, "Do not shrink. Do not be afraid of me. See how my eyes look at you. I too was made in His image. I give you the rose" (66). Like the dwarf, Dan seeks a recognition, an acceptance that transcends race, class, and physical deformity.

In his memoir *Black Boy* (1945), Richard Wright also links staged fighting with freakishness to capture the degrading treatment of black men in American society. Wright initially presents Shorty as a type of racial freak, describing him as "the round, yellow, fat elevator operator. He had beady eyes . . . , the complexion of a Chinese, a short forehead, and three chins; psychologically he was the most amazing specimen of the Southern Negro I had ever met" (259–260). Shorty's blackness is made more exotic by his "Chinese" features and unusual body. Despite Shorty's intelligence and passion for reading, Wright explains that "in the presence of whites he would play the role of a clown of the most debased and degraded type" (260). Day after day he demands a quarter to operate the elevator, humiliating himself through dancing, humming, moaning, making faces, drooling, and then allowing white men to kick him. His behavior is reminiscent of a cakewalk dance, which African slaves used to parody whites and which later became part of minstrel shows:

> "But this black sonofabitch sure needs a quarter," Shorty sang, grimacing, clowning, ignoring the white man's threat.
> "Come on, you black bastard, I got to work," the white man said, intrigued by the element of sadism involved, enjoying it. . . . "What would you do for a quarter?" the white man asked, still gazing off.
> "You can kick me for a quarter," he sang, looking impishly at the white man out of the corners of his eyes.
> The white man laughed softly, jingled some coins in his pocket, took out one and thumped it to the floor. Shorty stooped to pick it up and the white man bared his teeth and swung his foot into Shorty's rump with all the strength of his body. (261)

Shorty's performance, which he justifies by claiming he has a "tough ass," elicits money from white men who enjoy seeing this humiliating act. Like a carnival barker, Shorty sells himself as an attraction—talking, prodding, coaxing customers into a kick "for just a quarter, just two bits!" And like his unusual, exotic body and clown-like behavior, this exchange of money links his performance with that of a sideshow.

Despite the white man's frustration, he approves of Shorty's behavior because it reinforces the man's racist assumptions about African Americans. In fact, Shorty's behavior and words sanction this racism:

> "Yeeeess, siiiiir," Shorty sang; but first he picked up the quarter and put it into his mouth. "This monkey's got the peanuts," he chortled. . . .
> "You're all right, Shorty, you sonofabitch," [the white man] said.
> "I know it!" Shorty screamed, then let his voice trail off in a gale of wild laughter. (261)

Shorty's social acceptance, in other words, is predicated on the ways in which he reinforces stereotypes about blacks (i.e., by acting wildly and referring to himself as a monkey). And Wright describes his own "disgust and loathing" for this elevator freak show. He resents blacks who disfigure and debase themselves because such behavior does not change social inequalities and injustices. It only reinforces them.

Ironically, Wright is later coerced into an equally degrading performance when he acquiesces to a fight staged for his white bosses and coworkers. Even though he and Harrison sidestep the foreman's attempts to trick them into a knife fight, they eventually agree to a boxing match for money: "The fight was on, was on against our will. I felt trapped and ashamed. . . . We fought four hard rounds, stabbing, slugging, grunting, spitting, cursing, crying, bleeding. The shame and anger we felt for having allowed ourselves to be duped crept into our blows and blood ran into our eyes, half blinding us. The hate we felt for the men whom we had tried to cheat went into the blows we threw at each other" (276). Each fighter projects his own self-loathing, hatred for whites, and personal shame onto the other. At this moment, Wright realizes that he, like most African Americans, is often coerced by white society to engage in acts of self-destruction and humiliation. Like Shorty, Wright's behavior and damaged body make him a kind of spectacle—not as a matter of choice but as a result of living within a racist society.[20]

Ralph Ellison actually announces his interest in freak shows in the first paragraph of *Invisible Man*: "I am invisible, understand, simply because people refuse to see me. Like the bodiless heads you see sometimes in circus sideshows, it is as though I have been surrounded by mirrors of hard, distorting glass" (3). This foregrounded connection between African Americans and sideshow figures permeates the text. For Ellison, distorted and freakish black bodies are visible signs for the self-destructive behaviors that alienate black men from each other, their Southern African-American roots, and middle-class white

America. The novel begins with a type of boxing match—the battle royal—that makes a freakish spectacle out of the participants. Before the match begins, a naked blond woman stands in the center of the ring surrounded by ten boxers: "The hair was yellow like that of a circus kewpie doll, the face heavily powdered and rouged, as though to form an abstract mask, the eyes hollow and smeared a cool blue, the color of a baboon's butt. . . . Her breasts were firm and round as the domes of East Indian temples" (19). In some respects, her doll-like hair, grotesque makeup (baboon-blue), and exoticized description transform the white woman into a freak exhibit; the black audience can look at her but not touch. Yet her sensual dance causes the white men to cross the line between viewer and spectacle. They reach out, pressing their fingers into her flesh, and before she can leave the room, they start tossing her up in the air.

The young narrator, however, cannot see the connections between his own public identity and the objectification of the white woman. Ironically, he responds in a way typical of freak show audiences—with a mixture of disgust and attraction. "I wanted at one and the same time to run from the room, to sink through the floor, or go to her and cover her from my eyes and the eyes of others with my body; to feel the soft thighs, to caress and destroy her" (19). Yet this response to her act mirrors the duality that whites feel about the narrator's performances as boxer and speaker. On one level, the humiliation of the battle royal can be measured through his physical injuries: his "right eye [was] popping like a jack-in-the-box"; his nose and mouth bleed like the dwarf's in "Box Seat"; and his hands and back are scorched by the electrified rug. Here whites' revulsion for the freak is manifested in the brutality they inflict on him (as well as the brutality they force African Americans to inflict on each other), for these injuries temporarily mark and disfigure his body. They are a type of vulgar makeup that transforms him into something freakish. Although the narrator still gives his rehearsed speech, believing "that only these men could judge truly my ability" (25), he functions as a novelty act for them. Ultimately, his opportunity to go to a black state college is a meaningless gesture because it does not change existing intellectual hierarchies.

Fighting actually frames the *Invisible Man*. The culminating event in the novel, a race riot based on the 1943 Harlem uprising, is precipitated, in part, by Clifton's fight with and death at the hands of a white policeman. Disillusioned and on his own, Clifton leaves the Brotherhood, the Communist Party in Harlem, and tries to make money as a street performer—manipulating Sambo dolls that play to white stereotypes about African-American bodies:

> A grinning doll of orange-and-black tissue paper with thin flat cardboard disks forming its head and feet and which some mysterious mechanism was causing to move up and down in a loose-jointed, shoulder-shaking, infuriatingly sensuous motion, a dance that was completely detached from the black, mask-like face. It's no jumping-jack, but *what*, I thought, seeing the doll throwing itself about with the fierce defiance of someone performing a degrading act in public, dancing as though it received a perverse pleasure from its motions. (431)

Because of this performance with the Sambo doll, Clifton learns that promoting degrading images of African Americans is profitable; like Shorty from *Black Boy*, he embraces this self-effacement with "fierce defiance." It serves both as a means to an end and as an act of resistance. He can capitalize on white interest in seeing blacks demean themselves without accepting these images. As the one operating the doll, he controls the act while distancing himself from the stereotypes embodied by it. Even though the narrator despises this contribution to racial stigmas about blacks on ideological and social levels, Clifton realizes that the Brotherhood ultimately wants to pit blacks against each other. He sees white society as controlling, as holding the strings of African Americans.

The narrator's blindness to Clifton's plight highlights his own role as a puppet for white men and the Brotherhood. As the narrator tries to confront him about the dolls, Clifton must run from the police; in his hurried escape "the doll [goes] over backwards, wilting into a dipping rag of frilled tissue, the hateful head upturned on its outstretched neck still grinning toward the sky. The crowd turned on me indignantly. The whistle came again. I saw a short pot-bellied man look down, then up at me with amazement and explode with laughter, pointing from me to the doll, rocking" (433). For the audience, the narrator is indistinguishable from the freakish doll; he too is an object of derision, a spectacle like the naked woman in the boxing ring in chapter 1. His association with the Sambo doll also recalls the battle royal when someone called out to him: " 'That's right, Sambo,' a blond man said, winking at me confidentially" (26). This early moment, followed by the boxing match, parallels Clifton's use of the Sambo doll and his subsequent fight with a police officer. Clifton "spun on his toes like a dancer and swung his right arm over and around in a short, jolting arc, his torso carrying forward and to the left in a motion that sent the box strap free as his right foot traveled forward and his left arm followed through in a floating uppercut" (436). Clifton is a performer in this impromptu street fight which seems almost choreographed, suggesting that the outcome is part of a large dance in which he must die for this transgression. Unlike the Bellows's *Both Members of This Club,* no illusion of equality exists here. The streets of New York offer an unfair and destructive arena for black men without the pretense of "sport" or "membership." The confines of the boxing ring in this novel and in the painting (the black fighter is surrounded by whites as well as ropes) represent white control of blacks in society more broadly. And the stakes for the black man are death (Wright's and Ellison's narrators fear dying in arranged fights, for example). Ultimately, these grotesque bodies act as a framing device in *Invisible Man,* suggesting that African Americans are forced to respond with violence to their entrapment.

This view of the black body as spectacle eventually became a source of guilt for many whites, feelings that arguably contributed to the decline of the freak show. In the short story "Keela, the Outcast Indian Maiden" from *A Curtain of Green* (1941), for example, late-modernist author Eudora Welty captures some of the latent guilt troubling freak show audiences. Steve, a former carnival barker and the narrator, seeks out a clubfooted black man (Little Lee Roy) who years earlier was forced into performing geek acts[21] while dressed as a savage Indian woman. Burdened by years of guilt after discovering that Keela was actually a disabled black man, Steve journeys to find him as an act of atonement. To lessen his role in Keela's construction as a freak, Steve claims to have been duped by the carnival, but when his temporary travel partner questions his inability (years earlier) to recognize Keela's gender and race, Steve reacts violently: " 'Bet I could tell a man from a woman and an Indian from a nigger though,' said Max. . . . [Steve] reached out and without any warning hit Max in the jaw with his fist" (66). By protesting Steve's version of events, Max questions his attempt to deny any culpability for the racist brutality inflicted on Keela. At this moment, fighting does not reinforce racist attitudes about blackness as it did in Toomer, Wright, and Ellison; it becomes Steve's strange way of asserting claims of racial tolerance and compassion. The mark left on Max is meant to be a sign of Steve's innocence, but the injury is only temporary. It fails to convince Steve—or anyone—that he wasn't complicit in the spectacle of Keela's body.

For years Steve has convinced himself that he did not know the truth—a common stance for freak show audiences to assume. As discussed earlier, Barnum often used the idea of "not knowing" to promote exhibits—publicizing scientific debates over the legitimacy of the "Fejee Mermaid" and "What Is It?" and even advertising some of his own exhibits as humbugs.[22] The question of authenticity in freak exhibits was a significant part of their allure because ambiguity challenged nineteenth- and early-twentieth-century audiences to decide the truth for themselves. By 1941, the time Welty's story was written, Steve, who had moved from itinerant showman to perpetual hitchhiker, represented a period that could no longer hide behind questions of humbug.[23] After the discovery of Keela's identity—as well as his humanity—the carnival owners are sent to jail, and Steve attempts to come to terms with the ways in which his spiel made him complicit in Keela's exhibition.

On a performative level, Steve's language shapes the audience's understanding of Keela ("Ladies and gents! Do not try to touch Keela, the Outcast Indian Maiden—she will only beat your brains out with her iron rod, and eat them alive!" (62)), but the effectiveness and power of his language are contingent on both Keela's silence and his own scripted behavior. Even though Steve sees his participation as a type of helpless meanness resulting from the carnival owner's deception, he acknowledges that he "was the cause for it goin' on an' on an' not bein' found out—such an awful thing. It was me, *what I said* out in front through the megaphone" (61; my emphasis). Welty, in other words, sees language—the way a barker's spiel and freak advertisements constructed difference and presented it to others—as equally responsible as coercion for the abuses in freak shows. Even though "Keela, the Outcast Indian Maiden" is exposed as a fraud by a Texan who opens his palms to Keela in a gesture of acceptance, his humanity remains in question until he speaks: "They made it stay in jail to see if it could talk or not, and the first night it wouldn't say nothing. Some time it cried. . . . And it could talk—as good as me or you" (64). From the bars of the exhibit to a jail cell, Keela is detained in both "cultures" (sideshow and legal) because of his race, suggesting the persistent racial biases of modernist culture; outside of the freak show, Keela's status as savage is still suspect. Ultimately, it is language that frees him from his identity as Keela. His ability to speak removes Steve's and the carnival's former linguistic control and enables him to become (once again) Little Lee Roy—someone who can voice his own history.

Welty's story also captures modern America's gradual rejection of such entertainment by enacting a kind of *de*freaking show in which we "watch" Keela move from freak to human being:

> And they undressed it an' found out it wasn't no outcast Indian woman a-tall. It was a little clubfooted nigger man. . . . Washed its face, and it

was paint all over it made it look red. It all come off. And it could talk—as good as me or you. But they told it not to, so it never did. They'd tole it if anybody was to come near it they was comin' to get it—and for it to hit 'em quick with that iron bar an' growl. . . . I was yellin' outside, tellin' 'em to keep away, keep away. You could see where they'd whup it. They had to whup it some to make it eat all the chickens. (64–65)

Welty invokes so many freak conventions through Keela (savage, exotic other, disabled, geek, hermaphrodite) that he completely embodies and symbolizes the freak show. As a result, the stripping action in jail exposes not only the artifices of freakishness but also its inherently brutal prejudices. Despite the revelation of Keela's humanity, Steve still refers to him as "it"—unable to let go of his objectification and construction as a freak. His desire to look also intensifies at this moment, suggesting that his quest is motivated, in part, by a desire to look at the real Keela. He admits that before the exhibit closed he watched Keela "a thousand times" (60), being both fascinated and repulsed by his savage exoticism and geek act. But his present desire to look is a self-indulgent form of pity ("I was goin' to give him some money or somethin', I guess, if I ever found him, only now I ain't got any" [67]). The narrative makes clear that Steve does not want to speak to Lee Roy, only to stare one more time. When Max gives Lee Roy money at the end, sending him inside, he literally enacts white America's reaction to a shameful history of racial prejudice—offering money or "charity" as a gesture of atonement. Lee Roy, in effect, is still a freak, but his act has changed. His new audience pays him to go away.

"Keela, the Outcast Indian Maiden" concludes with two acts of silence. First, Max silences Steve when they leave Lee Roy: " 'I didn't go ask you a question. . . . You eat, and I'll listen to the juke box' " (68). Then the story offers a second ending in which Lee Roy speaks articulately for the first time:

> "Today while all you all was gone, and not a soul in de house," said Little Lee Roy at the supper table that night, "two white mens come heah to de house. Wouldn't come in. But talkes to me about de ole times when I use to be wid de circus—"
>
> "Hush up, Pappy," said the children. (68)

Lee Roy's humanity, as captured in this family meal, is juxtaposed with Steve's and Max's perception of his behavior (his inexplicable guffawing) throughout the story. His family's need to erase any connection with the freak show is also a way to preserve his dignity and humanity. Not to speak of this history is to reject it, and silence affirms the status of the present as distinct from the past.

"Who's Passing for Who?": The Performance of Race in Cather, Fitzgerald, Faulkner, and Larsen

One night in a smoke-filled New York bar, three white schoolteachers—a woman and two men—from Iowa were introduced to Langston Hughes and a friend. Excited about meeting Negro artists, they bought round after round of drinks, talked of novels and paintings, and listened eagerly to stories about avant-garde life in Harlem. Suddenly, at an adjacent table, a black man rose angrily and struck a blond woman. Within seconds, one of the Iowa men jumped up in her defense and hit him: "Keep your hands off that white woman," he demanded. At this point, a waiter quickly explained that the blond was actually "colored," and the white man sheepishly dropped his chivalric stance—lowering his fists and mumbling an apology.

A few moments later, the friends of this failed Lancelot told Hughes that, as a matter of fact, they too had been passing—masquerading as white for over ten years. "Then everybody laughed. . . . All at once we dropped our professionally self-conscious 'Negro' manners, became natural, ate fish, and talked and kidded freely like colored folks do when there are no white folks around." The next morning, after partying all night, the Iowa woman shocked Hughes again by telling him, "We're white. We just thought we'd kid you by passing for colored a little while—just as you said Negroes sometimes pass for white." Unsure of the truth, Hughes felt betrayed: "Whatever race they were, they had had too much fun at our expense—even if they did pay for the drinks."

The ambiguity in Hughes's essay, "Who's Passing for Who?" (1952), points to both black and white anxieties about passing. What happens when the body no longer provides a visible marker for difference? As I have discussed in this chapter, a tremendous amount of energy was put into constructing the black body as a spectacle. Whether it was through the language of science or the sales pitch of a sideshow barker, white America needed to see racial difference as absolute. The body on stage (or in the ring) needed to be "Othered" in every way—racially, culturally, intellectually, and morally. In the context of freak show and lynching photography, the construction of blackness as barbaric helped reinforce commonly held beliefs about the inferiority of non-Anglos. Throughout the late nineteenth and early twentieth centuries, freak shows constructed racial difference into something freakish—a connection that writers used literally and metaphorically—and for many, this transformation of the black body into a spectacle temporarily assuaged fears about immigration and miscegenation. But passing undermined white hopes of maintaining racial hierarchies built on visible difference. If race could be ambiguous, then the culture of hatred based on skin color was flawed.

A great deal of modern literature explores the implications of passing. In the writings of Willa Cather, F. Scott Fitzgerald, William Faulkner, and Nella Larsen, for example, passing repeatedly appears as an important theme for the loss of cultural identity within both black and white communities. In these texts, the racially ambiguous body is often presented as freakish in order to portray a society that regards miscegenation with fear and disgust. It embodies the visible breakdown of racial hierarchies. And it exposes the hypocrisy of politics and social attitudes based on race.

Cather's *My Ántonia* (1918), a retrospective narrative about Jim Burden's lifelong relationship with Ántonia Shimerda, is preoccupied with the presence of ethnic and racial difference in America. Early in the novel, the teenage farm boys of Black Hawk are captivated by the exotic beauty of Ántonia and the other immigrant girls: "Physically they were almost a race apart, and out-of-door work had given them a vigour. . . . a positive carriage and freedom of movement and made them conspicuous among Black Hawk women. . . . When one danced with [daughters of well-to-do families], their bodies never moved inside their clothes" (149–150). For the mothers of the town, these country or "hired" girls *were* a race apart: "All foreigners were ignorant people who couldn't speak English" (151). Jim dismisses these prejudices, attributing them to class anxieties: "The country girls were considered a menace to the social order. Their beauty shone out too boldly against a conventional background. But anxious mothers need have felt no alarm. They mistook the mettle of their sons. The respect for respectability was stronger than any desire in Black Hawk youth" (151). But the novel's preoccupation with ethnicity suggests that Jim is mistaken; though the community willingly helps these girls assimilate into American culture (primarily hiring them as house girls), social respectability demands that these boys marry into their own class and ethnicity.

These concerns about race are most clearly demonstrated by the pleasure people derive from the performance of Blind d'Arnault—an African American who is perceived as a type of minstrel-freak. Before the disfigured mulatto pianist Blind d'Arnault performs, Cather presents minstrelsy as an active part of the traveling entertainment that passed through the sleepy town of Black Hawk. In the Harling house, for example, "[Sally] sat down in her hat and coat and drummed the plantation melodies that Negro minstrel troupes brought to town" (119). Blind d'Arnault, however, doesn't embody the positive connotations of this earlier scene; instead, his physical deformities ("ugliness" and blindness) link him more explicitly to the tradition of freak shows:

> He was a heavy, bulky mulatto, on short legs, and he came tapping the floor in front of him with his gold-headed cane. His yellow face was lifted in the light, with a show of white teeth, all grinning, and his shrunken, papery eyelids lay motionless over his blind eyes. . . . He had the Negro head, too; almost no head at all; nothing behind the ears but folds of neck under close-clipped wool. He would have been repulsive if his face had not been so kindly and happy. (139)

His exaggerated smiles and physical deformities make him a kind of freak exhibit, emphasizing his role as spectacle. Blind d' Arnault is based on the famous nineteenth-century pianist Thomas Greene Wiggins, better known as Blind Tom, whom Cather saw perform in Lincoln, Nebraska (figure 1.6).[24] According to Thomas Riis, his "precocious talents were made to order for the era of P. T. Barnum. A blind and possibly mentally impaired black boy, who gesticulated wildly and played like a virtuoso, Tom was quickly and deftly marketed as a freakish curiosity, an untutored 'idiot,' who nevertheless possessed rare and amazing powers" (35). Similarly, the audience for Cather's d' Arnault seems more interested in his extraordinary body and mulatto background than his performance. His caricatured face, freakish body, yellow skin, and convulsive movements not only make him a spectacle, but they also make him safe—the clearly identifiable Other.

Throughout his fiction, Fitzgerald presents fears about difference and miscegenation that are far more acute. Tom Buchanan in *The Great Gatsby* (1925) laments that "it's up to us, who are the dominant race, to watch out or these other races will have control of things" (13), and later in the novel he rants: "Nowadays people begin by sneering at family life and family institutions, and next they'll throw everything overboard and have intermarriage between black and white" (130). For Tom, miscegenation threatens to destroy the class and racial hierarchies that privilege whiteness.

This Madison Grant-like paranoia also surfaces in *Tender Is the Night* (1934), which Fitzgerald began writing in 1925. In this story of Dick Diver's disintegrating marriage and psychiatric career, Fitzgerald

Germon   914 Arch St. Phila.

Figure 1.6 Blind Tom—Musician (1865). Photograph by Charles Eisenmann. In this *carte de visite*, Blind Tom poses in the tradition of nineteenth-century portraiture (typically reserved for middle- and upper-class white society), but just as his race excludes him from these circles, his closed eyes, curly hair, and baggy clothes are out of place as well. Courtesy of the Becker Collection, Special Collections Research Center, Syracuse University Library.

uses the freakish body to express Dick's latent racial fears.[25] After the murder of Jules Peterson, an African American who helps one of the Divers' friends, Dick describes "the face, harassed and indirect in life, [as] gross and bitter in death; the box of materials was held under one arm but the shoe that dangled over the bedside was bare of polish and its sole was worn through" (110). His body, found on Rosemary's bed (the young actress with whom Dick is having an affair), has stained her sheets with blood, suggesting the sexual threat that black men supposedly presented to white women.[26] And Peterson's association with the shoe-repair business, as evident by the polish near his body, alludes directly to blackface. (Blackface was traditionally performed by white men who used burnt cork, greasepaint, and shoe polish on their faces to appear as African Americans.[27])

This conflation of minstrel and freak is not surprising, given that they often appeared on the same stage. In the Lecture Room of Barnum's American Museum, for example, the variety of acts that made up an afternoon program included freak exhibits and minstrel acts, and even Barnum, who was always putting himself on display for the public, performed in blackface:

> I blacked myself and sung the advertised songs, 'Zip Coon,' etc., and to my surprise was much applauded. . . . One evening after singing my songs I heard a disturbance outside the tent and going to the spot found a person disputing with my men. I took part on the side of the men, when the person who was quarrelling with them drew a pistol and exclaiming, 'you black scoundrel! how dare you use such language to a white man,' and proceeded to cock it. . . . Quick as thought I rolled my sleeve up, showed my skin, and said, 'I am as white as you are, sir.' He dropped his pistol in positive fright and begged my pardon. (90)

Although Barnum uses this anecdote to illustrate his quick wit and ingenuity, it highlights the "positive fright" whites felt about passing and the fluidity of racial boundaries. And in the literary imagination of the early twentieth century, minstrel-freak figures appear as a desperate fantasy on the part of many whites to "see" racial difference on the body.[28]

Fitzgerald specifically illustrates this mixture of minstrel and freak traditions through the image of Peterson's damaged, black body. But the connection to freak shows doesn't stop there. In addition to Peterson's contorted face, his body is associated with violent images of Native Americans and put "on display" in the hotel corridor. Peterson's exoticization, along with his staging, link him to the traditions of the freak show as well. Dick's explicit comparison of Native Americans and African Americans suggests that all minorities or oppressed groups are seen as dangerous by members of dominant cultures.[29] When Abe North (a name that alludes to the abolitionist movement and, in the context of Dick's racism, to the ultimate failure of the North to provide true equality and freedom for African Americans after the Civil War[30]) first brings Peterson to the hotel room, Dick explains: "[He] was rather in the position of the friendly Indian who had helped a white" (106), and after the murder Dick concludes "that Abe's first hostile Indian had tracked the friendly Indian and discovered him in the corridor . . . had hunted him down and slain him" (110). This association with Native Americans links Dick's rhetoric to that of sideshow managers who presented non-whites as exotic others. The fantasy here not only parallels such exhibits, but it also enables Dick to dehumanize Peterson more easily—to remove any responsibility on his part for the death. When Dick has seen enough, he simply wants to get rid of Abe and his trouble with "the Negroes": "[He] regarded [Peterson] politely—interest formed, dissolved, he turned to Abe: 'You go to some hotel and go to bed. After you're all straight Mr. Peterson will come and see you' " (107). To prevent any involvement in this "nigger scrap," Dick "dragged the body quickly into a plausible position in the corridor" (111), and then had the hotel manager-owner dispose of it, claiming that " 'we came on a dead Negro . . . in the hall . . . Of course I must ask you to keep my name out of it. I don't want any French red tape just because I discovered the man' " (111). Though Dick justifies his actions in the name of protecting Rosemary's reputation, he clearly wants his world to remain unencumbered by racial problems. He controls the threat that Peterson represents by using some of the interpretive conventions of freak shows and literally putting Peterson's body on display in "a plausible position in the corridor."[31]

William Faulkner takes the problem of racial ambiguity to an extreme through his character Joe Christmas in *Light in August* (1932). Throughout the novel, Joe's ethnic identity remains uncertain, and questions about whether or not he is part African American preoccupy both white and black characters. Even Joe himself is unclear about his origins: " 'I think I got some nigger blood in me. . . . I don't know. I believe I have' " (184). Like Toomer's "Box Seat" and Welty's "Keela, the Outcast Indian Maiden," this novel specifically links its main character with the circus and puts the reader and other characters in the place of a freak show audience, inviting them to participate in "discovering" the truth about Joe. As the town interprets his behavior as a violent assault on whiteness (he both has sex with the white Joanna Burden and kills her), they need to label him "black." Only when imposing this racial identity can they justify killing him for overstepping the interracial taboos of miscegenation and passing.

In part, the confusion about Joe's ethnic identity stems from his origins in the circus. Doc Eupheus Hines, Christmas's grandfather, tells Byron Bunch that his daughter was impregnated by a Mexican working in the circus. Later, however, the circus manager claims the man was actually black:

> When the trial was over and the circus owner come back and said how the man really was a part nigger instead of Mexican, like Eupheus said all the time he was, like the devil had told Eupheus he was a nigger. . . . and all the folks knowing it and me trying to get Eupheus to lets move away because it was just that circus man that said he was a nigger and maybe he never knew for certain. (357)

Just as freak exhibits obscured and falsified the actual identity of their performers, no one could verify the ethnicity of either Joe's father or Joe himself. Like Welty's Keela and Morrison's Wild African Savage, the father's role in the circus depended in part on the obfuscation of his actual ethnicity; he needed to pass as Mexican.

Even though white characters in the text are forced to judge Joe according to his actions because his race is unclear, they eventually use blackness as a way of explaining his violent acts. Bobbie, his prostitute girlfriend, for example, refers to him as black only after he assaults his abusive father and possibly kills him: " 'Bastard! Son of a bitch! Getting me into a jam, that always treated you like you were a white man. A white man!' " (204). This violent act (which jeopardizes her profession as a prostitute) clearly changes her perception of him. Similarly, Bobbie's pimp has Joe beaten up, marking his body in the hopes of finding some visible reassurance of his blackness: "*We'll find out. We'll see if his blood is black*" (205). Not only does Joe's swollen and bloody face literally darken him, but, as evident in the other works discussed in this chapter, this comment about black blood reveals a white need to see the differences between black and white as inherent.

When the town of Jefferson hears about Miss Burden's murder and the final shootout with Christmas, they attribute these crimes to blackness: "Among them the casual Yankees and the poor whites and even the southerners who had lived for a while in the north, who believed aloud that it was an anonymous negro crime committed not by a negro but by Negro and who knew, believed, and hoped that she had been ravished too: at least once before her throat was cut and at least once afterward" (271–272). For them, Joe's blackness enables these hateful fantasies about murder and rape—fantasies that ultimately "remove" his white characteristics. Joe becomes a representative of all African Americans, for the town needs this interpretation to justify his acts and his death. The frightening implications of passing can be controlled if Joe's character can be interpreted as black. Even one of the most respected intellectuals of Jefferson, Gavin Stevens, offers a similar reading of Joe's character:

> Because the black blood drove him first to the negro cabin. And then the white blood drove him out of there, as it was the black blood which snatched up the pistol and the white blood which would not let him fire it. . . . It was the black blood which swept him by his own desire beyond the aid of any man, swept him up into that ecstasy out of a black jungle where life has already ceased before the heart stops and death is desire and fulfillment. And then the black blood failed him again. . . . He did not kill the minister. He merely struck him with the pistol and ran on and crouched behind that table and defied the black blood for the last time, as he had been defying it for thirty years. (424–425)

Stevens interprets the final showdown, in which Christmas takes Reverend Hightower's pistol and lets himself be shot by Grimm, as an internal one. He believes black (evil) and white (good) blood have struggled for dominance in Joe, and that his passing was a lifelong struggle to suppress his blackness. No different than any of the other racist responses to Joe, he rationalizes Joe's death by making the violence of blacks inherent, regardless of visible signs.

In African-American fiction in the early twentieth century, passing often means the loss of self, for assimilating into white society usually requires some abandonment of racial and cultural heritage. Over time, this loss of identity can make recognizing the self as black a startling moment in which one's own body seems unfamiliar, even freakish. Nella Larsen's *Passing* (1929), for example, uses language alluding freakishness to explore black anxieties about passing as a loss of self.[32] Werner Sollors has recently argued that "Larsen ticks off a whole repertoire of recurrent thematic aspects of interracial literature such as fingernails as a racial sign, the curse of Ham, or the biracial mother's fear of giving birth to a darker-skinned descendant" (*NBW* 25). He interprets these recurring moments as thematic because "they inevitably refer us *out* of the novel and toward relationships with other texts and discourses" (25). I would like to add freakishness to this list of themes. Larsen specifically presents the fear of giving birth to a dark-skinned child as freakish, putting her text in the tradition of literature discussed in this chapter. Larsen's characters struggle with feelings of shame and remorse for hiding their racial identity. Both the narrator, Irene, and her friend Clare are able to pass, but Clare depends on passing to maintain a white, middle-class lifestyle. Eventually, after years of rejecting her African-American roots and culture, she reestablishes ties with her former friend Irene who lives as a black woman. For women like Clare, dark skin color is dangerous. When she talks about the possible dangers of having a dark child, she explains that "it's only deserters like me who have to be afraid of *freaks of nature*" (169; my emphasis). The term "freaks" labels[33] blackness as something abnormal and repulsive, and as Gertrude (another passer) explains: "Nobody wants a dark child."

Later in the novel, at the Negro Welfare League dance, Irene uses similar labels to protect Clare, but in doing so she reveals a detachment from her own African-American identity. While Clare dances with various black men, Hugh Wentworth comments that " 'all the ladies of my superior race who're lured up here . . . are always raving about the good looks of some Negro, preferably an unusually dark one. . . . Do you think he's—er—ravishingly beautiful?' " (205). Wentworth's rhetoric (which is also reminiscent of Madison Grant's and Tom Buchanan's) speaks to his own fears about the lure of blackness for white women. Irene assuages his concern by dismissing this notion and explaining that white women are excited only by novelty and the strangeness of difference: " 'the sort of thing you feel in the presence of something strange, and even, perhaps, a bit repugnant to you; something so different that it's really at the opposite end of the pole from all your accustomed notions of beauty' " (205). With the same type of justification used by freak show managers, Irene constructs blackness as exotic and presents African-American culture as something that does not threaten existing racial hierarchies. In other words, Irene has appropriated the language of nativists, eugenicists, and freak show mangers. She labels dark skin as "repugnant," but her interpretation of blackness here is a rejection of self. Irene has set herself above Clare in moral terms because she does not pass as a way of life. Yet by viewing blackness as grotesque, she has aligned herself completely with white notions of beauty and superiority, and like Clare, she has lost contact with her racial heritage.

In the first half of the twentieth century, modernist literature often expressed and tried to come to terms with racial anxieties by constructing the black body as a freakish spectacle. Freakishness became a powerful artistic tool for capturing these fears about racial difference, miscegenation, and passing. Though freak shows were failing to mitigate these concerns, many clung to the modes of construction that they offered to reaffirm prejudices and to maintain cultural and social distinctions between different ethnic groups. As many of these authors show, however, freakishness exposes the superficiality of such distinctions. It captures some of the feelings of hatred, fear, and shame motivating many relationships between blacks and whites—feelings that remain a cruel legacy today.

*   *   *

Broken Glass

Bootlegging kept us from going without food. By 1933 Mother had made enough money selling liquor to open a bar, Doyle's. It was a small building on 26th and Reed in South Philadelphia.

I was fifteen. I served drinks.

Every afternoon dozens of tired, unemployed men talked of work and sex and endless days without food. They drank to keep from going home. They sang to remember the green grasses of a far-away land. And they fought each other to forget about themselves—about their failure as fathers, as husbands, as men.

I served them all—well, all the Irish. The Italians, Chinese, and blacks mostly stayed in their own neighborhoods, but sometimes one would come in for a drink. That's when the bar became silent. Even the smoke seemed to clear.

Early on I had learned how to get rid of unwanted customers—taking their money, filling a glass, then dropping it on the bar. Beer or whisky spilling. Broken glass glimmering like cheap jewelry in the dim light.

They rarely came back.

One afternoon, a black man walked into the bar with a ten-dollar bill. He ordered a cold beer and watched as I poured. Everyone else was looking at me too. The place was real quiet like a library. Even Mom's brother, Tommy Doyle, stopped singing.

Then I carried the glass over to the counter and broke it right in front of him. The beer spilled everywhere.

He didn't move though. He just ordered another one. Then another. Glass after glass breaking until I lost count. Finally, he stood up—out of money and tired of the game, I guess—and he asked without waiting for an answer: "How many times must we pay?"

He walked slowly out into the street.

Lying in bed as she told me this story sixty-five years later, my grandmother cleared her throat: "He probably stole the money. Niggers are all the same."

She laughed, then winced from the pain in her now unreliable body. Reaching for a glass of water on the nightstand, she accidentally knocked it onto the wood floor, where it shattered into dozens of sharp pieces.

I rushed to pick up the shards, placing them in my palm one at a time. "It's all right. I'll take care of it," I told her.

But in truth I was afraid. As I reached for those translucent fragments, I was afraid that one would cut deeply into my pale skin.

*   *   *

War-Injured Bodies: Fallen Soldiers in American Propaganda and the Works of John Dos Passos, Willa Cather, Ernest Hemingway, and William Faulkner

Innocent Americans had been killed, and the president of the United States was determined to go to war. "The world must be made safe for democracy," he told Congress in a special session. "We . . . shall bring peace and safety to all nations and make the world at last free." As the path to war became increasingly clear, dissenting voices in the administration resigned. The national debt increased more than twenty-fold, and civil liberties were curtailed in the name of patriotism.[1]

I am, of course, talking about President Woodrow Wilson and the years leading up to U.S. involvement in World War I. In order to build public support and to suppress antiwar sentiment, Wilson created the Committee on Public Information (CPI). With the aid of more than 150,000 employees, this committee designed posters, films, scholarly pamphlets, and news reports that depicted the enemy as both a military and ethnic threat. Anything German became suspect and dangerous. Even the temperance movement capitalized on this newfound jingoism, claiming that German breweries in America were distributing beer to compromise the readiness of U.S. troops and the job performance of the workforce. This climate of growing intolerance (which helped pass the Eighteenth Amendment in 1919) was also evident in the monstrous images used to characterize the enemy.[2] These images conflated all types of ethnicities and physical abnormalities to make the Other as freakish as possible, to make difference synonymous with disloyalty and all things un-American. In the mode of freak show exhibits, propagandists used the damaged and/or exoticized body to heighten contemporary fears about race and to justify U.S. involvement in international affairs more broadly.

World War I only exacerbated racial tensions in the United States. As James Abrahamson explains, "Unlike previous major wars, World War I . . . heightened rather than quieted racism. In 1919, lynchings of Afro-Americans—ten of them ex-soldiers and several of them still in uniform—disgraced the United States at almost twice the 1917 rate" (125). European immigration was also considered a serious threat to national security. According to Serge Ricard, "ethnic diversity was felt to be incompatible with national unity. The gospel of undiluted Americanism soon appeared as the most authentic expression of patriotism, and 'hyphenated Americanism' was made to sound like a contradiction in terms" (20).[3] Many propagandists exploited these racial fears by using some of the more sensational dimensions of exotic freak show exhibits to depict the enemy. On posters, the German soldier might appear with Asian features or as a dark beast in military uniform. In these ways, propagandists were attempting to justify America's war effort in terms of racial preservation, suggesting that U.S. involvement abroad (in these and other imperial endeavors) would preserve a homogeneous national identity.

In the aftermath of World War I, the racial Other was not the only problem. Disabled veterans had returned from the front lines, and their damaged bodies started to become a painful reminder of something the country wanted to forget. As historian Thomas Britten explains, after the United States rejected the Treaty of Versailles in 1919, "widespread disillusionment replaced the postwar euphoria, and American veterans confronted the realization that their sacrifices had failed to usher in the era of world peace that President Wilson had envisioned" (159). Amid this disillusionment, the wounded soldier (as well as his horrifying stories of military engagement[4]) undermined America's vision of itself as a powerful and indomitable empire, reinforcing popular distrust for U.S. imperialism. Instead of signs of an ennobling sacrifice, much of the nation saw these injuries as a representation of America's disastrous encounter with the foreign.

Accordingly, the prewar use of difference would sharply contrast literary depictions of the body after Armistice. Rather than demonizing the enemy, postwar fiction tends to focus on the costs of war for those who fight. Writers such as John Dos Passos, Willa Cather, Ernest Hemingway, and William Faulkner examined this conflicted response to the war, in part, through the injured body. In these works, visible wounds represent physical and psychological trauma, not heroism and valor. They are emblematic of the ugly, self-destructive, and thankless aspects of battle. As William Leuchtenburg explains in *The Perils of Prosperity, 1914–1932*, "American foreign policy in the 1920s was built on disillusionment with World War I—a dirty, unheroic war which few men remembered with an emotion save distaste. . . . The war left a determination in millions of Americans never to fight again. . . . Even more important, it left a deep cynicism about American participation in European affairs" (104). War fiction of the 1920s taps into this cynicism by linking wounded soldiers with the spectacle of freakishness—applying some of the same tools that propagandists had used to construct the enemy as a freak to the returned soldier.

Injured veterans had been part of freak shows since the nineteenth century. In Barnum's American Museum, for example, "the second floor contained exhibits of the greatest variety: a fortune teller, a *one-armed Civil War veteran* who guessed weight . . . .Present also was a fat girl, the lightning calculator, giantesses and dwarfs, and other popular curiosities" (N. Harris 165; my emphasis). The deformed soldier in this context is equated with the other freaks on display. Ostensibly, his ability to guess weight makes him an attraction, but like the fat girl and the dwarfs, his success as an exhibit depends on the spectacle of his body. In twentieth-century literature, the connection between freakishness and wounded veterans highlights the alienation and isolation felt by many of these men—whose damaged bodies now excluded them from mainstream society. These images are in sharp contrast with propaganda posters that had routinely presented both the enemy as monstrous and enlistment as a moral act—showing proud, muscular, youthful white bodies as emblematic of America's military strength and courage.[5] Instead, these literary texts portray a war that shattered the strong, young body and a society whose social prejudices about disability hampered true healing for these men.

MONSTROUS IMAGES: THE FREAKISH FOREIGNER

As discussed in Chapter 1, many sideshows constructed African Americans as exotic freaks. Robert Bogdan points out that "white Americans . . . [did want] to see the warriors, the bestial Africans, and the pygmies. Showmen thus had a mandate to mold the presentations of the Africans they exhibited to justify slavery and colonialism"

(187).[6] In part, these presentations reinforced racial prejudices in order to assuage popular anxieties about difference. The stage could contain the racial Other, the ethnic threat; it made the nonwhite body safe through the trappings of a freak show. WWI propagandists recognized the power (as well as the draw) of these sideshow images, and they used many of the same techniques to enfreak the enemy.[7] Unlike freak show entrepreneurs, however, they didn't want to contain the threat. They wanted to remove the safety net that freak shows offered and to depict the Other as unleashed on American soil.

Using a circus-like drawing of a gorilla to represent Germany, for example, propaganda artist H. R. Hopps[8] links the enemy with American fears about miscegenation. Hopps enhances the German threat by casting it as black and as sexual—a titillating image designed to make white men both angry at the fear of conquest and sexually aroused by its voyeuristic overtones. A salivating gorilla with blood-stained hands, ferocious orange-yellow eyes, and an open mouth has landed on American shores. His right hand clutches a bloody club engraved with the German word "Kultur," while a helpless white woman succumbs to his powerful grip in the other. Her golden locks and right hand cover her face as she dangles between his legs; torn clothing exposes her breasts. In the background, a devastated Europe provides a haunting vision of what could happen to America if the viewer fails to enlist in the U.S. Army (figure 2.1).[9] In a move akin to what Barnum did with the African-American pinhead in "What Is It?," Hopps's 1917 picture transforms this German soldier into a dark, savage gorilla with a blond mustache—a violent version of Barnum's man-monkey and most probably an allusion to Kaiser Wilhelm. Because the enemy in this case was also white, he needed to be depicted as a beast in order to elicit the strongest possible anti-German response. The blond woman's position between his legs, her nudity, and the bloody finger wrapped around her waist also suggest sexual violation. The woman's faceless, naked body encourages the male gaze, giving her no way either to look back at the viewer or to cover herself. Because this gaze is also a violation, it invites *white* men to take control of both her and her despoiler in the name of her virtue.

Given the racial climate in the United States at the time, it is not surprising that Hopps exploits mainstream prejudices in this way.[10] The blond hair on this black body plays into the miscegenation taboo, and it equates German culture with African-American culture. Just as the term mulatto, which means "little mule" in Spanish, reinforces a degrading connection between African Americans and animals, the biracial implications in this figure are designed to be equally dehumanizing. It's much easier to kill the enemy if he can be seen as an

Figure 2.1 "Destroy This Mad Brute" by H. R. Hopps (1917). Hopps casts the German threat as a racial one in this poster. Notice the details that suggest sexual violation—her partial nudity, her position between his legs, and his blood-soaked finger around her waist. All of these elements play into contemporary anxieties about miscegenation. Courtesy of the Hoover Institution Archives, Stanford University.

animal. The carnival overtones further trivialize German cultural accomplishments; the word "Kultur," for example, is surrounded by ironic quotation marks and covered in blood. Like a beast at a carnival, German culture is presented as brutal—something that should be caged, controlled, and even destroyed.

Ellsworth Young's poster "Remember Belgium: Buy Bonds Fourth Liberty Loan" (1918) also casts the enemy as dark and misshapen. Here a German soldier drags a young girl from her burning village. Though this image is not racially charged (both the soldier and the girl are sketched in gray as if visible only through a smoky haze), it does use tactics similar to Hopps's picture. Young, for example, presents the threat in terms of gender. Germany is characterized as a male aggressor that assaults defenseless women and children. He also uses an inhuman figure to represent Germany more broadly. The soldier has no face, and he wears a bulky uniform that gives his body little definition. Even his pointed helmet, boxy profile, and open stance seem more skeletal than human. Like Hopps's gorilla, this warrior is a metaphor for the enemy—suggesting his callous brutality, destructiveness, and relentless drive. Young enhances the poster's metaphoric possibilities by making the girl and landscape ambiguous as well. Though the text tells us that its subject is Belgium, Young doesn't provide any geographic markers, implying that no one—no place—is safe from German aggression.[11]

The use of exoticized and extraordinary bodies in World War I propaganda left a powerful legacy for propagandists in subsequent years, and I would like to touch on two examples here. During World War II, Nazi propagandists, who notoriously represented Jews as freakish monsters (depicting exaggerated physical features, excessive weight, hairiness, and other stereotypes), reprinted Hopps's gorilla poster in 1939, superimposing the following text:

> "If Germany were exterminated from the world tomorrow, day-after-tomorrow there wouldn't be a single Englishman on the entire globe who wouldn't become richer." So wrote the British paper, "Saturday Review," over forty years ago. And when they assaulted us 25 years ago, they wrote on their rotten, slanderous poster: "Destroy This Mad Beast"—They meant the German People!!! Forget?? Not a second time!!!

Reprinting this poster is certainly a testament, albeit an ironic one, to the power of this image; like the original, its underlying message reinforces divisive ideas about cultural difference. Although the ostensible concern here is economic (the British plan to become wealthy at the expense of Germany), the original image and text ("Destroy This Mad Beast") make German culture the target. This war, the 1939 reprint implies, is about preserving a distinct German identity—one that England and the United States threaten.

Other posters from this period employ techniques similar to Hopps's, attacking the enemy (in this case the United States) in terms of race and culture.[12] In the 1944 poster "Kultur-Terror" by Leest Storm, a hideous American monster demolishes the cultural artifacts of Europe (figure 2.2). In the background, the Statue of Liberty, which appears almost indistinguishable from the skyscrapered landscape of America, is juxtaposed with a mishmash of sophisticated European architectural styles (a fountain in a piazza, churches, and castles). This image suggests the superiority of Europe's historical and aesthetic traditions when compared with the tawdry, prefabricated, and duplicated architecture of America. Within this smoldering European town, people are running from a four-armed monster that holds a bag of money, a record, manacles, a machine gun, and a hangman's noose. Other fragmented images of American culture make up this creature as well—a shapely female leg (adorned with a ribbon reading "World's Most Beautiful Leg"), a mechanized male leg with a blood-stained bomb, a drum-stomach, a greedy caricatured Jew who won't let go of his money, and a Star of David loincloth. Once again, but on the other side of the Atlantic, ethnic difference and race are the primary terror to Anglo-Saxon purity. At the center of the poster, dark blue arms flex above the beast's cage-chest where two black caricatures dance the jitterbug. The racism here is double-sided. Blacks are unfairly imprisoned by this creature who wears a Ku Klux Klan hood, but they also live in its heart. Blackness, in other words, exists at the core of America, and this mixed image of oppression and centrality points to the country's hypocrisy about race. Furthermore, two women rest on the beast's dark shoulders: a white woman adorned with a "Miss Victory" ribbon and a Native American in full headdress wearing a "Miss America" ribbon. Storm ironically gives the "Miss America" label to a Native American, a subtle reminder of the United States' ethnic impurity and the vicious treatment of its indigenous people. Storm's poster suggests that America—with its oppressive racial history and superficial culture—has become a kind of monster. It is a hybrid of disparate parts that has no appreciation for the traditions and cultural purity of Europe.

Figure 2.2   "Kultur-Terror" by Leest Storm (1944). The text at the bottom reads: "The USA claims it will save European Civilization." Courtesy of the Hoover Institution Archives, Stanford University.

One of Ours?: Reading Injured Bodies in John Dos Passos and Willa Cather

In books and stories about the war, many writers in the 1920s explored the metaphoric possibilities of freak shows and freakishness not to demonize the enemy but to suggest that the ethnic hatreds and physical atrocities brought on by war had a destructive impact at home. In John Dos Passos's *Three Soldiers* (1921) and Willa Cather's Pulitzer Prize-winning novel *One of Ours* (1922), the damaged soldier's body represents the loss of community, ethnic identity, and the self. As I demonstrated above, the government tried to ensure that physical injuries were considered a noble sacrifice for one's country, markers of courage and strength in battle; but in actuality, after the war, the visibly scarred and damaged body guaranteed exclusion.

Dos Passos captures this exclusion by depicting military service as degrading and demoralizing men. In order for John Andrews, one of the white protagonists of *Three Soldiers*, to avoid this dehumanization, he hopes that his injuries from battle will get him out of the service: "Perhaps he was badly enough wounded to be discharged from the army. That meant that he . . . who had let himself be trampled down unresistingly into the mud of slavery, who had looked for no escape from the treadmill of death, would live" (166). Andrews sees physical injury both as a possible escape from the slave-like conditions of army life and as a way to preserve his dignity in the eyes of others. When he is not discharged, however, Andrews assumes French ethnicity to break ties with the American military. His life in Paris as part of a school detachment (a program established by the United States to allow soldiers to study and/or receive additional training during the war) eventually enables him to disassociate from the army because he starts passing as French, speaking French fluently and using the name Jean André. He also abandons his uniform and goes AWOL—acts that make him, by U.S. law, a criminal. By discarding the clothes and language that would mark him as an American, Andrews adopts a different physical and cultural identity to escape his connection with the war. This decision ultimately makes him a kind of Other, aligning him with defectors and outcasts.

Dos Passos explicitly invokes freak show imagery to capture Andrews's subsequent marginalization. After Andrews abandons his symbolic and literal connections to the U.S. military, he encounters a freakish community of AWOL soldiers who live in a dilapidated gin mill on the rue des Petits-Jardins. The place is run by freak figures: a maid/prostitute referred to as a "dawg-faced" girl (337) and the owner, "Chink," who is "a stout man in a dirty white shirt stained to a brownish color round the armpits . . . His face was flabby, of a greenish color; black eyes looked at Andrews fixedly through barely open lids, so that they seemed long slits above the cheekbones" (332). These physical descriptions (of ugliness, obesity, and Asian ethnicity) and epithets (such as "Chink" and "dawg-faced girl") transform these peripheral figures into freaks. (Jo-Jo the Dog-Faced Boy, for example, was one of Barnum's most famous exhibits of this kind.) Like sideshow performers, they are given no "real" names but are defined only by their physical and ethnic characteristics. Dos Passos then juxtaposes these figures with the AWOL community to suggest how the war has made spectacles out of these men.

The freakishness of these soldiers is not always manifested in physical injuries, but in every case they have been emasculated by their experiences and ostracized for their choices. Even those without bodily wounds are hiding from the outside world. Slippery, the pristine soldier, "was dressed as a second lieutenant, his puttees were brilliantly polished, and he smoked through a long, amber cigarette-holder. His pink nails were carefully manicured" (337). As his name suggests, there is slippage between his perfectly clean uniform and his need to hide in this dingy room. His uniform is no longer an image for the strength and masculinity befitting a U.S. soldier, but one of femininity—the outfit for an effeminate gentleman with manicured fingernails. As these descriptions imply, Slippery does not get dirty by engaging in war; instead he abandons service because he cannot live up to the physical expectations of military service.

In another example that inverts the codes of bravery and courage typically associated with the military, deserter Al's injuries, which are the most explicitly described wounds in the novel, suggest that he must have been harmed in battle: "A piece of toweling, splotched here and there with dried blood, was wrapped around his head, and a hand, swathed in bandages, was drawn up to his body. The man's mouth took on a twisted expression of pain as he let his head gradually down to the bed again" (333). We subsequently discover, however, that he was injured not in combat but in the act of running away: " 'I'm almost crazy with this hand. One of the wheels went over it. . . . I cut what was left of the little finger off with a razor.'. . . You see, my foot slipped when they shunted a car I was just climbing into, an'. . . I guess I ought to be glad I wasn't killed' " (333–334, 338). An ironic inversion emerges here between experience and signifier. He has the mark of battle but has not earned it. Al's wounds, therefore, are a public sign of disgrace, of his desertion from the army. The ambiguities about Slippery's perfect uniform and Al's injuries reveal an artificiality underlying propagandistic images of a soldier's strength, invulnerability, and commitment. In refusing to sacrifice their lives for the war, these men have become freakish, a transformation that Andrews recognizes as one of the costs of dissent and difference.

Willa Cather's *One of Ours* also uses freakishness to undermine idealized notions about the war. Throughout the first half of the novel,

Cather weaves together images of sideshow freaks with descriptions of the Wheeler family, centering the first three chapters around Claude Wheeler's desire to see a circus. Claude's sense of freakishness reflects both his perception of the Weaver family and his own feelings of displacement—from his family and community.[13] We first see Claude's "red hair standing up in peaks, like a cock's comb" (3) on his head, which is "so big that he had trouble in buying his hats, and uncompromisingly square in shape; a perfect block-head" (16). Similarly, his gigantic father is "a very large man, taller and broader than any of his neighbors" (5). These exaggerated portraits seem more fitting for sideshow performers than one's own family, and Claude explicitly makes this connection when he links his father with a circus performer: "Mr. Wheeler was . . . chaffing with a little hunchback who was setting up a shellgame" (10). Not only are shellgames the kind of entertainment found at carnivals, but pairing Mr. Wheeler's enormous height with the "little hunchback" also accentuates the difference between these bodies in a very Barnum-like manner.

Other aspects of the setting transform the Wheeler farm into a type of freak show as well. Bayliss, Claude's materialistic brother, was "thin and dyspeptic . . . [and] from [his] drawl one might have supposed that the boy was a drunken loafer" (9–10).[14] The farm hands, Dan and Jerry, are the "dirtiest hired men in the country," and Jerry's neglect of Molly, an old mare, has made her "wretchedly thin, and her leg swollen until it looked like an elephant's. . . . Her scaly, dead-looking foot lifted just a little from the ground" (4–5). Claude's perception of Molly's injury as grotesque not only reflects his disgust for her neglect, but like the associations he makes between family and freak shows, it also suggests his anxieties about fitting into a community he abhors. Even though he waits anxiously to see the circus in the first three chapters, the reader never does get to see the show; we hear about it only in a passing reference from Claude when he tells Mahailey about "the clown, elephant and the trained dogs."[15] By not showing us the circus, Cather keeps the reader's attention on the Wheeler family and on Claude's perception of his own world (and his place in it) as distorted and freakish.

In the second half of *One of Ours*, Cather juxtaposes these earlier images with the display of injured or dying soldiers. Critic Frederick Griffiths has discussed the parallelism in both halves of the novel as "a balanced symmetry of peace and war with a whole series of mirror image reversals between the two; the images of the first part tend to repeat themselves more concretely in the second" (268). I would like to suggest a parallel between this early carnival imagery and the subsequent images of disfigured soldiers as well. In the fourth section of the novel, an epidemic of influenza breaks out on the steamer *Anchises*, killing hundreds of soldiers and exposing Claude to his first war casualties. Corporal Tannhauser's death, for example, is described vividly: "His congested eyeballs were rolled back in his head and only the yellowish whites were visible. His mouth was open and his tongue hung out at one side. From the end of the corridor Claude had heard the frightful sounds that came from his throat" (243). Surrounded by sickness, death, and grotesque bodies, Claude surprisingly begins to thrive. For the first time in his life, he has found a sense of purpose, having distanced himself from the sense of estrangement he felt while living on his family's farm in Nebraska:

> Life had never seemed so tempting as it did here and now. He could come up from heavy work in the hospital, or from poor Fanning and his everlasting eggs, and forget all that in ten minutes. . . . He awoke every morning with that sense of freedom and going forward. . . . Other fellows were sick and dying, and that was terrible,—but he and the boat went on, and always on. (251–252)

Despite the casualties, America's participation in the war and its role as a world power give meaning to the lives of Claude and other young men.[16] At a time when the explosive growth of urbanization threatened the values of rural America,[17] Claude describes it literally as "a miracle" for "all the Wheelers and the rough-necks and the low-brows" (253). For Claude, the war provides lower- and middle-class rural America an escape from the pedestrian. As a result, he needs to distance himself from its harsh costs, namely suffering and injury, in order to see his and America's role in the war as meaningful and ennobling.

At this point, Cather introduces a figure to tie freakishness more explicitly to the representation of soldiers' bodies in her text. When the doctor convinces the Chief Steward to relinquish some of the stolen supplies to save Fanning (one of the many sick soldiers onboard), he sends a messenger to deliver the eggs: "There was a scratching at Claude's door. . . . [The messenger] was unwashed, half-naked, with a sacking apron tied round his middle and his hairy chest splashed with flour. He never spoke, had only one eye and an inflamed socket. Claude learned that he was the half-witted brother of the Chief Steward, a potato-peeler and dish-washer in the galley" (257). The juxtaposition of the abused and mistreated brother with Fanning's decaying body suggests that the suffering of war can transform the body into something freakish. The brother, a wild beast who hides in the bowels of the ship, embodies some of the horrifying possibilities for these soldiers. His disfigured body has made him an outcast—someone to be hidden from mainstream society. And as Cather had seen after the war, this fate would not be uncommon for the severely wounded soldier. The Steward's brother, in other words, raises questions about the body as spectacle, foreshadowing the role of injured soldiers in the remainder of the text.

When the ship finally arrives in France, Claude perceives this seaside town as a type of carnival. Here, he becomes obsessed with the spectacle of both racial otherness and physical deformities:

> Claude was wandering alone in a brightly lighted street full of soldiers and sailors of all nations. There were black Senegalese, and Highlanders in kilts, and little lorry-drivers from Siam—all moving slowly along between rows of cabarets and cinema theaters. . . . The sidewalks were crowded with chairs and tables. . . . From every doorway music-machines poured out jazz tunes and strident Sousa marches. The noise was stupefying. . . . Claude stationed himself before a movie theater . . . and stood watching people. (269)

For Claude this surrounding with its bright lights and deafening noise is a type of carnival/sideshow in which two types of people become exhibits. First, amidst the backdrop of cinemas and cabarets, he stares at the exotic—the Senegalese and lorry drivers from Siam. Though they are all soldiers, Claude makes subtle distinctions based on race and culture to establish a self/other dichotomy: "Highlanders *in kilts,*" "*black* Senegalese," and "*little* lorry-drivers." Interestingly, this scene is also wholly American. All of the music is either jazz or patriotic tunes by Sousa; nothing of French culture is present. Though this type of diversity may be unfamiliar to Claude given his rural upbringing, it is very much an image of modern American heterogeneity.

Then Claude sees a disabled soldier, and his reaction suggests that disability doesn't ennoble the soldier—it transforms him into a spectacle:

> The man wore the American uniform; his left arm had been amputated at the elbow, and he carried his head awry, as if he had a stiff neck. His dark, lean face wore an expression of intense anxiety, his eyebrows twitched as if he were in constant pain. . . . Without realizing what he did, Claude followed them out of the crowd into a quiet street, and on into another. (269)

Claude follows, Cather implies, because he wants to look at this disfigured body, and his behavior parallels that of a doctor who has been observing this soldier as the subject for a book: " 'He's a star patient here. . . . This psychopath, Phillips, takes a great interest in him and keeps him here to observe him' " (272). Both men are drawn to this body, and Cather uses this symmetry to suggest that there is little difference between staring at him on the street and making him an object for scientific exploitation.

When Claude learns about the doctor's book, he wants to help the soldier escape, in part, because he needs this soldier to represent the nobility of military service. Claude doesn't want to face the possibility that the injured soldier could be seen as a spectacle. As a result, while visiting Fanning in the hospital, he starts to see death as preferable to disability and illness: "One poor fellow, whose face and trunk were wrapped in cotton, never stopped moaning, and as he was carried up the corridor he smelled horribly. . . . To shed bright blood, to wear the red badge of courage,—that was one thing; but to be reduced to this was quite another. Surely, the sooner these boys died, the better" (271). Claude still sees the war as a something honorable, but the wounded body calls that into question. War is not ennobling here but disabling. These men have been "reduced," and this transformation of the body into a spectacle is too much for Claude to bear.

Cather ends the novel with Claude's death in battle and his mother reflecting on the ramifications of postwar disillusionment for U.S. veterans. Though her son "died believing his own country better than it is" (370), she feels regret about those American soldiers who either wander through Europe "lost" or return home to a country that does not want to be reminded of war: "One by one the heroes of that war . . . die by their own hand. . . . [They] were the ones who had hoped extravagantly,—who in order to do what they did had to hope extravagantly, and to believe passionately" (370). This extravagant hope, which Claude championed throughout the text, could only survive by denying the realities of suffering, disability, and death.

THE HEALING: INTERPRETING DISABILITY AT HOME

Cather's vision of postwar America—filled with disillusionment, isolation, and suicide—doesn't offer much hope for healing. But America had to find ways to heal, and recovering from disability became one of the themes of propaganda posters and postwar literature. Healing meant forgetting about years of devastation, and in America, which didn't have ruined cities and ravaged lands at home, this was somewhat easier to do.

To overcome some of the negative associations with disability, posters—from Europe and the United States—ennobled these soldiers both as a means to solicit national patriotism and to mitigate earlier images of monstrous war bodies. This emphasis on seeing the extraordinary body as heroic suggests concerns about the marginalization of disabled veterans after the war, and the need to challenge some of the social stigmas accompanying disability, such as weakness, dependence, and even freakishness. While some of these men needed assistance, their heroic sacrifices for freedom deserved respect and acceptance. Propagandists responded by presenting the disabled veteran not as a burden but as a figure of strength and communal relevance.

In a somewhat flamboyant display of bravado, A. Ortelli's 1918 poster for Italian veterans read: "For the Fatherland my eyes! For the Peace your money" (figure 2.3). Between these phrases stands a fully dressed soldier with his head bandaged and blood seeping through the gauze covering his eyes. His open stance and clenched fist communicate ongoing defiance and pride. The facelessness of this soldier enables him to represent Italy quite broadly, and specifically its determination to recover from the war.

By contrast, in the United States, Albert Sterner's 1918–1919 drawing for the Permanent Blind Relief Fund is more bleak, and it reflects a tendency to respond to disability with empathy instead of more intellectual understanding (figure 2.4). It captures a haunting vision of darkness and dislocation—a sighted man's vision of blindness. A shrouded specter, who is as expressionless and mournful as the blind man, tentatively guides him forward. Debris and darkness enclose the landscape; a thin, lighted window to the right of the men provides the image's only light. Physically, the soldier looks unharmed; his eyes seem simply closed. But the sign beneath reveals otherwise: he is blind. Despite the starkly different tone, both posters present fit, heroic bodies, suggesting that blindness is not *dis*abling. Although these men can and should be considered important and useful members of society, the tone of Sterner's work implies society's reluctance to embrace them.

Georges Dorival's poster tries most explicitly to find a space for disabled veterans in French society (figure 2.5). In it, two decorated soldiers shake hands. The officer has lost an arm; the *poilu* (a term for front-line French soldiers, literally meaning "shaggy" or "hairy") is missing a leg. Clearly, the underlying message of the poster is that of

Figure 2.3 "Per la patria I miei occhi. Per la pace il vostro denaro" by A. Ortelli (1918). The soldier's muscular frame and bold stance suggest that disability is not a weakness. The perspective of the drawing also invites the viewer to look up at the soldier's face, suggesting that his sacrifices are something to admire and respect. Courtesy of the Hoover Institution Archives, Stanford University.

Permanent Blind Relief War Fund 590 Fifth Ave

Figure 2.4 Permanent Blind Relief War Fund by Albert Sterner (1918–1919). The dark, haunting landscape and shrouded figure capture a sighted man's vision of blindness. This poster asks the viewer to empathize with the fear and uncertainty that blinded veterans must have been experiencing. Courtesy of the Hoover Institution Archives, Stanford University.

utility. Despite the rigid class hierarchies presented by associating the officer with urban culture and the *poilu* with agriculture, the latter holds a scythe that makes him a productive member of his community. Likewise, the smokestack behind the officer suggests that he is somehow part of the city's ongoing productivity. A new community is also being formed here, one that may erase class to a certain extent. Even if nondisabled citizens remain unwilling to accept them, the General Association of Injured Soldiers offers some type of community.

Some American literature in the mid- and late 1920s also dealt explicitly with postwar experiences of injured soldiers attempting to find a place back home. William Faulkner's *Soldiers' Pay* (1926) and a number of works by Ernest Hemingway, for example, ennoble the wounded veteran, in part by suggesting that prejudices about disability trivialize the sacrifices made by those who fought in the war.

From the collection *Men Without Women* (1927), Hemingway's "In Another Country" presents complete physical recovery as the

Figure 2.5 "L' association générale des multilés de la guerre" by Georges Dorival (1917). These decorated soldiers are presented as capable and essential members of French society (urban and rural). In the center of the poster, they clasp hands, suggesting the need for community and acceptance. Courtesy of the Hoover Institution Archives, Stanford University.

only means of removing some of the social stigmas surrounding disfigurement and military service. This text, his first story explicitly about World War I—other than the vignettes from *In Our Time* (1925)—deals with unrealistic postwar attempts to cure wounds through ineffectual machine technology. Every afternoon the narrator attends a rehabilitation session in an Italian hospital and describes the seemingly pointless therapy applied to his and the other soldier's bodies: "[His leg] dropped straight from the knee to the ankle without a calf, and the machine was to bend the knee. . . . But it did not bend yet, and instead the machine lurched when it came to the bending part" (206). Similarly, the Italian major, who gives the speaker grammar lessons, "had a little hand like a baby's . . . which was between two leather straps that bounced up and down and flapped the stiff fingers" (207). The goal of these machines and of the "improved" images the doctors show the patients is visible restoration, a removal of the stigma of bodily difference by erasing the history of injury: "The doctor went to his office in a back room and brought a photograph which showed a hand that had been withered almost as small as the major's, before it had taken a machine course, and was a little larger" (207).

Through these details, Hemingway suggests that removing such physical markers was considered necessary for social acceptance outside of the military and for normality in general. The narrator actually witnesses some of the mainstream prejudices facing these soldiers firsthand:

> Another boy who walked with us sometimes . . . wore a black silk hand-kerchief across his face because he had no nose then and his face was to be rebuilt. He had . . . been wounded within an hour after he had gone into the front line for the first time. They rebuilt his face, but he came from a very old family and they could never get the nose exactly right. He went to South America and worked in a bank. But this was a long time ago, and then we did not any of us know how it was going to be afterward. We only knew then that there was always the war. (207)

For these men, the war will always exist in their injuries as well as in the social ostracism implied by the heckling (which is directed at both their status as officers and their damaged bodies) and this man's need to move to South America. Injured soldiers, the narrator implies, learned after the war that they were not welcome, and no degree of physical reconstruction could change this. For Hemingway's wounded boy soldier, he has lost the physical features that link him to his family, and they reject him as a result. His body becomes a mark of familial disgrace. Like Al in *Three Soldiers*, this boy cannot escape his physical badge of dishonor, and Hemingway uses this connection between disfigurement and familial rejection to show how the injured body was sometimes grounds for exclusion. War irrevocably changed the soldier—in ways that ostracized many of these men from the very society they fought for.

Faulkner's *Soldiers' Pay* uses the treatment of disabled veteran Donald Mahon to critique social responses to disability and the American tendency to privilege self-centered individualism over communal sacrifice. In the context of this novel, freakishness becomes a metaphor for the psychological, emotional, and physical "deformities" of nondisabled characters. Before the war, Margaret Powers, who has taken it upon herself to care for Mahon, recalls prewar excitement: "You remember how it was then—everybody excited and hysterical, like a big *circus*" (158; my emphasis). Faulkner himself joined in this countrywide enthusiasm, enlisting in Canada's Royal Air Force, but he had not completed training before the war ended. Subsequently, he falsified his rank, wore the clothing of an RAF officer, claimed to have flown in battle, and manufactured a limp and a head injury.[18] He even told stories to his brother "of celebrating armistice by doing aerial stunts while drunk and finally crashing upside down into a hangar" (Wulfman 29–30). This deception is interesting on many levels. To convince people of his wartime experiences, Faulkner felt the need to fabricate evidence, to make his body a visible sign of heroism and valor. But he could also remove that sign when social attitudes about the war became far more negative. He had manufactured a way to "experience" the war without the trauma of battle or the lasting stigma of disability.

Yet this role-playing also exposes the disparity between his hope for recognition as a military hero and the reality of postwar life for veterans—a conflict that preoccupies *Soldiers' Pay*. In this novel, injured soldiers like Mahon and James Dough (a veteran with an artificial leg and a "festering arm" [186]) were not heroes; they were considered burdens. As Joe Gilligan, another of Mahon's caretakers, explains to the train conductor who threatens to throw off the soldiers: " 'Men . . . he don't want us here. And this is the reward we get for giving our flesh and blood to our country's need. . . . You have refused the hospitality of your train to the saviors of your country' " (8). Joe begins to realize that a soldier's pay is being seen not as a savior but as a problem. Like Cather's image of those who returned home only to kill themselves, Faulkner uses freakishness to suggest that there is something wrong with a country that rejects its own, particularly after they have given up part of themselves for it.

Joe becomes increasingly disgusted with the town's reaction to Mahon's blindness, terrible facial scar, and withered hand: " 'G'wan now, beat it. Show's over' " (145). Though this is now a dead metaphor in American speech, the phrase "show's over" is a fitting reference for the town's initial desire to stare at Mahon's body. As Joe tells Margaret, " 'That damn Saunders hellion brought his whole gang around to see the scar. We got to stop this . . . can't have these damn folks in and out of here all day long, staring at him' " (146). The scar has become a town attraction, and like freak show audiences, the community reacts to Mahon's mortal injuries with both curious interest and revulsion:

> Curious, kindly neighbors came in—men who stood or sat jovially respectable, cheerful: solid business men interested in the war only as a by-product of the rise and fall of Mr. Wilson, and interested in that only as a matter of dollars and cents, while their wives chatted about clothes to each other across Mahon's scarred, oblivious brow; . . . girls that he had known, had danced with or courted of summer nights, come now to look once upon his face, and then quickly aside in hushed nausea, not coming any more unless his face happened to be hidden on the first visit (upon which they finally found opportunity to see it); boys come to go away fretted because he wouldn't tell any war stories. (145)

Though this catalogue reinforces his status as spectacle, it also presents the ways Mahon fails as an exhibit: the men talk only of finances related to a war that doesn't interest them; their wives can't gossip about the most interesting news in town—his deformity; the young girls don't return when they see he is no longer a potential suitor; and the boys want stories he cannot tell. In other words, Mahon does not encourage repeat business, for his severely scarred body (as well as his inability to sensationalize the war for the young boys) makes the townspeople tired of looking—once the initial thrill is gone.

Public curiosity about Mahon's sexuality also links him to the tradition of freak exhibits. Sexuality was always a crucial component to freak shows. As Leslie Fiedler argues,

> all Freaks are perceived to one degree or another as erotic. Indeed, abnormality arouses in some "normal" beholders a temptation to go beyond looking to *knowing* in the full carnal sense the ultimate other. That desire is itself felt as freaky, however, since it implies not only a longing for degradation but a dream of breaching the last taboo against miscegenation. (137)

Fiedler, in other words, believes that desiring to know the other on sexual and intimate terms makes the viewer a type of freak. Similarly, Faulkner suggests a freakishness in those characters who want to know if Mahon could still be Cecily Saunders's husband in a carnal sense. Like the question that surrounds Jake Barnes's injury in Hemingway's *The Sun Also Rises* (1926), a curiosity about Mahon's sexual function drives the text. For example, the young girls whom Mahon courted before the war return to see his body and never come back; Cecily's parents talk around the implications of his injuries: "The idea of driving your daughter into marriage with a man who has nothing and who may be half-dead, and who probably won't work anyway. You know yourself how these ex-soldiers are" (95). Clearly for Mrs. Saunders, any explicit discussion about his sexual impotence is taboo; instead, his wounds allow her to use commonly held social biases to justify why her daughter should not be bound to marry him. Although, before the war, Cecily wanted to be married to a veteran ("to be engaged to a man who will be famous when he gets here—oh, it seemed then that I did love him" [83]), she has an affair with George in his absence. She also screams and faints at her first meeting with the invalid Mahon, completely rejecting the idea of marriage: "About being engaged to him? How can I, with that scar? How can I?" (127).

Many of the characters associated with Mahon are also marked by sexual excesses (romanticism, abstinence, lewdness) that prevent them from forming romantic relationships and that thus become freakish. Cadet Julian Lowe, for example, feels that he has fallen in love with Margaret, romanticizing their love with Petrarchan excess (until he moves out west and meets a younger woman). Idealistic about the war and romance, he assumes that Margaret loves Mahon because of his scar: "Oh Margaret . . . I would have been killed there if I could, or wounded like him, don't you know it?" (48). Lowe clearly sees this war wound as a mark of chivalric honor that is not attached to any realistic vision of battle or of Mahon's experiences upon returning. Margaret, however, cares for Mahon as a gesture of atonement to her dead husband, who was killed at the front. Traumatized by both the loss of her husband and the circumstances surrounding their impulsive marriage, she is unwilling to love anyone else. This self-repression is manifested, in part, in the disfigurement of her own body—other characters describe her mouth as looking like a scar, for example. These painful experiences and her responses to them have become visible on her body.

Januarius Jones, a college-student wastrel who hangs around the Mahon household in order to flirt with Cecily, is most explicitly linked to freak show strategies of physical otherness and sexual ambiguity. A heavyset, vile man, Jones flirts offensively with Cecily and is described as having "yellow unwinking eyes—like a goat's" (79). As a matter of fact, Cecily compares him to a variety of animals—"Jones' yellow, fathomless eye, like a snake's" (215) and his fat body reminds her of "a worm" (216)—and she even feminizes his body: "The feminine predominated so in him, and the rest of him was feline: a woman with a man's body and a cat's nature" (218). As I have shown, freak show audiences were drawn to ambiguity, and hermaphrodite exhibits, which I discuss in chapter 4, challenged the viewer to guess (and in some cases to pay extra) to "discover" their true sex. In addition to his sexual ambiguity, Jones is also associated with exotic exhibits: "Januarius Jones, by nature and inclination a Turk, was also becoming an oriental" (280). Like an exotic exhibit, his difference is used to reinforce the superiority of those around him, acting as a foil for their clearly defined masculinity and strength. By lurking in corners, flirting with any available woman, and slithering away from fights, Jones reinforces the honor and integrity of war veterans. In other words, his characteristics and personality—sloth, obesity, licentiousness, sexism, cowardice, anger, and femininity—make him a freak; whereas, Mahon and other injured veterans are transformed into spectacles by the interpretation of others. These negative social responses to difference are responsible for the poor treatment of veterans. And by contrasting Jones with Joe, Faulkner suggests that society, in its attempt to forget about the war, has failed to recognize the physical and personal sacrifices of these veterans. Their honor, strength, and sacrifice should make them heroes, not spectacles.

Recalling World War I: Johnny Got His Gun

Dalton Trumbo moved to Los Angeles in 1925 to become a writer. He attended classes at the University of Southern California, worked long hours at a bakery, smoked several packs of cigarettes a day, and wrote feverishly. A few years later, he was contributing to the *Hollywood Spectator* and began working as a reader and screenwriter for Warner Brothers Studios. For the next fifty years, his reputation in Hollywood would be divided between his successes as a screenwriter, which included the films *Kitty Foyle* (1940), *Roman Holiday* (1953), *The Brave One* (1957), and *Spartacus* (1960), and his arrest for refusing to testify before the House Un-American Activities Committee in 1947. Trumbo was one of the Hollywood Ten, a group of writers and directors who went to jail for their leftist views and for refusing to state whether or not they had been members of the Communist Party. He was subsequently fired from Metro-Goldwyn-Mayer and blacklisted.

In addition to his prolific work as a screenwriter, Trumbo was a novelist. Not long after publishing his first book, *Eclipse*, in 1935, he read an article about a severely disfigured World War I veteran. This story became the inspiration for his second novel, *Johnny Got His Gun* (1939), which won the National Book Award. Trumbo's portrait of

the horrible human costs of war was published just after the start of
World War II. He would later adapt his book as a film in 1971—to
once again protest a contemporary war. The film version makes a vivid
connection between wounded veterans and freaks; in this way, *Johnny
Got His Gun*, which Dalton directed as well, provides an effective
conclusion for this chapter.

The film begins in the midst of battle. While burying a fellow soldier,
the protagonist, Joe Bonham, hears a shell screaming through the
black, rainy sky. He starts running blindly through barbed wire and
stagnant puddles. The piercing sound gets louder. It is everywhere. As
he dives into a muddy ditch, a white, burning brightness explodes
around him; then darkness. . . . At the hospital, he becomes
Unidentified Casualty Number 47; with no eyes, nose, teeth, jaws,
tongue, face, arms, or legs, he seemingly has no means to communicate.
Military doctors decide to keep him for study in a private room with
closed shutters, so others cannot see him. They cover his body and
face with sheets. But Joe can still dream, of his past and a possible
future—a future that includes a traveling sideshow.

Through an internal, extradiegetic monologue, Joe narrates his
experiences, which alternate between black-and-white hospital scenes
and flashback/fantasy-dream sequences. The latter reveal images from
his past (his first sexual experience with his girlfriend, Corinne, fishing
trips with his father, his father's death, and some of his early experiences in the war) and surrealistic fantasies (about Corinne's new life
without him, discussions with his dead father, and a distorted office
Christmas party before the war). As Joe gradually figures out what has
happened to him, he describes himself as a freak—"Me lying here like
some freak in a carnival show"—and he even recalls a family trip to
the circus. At the time, his father imitated a freak show barker, and in
one fantasy-dream, he imagines his father and mother advertising his
injuries in that manner: "He is the armless, legless wonder of the
twentieth century." They also sell tickets for fifteen cents and set up a
sign above the stage: "Joe Bonham, the self-supporting Basket Case."

On one level, this fantasy sequence works as a metaphor for Joe's
current situation, reflecting his fears about other people's reactions to
him. On another level, Joe, an extreme vision of the disabled soldier,
needs to perceive himself as "self-supporting," as a functional part of
society. And he believes that the freak show will offer him a way to
make money and maintain his autonomy. Despite his condition, the
fact that Joe considers the freak circuit his only option reflects widespread social attitudes about the injured body as freakish. This
metaphor suggests that the damaged body doesn't have a place in

American society, and this notion is reinforced by his audience, which consists of other carnival freaks (dwarfs and clowns) who watch and laugh. This inverted audience transforms the disabled veteran into the most extreme form of spectacle: a spectacle for other spectacles.

In the culminating scene of the film, Joe sees a dwarf carrying an American flag and leading a small freak troupe across the desert. Just as in the earlier traveling show, where Joe was displayed amid palm trees and water, the freak show becomes a distorted oasis. It gives the most extreme outcasts an opportunity to survive, but only on the fringes of civilization. Joe sees their movement across plains and deserts as an image of mobility and possibility. When this is denied to him, however, he wants to die. Using his head to communicate with the military staff via Morse code, he responds to their question "What do you want?":

> But maybe there's a way I can take care of myself. Yes, there is a way. All you have to do is put me on display, and people will pay to see me. Lots of people. Put me in a fancy coffin with windows in it, and take me out where people are spending money and having fun. Take me to the beaches and the county fairs and the Fourth-of-July celebrations and all the church bazaars. They've seen the pin-headed girl from Timbuktu and the dog-faced man who crawls on his belly like a reptile, but they're not real freaks. They were born that way; they were made that way by God. But this thing here in his fancy coffin was made by people. By you and me and the lady next door, and that takes a lot of planning and costs a lot of money. Advertise me as the only piece of meat in the world that can talk through the back of its head, and if that doesn't pull them in, then do me as the last man on earth who joined the army because the army makes men. So rally around the flag boys—your flag, their flag, anybody's flag—because the flag needs soldiers and the army makes men.

As Joe realizes, his status as a spectacle is based on perception ("by you and me and the lady next door"). A product of his society, he too recognizes and accepts social standards for normality and thus accepts his own abnormality. This passage also links freakishness to the costs of war: "Rally around the flag . . . because the flag needs soldiers and the army makes men." For Joe, the army makes "freaks"—men who sacrifice themselves for a country that later abandons them.

Like the war fiction of Dos Passos, Cather, Hemingway, and Faulkner, *Johnny Got His Gun* uses freakishness as an image for injured veterans to suggest that healing is impeded by prejudices and fears about the disabled body. Even though the implied subject at the time

of this adaptation is Vietnam, its parallel to the 1920s—to the period
it was originally written about—suggests longstanding ambivalences
in America about confronting and dealing with the physical costs of
war. In one of his flashback sequences, Joe recalls a discussion with his
father about his father's prized fishing pole. Comparing his son to the
pole, the father tells him that one day he too will be "unusual"; he
will make a difference: "You're going to make the world safe for
democracy. . . . For democracy any man would give his only begotten
son." Joe responds, however, by saying: "I wouldn't."

Perhaps his answer best encapsulates the public response to World
War I after Armistice. Wounded soldiers were a painful reminder of
America's involvement in the war and increasing participation in the
world. By the 1920s, these sacrifices seemed too great, and for
America the easiest solution was to forget the cost by ignoring those
who had lost the most from it.

*   *   *

The Wicked Witch

Witches live in the city of angels.

*They don't hide in dark caves or ramshackle huts. Perhaps if Los
Angeles had misty swamps, such things would be different. But even without
cauldrons, broomsticks, and ancient spells, you can find one. Actually, a
witch lived around the corner from my parents' house. Not any witch—the
quintessential witch of Hollywood. She was the voice of the wicked witch in
Walt Disney's* Snow White, *but outside the world of animation, no one
ever saw her—well, no one saw more than her hand.*

*Every Halloween when my brother and I were still young enough to
become goblins, ghosts, or superheroes for the night, we visited our neighborhood witch. Her house stood on a street lined with palm trees and shiny
new cars. The yard looked like a Japanese garden. Wooden bridges arched
over small streams and exotic flowers. There was even a wishing well in the
middle of it all. But on those moonless Halloween nights, this place seemed
more like a jungle crawling with unseen dangers. While Mom waited by
the fence, my brother and I, after several deep breaths, scampered up to the
towering front door and knocked.*

*A few moments of uneasy silence passed. Then her witch-voice and
wicked laugh screeched through the intercom:*

"Trick or Treat?"

"Treat," we called back.

*A pale hand, with thick, knotted knuckles and purple veins, pushed
through the mail slot. Her fingers curled open to reveal two small candy
bars in her palm. With lightning speed, we grabbed them and ran. On the*

other side of the fence, we could breathe easily again—though we never wondered if it was safe to take candy from a witch.

For the next couple of days, my brother and I would periodically lie down on his bedroom floor and size up the loot: 27 Milky Way bars, 19 Sweet Tarts, red licorice, and countless other candies that seemed as if they would last forever but never made it through the week. Then one day the sound came. A startling nasal whine filled the quiet morning skies. Through the bedroom window, we could see a thin iron tower standing above the nearby shopping district. Behind it, the Hollywood sign sat cheerfully in the hills under a hazy, light-blue sky. Mom told us it was a World War II air-raid siren. It was November 2nd—All Souls Day.

Living in Los Angeles, we had seen enough movies to picture kamikaze pilots ruthlessly bombing our neighborhood, but for the first time this sound made it seem possible. For several years in the early eighties, this siren wailed on All Souls Day, reminding our parents of wars they knew, wars their parents knew, and wars they hoped we would never know. Specters of a past we didn't understand casting shadows of a cold war without troops and kamikaze pilots.

Eventually the siren stopped—the souls ceased crying—and my brother and I ate our candy.

*   *   *

Every year when I visit during the holidays and take long walks through my old neighborhood, I pass the witch's house. A new generation of children ride bikes and run through the streets.

In her front yard, the wishing well is still there, but the house has changed. The façade has been painted. A new black Honda Civic sits in the driveway while young people bustle in and out of the front door. Loud music pours out of a stereo in the open garage.

So after all these years, the wicked witch is truly dead—her absence filled by rock songs, brash energetic voices, and fashionable cars. The tower is also gone. The siren silenced and the iron dismantled. There are no symbols left.

A few kids suddenly whirl past me on skateboards, jump, and then lurch out into the street. With the slapping of their boards against the pavement, I turn toward them. They will never be mesmerized by her deformed hand or feel goose-bumps raised by her voice. They will never hear a morning siren weep for the day of souls. Perhaps, the city of angels needs it this way—to take down the past and replace it with something new. To forget, so those who live here can rest a little more quietly when spirits try to walk the earth.

Worn, Damaged Bodies in the Great Depression: FSA Photography and the Fiction of John Steinbeck, Tillie Olsen, and Nathanael West

The Lord Jesus Christ: Who shall change our vile body, that it may be fashioned like unto his glorious body according to the working whereby he is able even to subdue all things onto himself.

—*Philippians 3:21*

Let me first assert my firm belief that the only thing we have to fear is fear itself—nameless, unreasoning, unjustified terror which paralyzes needed efforts to convert retreat into advance.

—*Franklin D. Roosevelt*

After seven years of unprecedented prosperity, the stock market crashed in late October 1929, precipitating the collapse of America's unstable economic system and the pervasive instability of the world economy. As unemployment grew, so did the lines for soup kitchens. People frantically withdrew money from local banks, causing thousands to close within a few years. Overproduction was making consumer goods too expensive for the workers producing them, and inflated prices and farming speculation created a surplus of agricultural goods that could not be sold at home or abroad. In short, chaos ensued. Out of this dust and despair emerged a figure whose charisma, eloquence, courage—and disability—galvanized a destitute public. Paraplegic Franklin Delano Roosevelt, whose disabling bout with poliomyelitis occurred eleven years before his presidency in 1932, possessed an unflagging optimism and strength that the public needed.

Social responses to the disabled body were complicated by Roosevelt's illness and the Depression. Disability had typically been treated as something shameful, to be hidden away or stared at as a spectacle in freak shows. Throughout the national crisis of the 1930s, however, the public readily interpreted Roosevelt's battle with paralysis as ennobling. During the 1928 Democratic National Convention, he was described as "a figure tall and proud even in suffering; a face of classic profile; pale with years of struggle against paralysis; . . . most obviously a gentleman and a scholar. . . . This is a civilized man" ("Franklin" 12). This interpretation was possible, in part, because Roosevelt masked his disability, and his gubernatorial campaign marked the beginning of a largely tacit agreement with the public and press about his body: "No movies of me getting out of the machine, boys,"[1] Roosevelt requested. Remarkably, the press obliged. Within a few years, the public would need to see their leader as having the strength to lift America out of the Depression, and they could believe this more easily if Roosevelt appeared healthy. Though much was done to minimize his disability, the public also found comfort in it, believing that Roosevelt's experiences with paralysis enabled him to empathize with their suffering. As historian Michael Parrish explains, "his withered legs also gave the aristocratic Roosevelt something in common with those many Americans who saw themselves as outcast or marginal people because of physical handicaps, economic deprivation, or racial and religious prejudice" (278). Part of his appeal as a leader, in other words, came from his own experiences with physical hardships, and for millions of Americans his ability to overcome great adversity buttressed their own struggles.

Roosevelt's paralysis, like the damaged bodies of many working-class men and women during the Depression, changed the way people viewed disability. The physical and psychological costs of the Depression were often visible on the body through illness, starvation, and physical injuries, and this made the extraordinary body on display at freak shows an unwanted reminder of social hardship. This unsettling connection between spectator and spectacle certainly prevented freak shows from maintaining some of the differences necessary to reassure audiences about their own bodies. And much literature in the 1930s explored this fluidity between self and other by juxtaposing bodies damaged by the Depression with freakishness. In many ways, the fiction of John Steinbeck, Tillie Olsen (in her novel *Yonnondio: From the Thirties*), and Nathanael West presents individual hardships as leading not to success and security, but a kind of freakishness. Like Gregor in Franz Kafka's "The Metamorphosis," working-class families in the 1930s were waking up to find that they had become monsters—dehumanized by the economic and social crises of the Depression. Along with the Farm Security Administration (FSA) photography of Dorothea Lange and Margaret Bourke-White's collection *You Have Seen Their Faces* (1937), contemporary fiction uses images of worn, damaged bodies not only as metaphors for eroded optimism and opportunity during the Depression, but also to challenge the perception and construction of disability as freakish.

EMBODYING A NATION: FDR AND THE IMAGE OF DISABILITY

Controversy continues to surround the Franklin Delano Roosevelt Memorial in Washington DC (figure 3.1). Prior to its unveiling in 1997, the National Organization on Disability (NOD) and several other groups demanded that the memorial include a statue of Roosevelt in a wheelchair. But the FDR Commission refused, claiming that the monument should honor the former president's desire and assiduous attempts to hide his paralysis from the public. After intense pressure from disability activists, however, Congress subsequently

Figure 3.1 Franklin Delano Roosevelt Memorial, Washington DC (2000). Photograph by Daniel Kurtzman. Before the addition of the new room, the representations of Roosevelt in the memorial mask his disability. Here, most of his body—and thus his disability—is hidden under the cloak.

ordered an addition to the monument that would feature a sculpture of Roosevelt in his self-designed wheelchair.[2] Some see this decision as an attempt "to juggle history to fit our 1990s political correctness";[3] others believe it sends an important message to the forty-nine million Americans with disabilities. According to Jim Dickson, the community affairs director of the NOD, "we need this statue to tell all the children with disabilities and all their parents that anything is possible."[4] In effect, these debates are about representing the past—about accepting disability as a positive part of American history and identity. FDR was a symbol of modern American life for almost two decades, and his accomplishments and appeal as a leader cannot be understood apart from his disability.

For both political and metaphorical reasons, Roosevelt wanted to keep the extent of his disability hidden from the public—a sleight of hand that required a willing media and public. As biographer Hugh Gallagher (*FDR's Splendid Deception*) explains,

> the veil of silence about the extent of the President's handicap required the unspoken acquiescence of everyone—Roosevelt, the press, and the American people. . . . Crippled or not, the nation wanted this man, with all his magnificent qualities, as its leader. So an agreement was struck: the existence of FDR's handicap would simply be denied by all. The people would pretend that their leader was not crippled, and their leader would do all that he could not to let them see that he was. (95–96)

But this unspoken contract of silence did not mean that Roosevelt denied his disability. In fact, nothing could be farther from the truth. Roosevelt recognized his symbolic importance for the nation. He embodied American strength, ingenuity, and triumph over adversity, and though he felt the need to appear stronger than he was, his struggles against paralysis resonated with millions of Americans. Whether visible or not, disability was a vital part of this message.

Roosevelt certainly battled polio alongside his efforts to lift the country out of economic depression, holding annual birthday events that raised millions of dollars for polio research and treatment. Though these Presidential Balls began as benefits for his disabled resort in Warm Springs, Georgia, Roosevelt later established the National Foundation for Infantile Paralysis to manage this work.[5] These examples suggest that paralysis was an active part of his identity as president, and, as his grandson Christopher Roosevelt recently remarked, "the reality is that he spent every single day of his life in the White House utilizing a wheelchair, and when he did appear before groups of individuals that had faced adversity, he used his disability to inspire them."[6] In light of ongoing debates about the Roosevelt Memorial, therefore, reservations about depicting him as a paraplegic are a testament to FDR's skillful manipulation of his public image, for even at the turn of the century, few people realize the extent of his disability. But ultimately this ongoing battle to acknowledge the significance of disability in his life reflects an ongoing desire to render disability a private, not a social or political, issue in America.

The silence surrounding Roosevelt's damaged body can also provide a way of rethinking and reevaluating images of the body in Depression fiction and art. The public's relationship to Roosevelt's disability in the 1930s suggests fears about the disabled body and what it represented in Depression society. As suggested earlier, the damaged body was an unwanted reminder of physical hardships, suggesting dependence and immobility at a time when people needed to find work wherever possible. Since the able body was the only tool that many people had for rebuilding their lives, its loss through impairment and illness was devastating, unthinkable. And in contemporary literature, writers often measured disillusionment through images of deteriorating bodies and freakishness.

Damaged Bodies in Olsen and Steinbeck

Early in his study *The Great Depression: America in the 1930s*, T. H. Watkins tries to capture the psychological impact of unemployment through the image of a damaged body. Retelling a story recorded by sociologist Thomas Minehan in 1932, Watkins describes Blink, a young tramp who was "so named because he had lost an eye when a live cinder blew into his face while he was riding an open car on the Santa Fe railroad. 'A bloody socket forms a small and ever-weeping cave on the left side of his face,' Minehan wrote. 'Tears streak his cheek, furrowing the dirt and coal soot, leaving a strange moist scar alongside his nose' " (60). For both Minehan and Watkins, Blink represents the hundreds of thousands of transients who hopped trains in the United States during the Depression, but his deformity goes without comment in both accounts—as if the body speaks for itself. These authors use Blink's physical appearance and anonymity as convenient metaphors for the widespread destitution facing America, but his body is not like the bodies of most other transients. The Depression had marked him, making his scarred face a symbol for the physical costs of unemployment, isolation, and transience. In this context, the Depression becomes a crippling force in both physical and psychological terms.

Depression writers also tapped into the metaphoric power of figures like Blink to suggest that deformity had become a way of life. In this fiction, freak shows do not appear per se, but they are alluded to when characters feel estranged from their own bodies and communities. The fear underlying this freakishness—being labeled or perceived as a freak—is the loss of self. When personal and psychological sacrifices become unbearable, characters begin to see themselves and others as freakish, suggesting that the suffering caused by the Depression ultimately transformed people into abject spectacles. Tillie Olsen's *Yonnondio: From the Thirties*, for example, maps the gradual disillusionment of one family through physical disfigurement. This novel tells the story of the Holbrooks's struggles to find a better life as they move from a coal-mining town, to South Dakota farmlands, to a West Coast industrial city. As their living conditions worsen, however, their bodies become increasingly disabled. And Olsen specifically frames the novels with two disabled figures, Sheen McEvoy and Erina, to present deformity as a palpable terror for working-class families.

At the outset of the novel, Mazie Holbrook, the eldest daughter and protagonist, attributes physical deformity to the working conditions of this Wyoming mining town. She is acutely worried about her father Jim's safety and the physical impact of mining on his body: "And no more can you stand erect. You lose that heritage of man, too. You are brought now to fit earth's intestines, stoop like a hunchback underneath" (5). These abusive conditions not only transform the miners into beast-like hunchbacks, but they also foster self-destructive frustrations. Jim eventually becomes violent at home, alienating himself from his wife and children. Only after another miner, Sheen McEvoy, tries to kill Mazie does Jim recognize his own transformation and the dangers that this environment poses to his family. McEvoy, the most visibly deformed figure in the town, suffered severe burns in an explosion "that had blown his face off and taken his mind" (10). When he tries to "sacrifice" Mazie to the mine by throwing her down a shaft, she is confronted with his damaged body, seeing it as an image for the possible fate of her father (or any miner): "His laugh, horrible as the cracked thin laughter of old breastless women watching youth, sent the night unsteady. . . . The red mass of jelly that was his face was writhing, like a heart torn suddenly out of the breast, and he laughed and laughed. . . . His body was hot and putrid" (11). For Mazie, he becomes a terrifying vision of the physical and psychological costs of abusive working conditions, but in the early 1920s, when the opening of the novel takes place, her family can still leave this place and build a life elsewhere.

As the family moves west, clinging to an American Dream that promises opportunity and hope, Mazie can see growing disillusionment on their deteriorating bodies:

> A man's face, heavy and sullen (strange and bright the blue of his eyes) moves here awhile and is gone: *Jim*; a woman's face, thinning, skin tightening over the broad cheekbones, the great dark eyes down a terrace of sunken flesh, fading until the eyelids shut over forever: *Anna*. A child's thin face looks up a moment, wondering dazed eyes: *Mazie*; a boy's face, scowl over the mouth, eyes hurt with the hurt of not understanding, then insane with anger; *Will*. On this face, half baby's, half child's, the breath of fever glows, closing the sober eyes; a tiny boy running along croons a song that is silenced; a tiny girl's fists beat the air, stiffening, stiffened: *Ben, Jimmie, Baby Bess*. (48)

They have become bodies that share a paralyzing pain, and the above description catalogues the ways in which they no longer "see" each other (eyes gone, eyelids shut, dazed eyes, eyes hurt, sober eyes). Physical pain impedes their ability to connect, isolating them from each other and from any external community.

Mazie ultimately copes with this alienation and the brutal conditions of city life by living in her own fantasy world, but even these visions become deformed. "Suddenly, she would see before her a woman with her mother's face grown gaunter, holding a skeleton baby whose stomach was pushed out like a ball, and behind was a wall like darkness and misshapen furniture. These had no reality, only the reality of nightmares, for only there had she seen such grotesqueness and crooked vision" (59). Mazie tries to dismiss these disabling visions as unreal, in part, because she fears identifying with them. But her body betrays her: "The pain, the darkening pain on everything. And, it seemed to Mazie that her limbs were crooked in sleep and a nightmare sweat were on her, for only there had she seen such grotesqueness and crooked vision" (72–73). As she sees herself increasingly marked by hunger and exhaustion, she cannot relegate the horrors of starving children, dilapidated surroundings, and injured bodies to her nightmares.

She must eventually confront the personal and physical costs of the Depression when she befriends the paralyzed Erina, whom the neighborhood girls compare to a freak exhibit. Mazie is both compelled and repelled by Erina's "twisted jerking body and the fits who dragged away Mazie's findings from the dump and moaned Suffer little children the Bible says Children suffer suffer. Her body is becoming Erina's body; she *is* Erina, stump arm ending in a little knob, the spasm walk, the drool" (112). Initially, Mazie uses Erina's body to reinforce her sense of normality and to feel better about her own shameful poverty. Even Erina's painful awareness of other girls' name-calling does not prevent Mazie from seeing her as a spectacle: " 'Jinella!' said Erina. . . . 'When she sees me she says here comes freak show, stink show, Miss Sewer from shantylicetown.' Her face quivered" (120). Mazie, who is considered ugly by the other girls, wants to empathize with Erina, but cannot stop staring—"fascinatedly unable to look away from the running sores on her legs and her pitiful arm. . . . She wanted to cry but she did not know what about. She wanted to hear Erina talk—but not have to look at her" (118, 120). Hearing Erina blame God for her deformity and talk about her beatings at home for being "born a cripple and epileptic" (126) may individualize her, but Mazie does not want to see what Erina's body symbolizes. In effect, Erina's body becomes a metaphor for Mazie's own sense of freakishness, a sign of the deteriorating effects of poverty.

Similarly, John Steinbeck explores some of the symbolic meanings attached to disabled bodies in his California trilogy, *In Dubious Battle* (1936), *Of Mice and Men* (1937), and *The Grapes of Wrath* (1939). Throughout these novels, migrant workers depend on their ability to do physical labor for survival. Whether a man is good at lifting heavy loads, picking apples, or fixing cars, he typically measures self-worth in terms of usefulness and a strong body. His dreams for a better life cannot be achieved without it. But these bodies eventually begin to break down under the strain of poverty and abusive working conditions, making disability an unsettling image for the physical costs of the Depression. Like the neighborhood girls' response to Erina, many of the workers in Steinbeck's fiction turn disability into a freakish spectacle as a way of denying their own frailty and the damaging impact of poverty.

In Dubious Battle presents bodies that have been transformed into spectacles to criticize the abusive working conditions at the time. The novel tells the story of a strike by migrant farmers in California's apple country facilitated by two Communist Party members, Jim and Mac. After traveling to the Torgas Valley where the powerful Growers' Association has forced apple pickers to take a pay cut, they persuade workers to strike, set up camp, and prevent trainloads of scabs and the police from defusing their protest. Mac, the more experienced strategist, repeatedly uses disfigured bodies as tools to encourage violent resistance among the workers and to help them overcome fears about the ramifications of striking. As Mac places these bodies on display, the novel suggests that isolation—as opposed to communal action—is part of the deforming process, for without unity, no strike (for survival or justice) can be successful. As the strike fractures (with men either running off or disappearing one at a time), Mac uses Joy's deformities and death, Burke's shattered jaw, and Jim's faceless body to inspire solidarity.[7]

Joy's body is the first to be exploited as a spectacle. At the beginning of the novel, he has been marked by both his resistance to unfair working conditions and his participation in the Communist Party: "His face was wizened and battered, his nose crushed flat against his face; his heavy jaw sagged sideways. . . . His head twitched several times. . . . He caressed one hand with the other. Jim saw that they were crushed and scarred" (24). Throughout the text, Joy is defined solely by his body, and his injuries are attributed to the fact that he acts outside of Party goals: " 'Didn't I keep on calling 'em sons-of-bitches till they knocked me cold?' . . . 'And if you'd kept your trap shut, they wouldn't have knocked you cold' " (25). As Mac's response suggests, Joy's damaged body, which has been abused because of his inability to control and repress his anger, symbolizes the dangers of individual action. Because his acts are isolated and impulsive, they don't have the power to change anything. Mac, however, invests Joy's body with meaning during the first pivotal moment for the strikers (confronting a trainload of scabs). "The misshapen, gnome-like figure faced the doorway and the men. The arms waved jerkily" (168). His body has become monstrous and grotesque,[8] and Mac exploits this by subsequently presenting his deformity as an image of what could potentially happen to these workers without organized resistance.

Joy remains mostly a silent and marginal figure, never speaking when he gets off the train, and Steinbeck uses this silence to make Joy's body a symbol for the abuse and deterioration of all working-class bodies. When Joy arrives with the scabs, he is immediately shot and killed by a vigilante sniper: "Joy had stopped, his eyes wide. His mouth flew open and a jet of blood rolled down his chin, and down his shirt. His eyes ranged wildly over the crowd of men. He fell on his face and clawed outward with his fingers. The guards stared unbelievingly at the squirming figure on the ground" (168). The guards recognize the power of his body as a metaphor for injustice and cruelty, and Mac immediately uses Joy's murder to inspire a riot by staging his body to motivate action. First, he has a platform built to make the body visible to everyone in the camp, but in order to decide whether or not to put the corpse on display, he opens the coffin to inspect the body: "A stubble was growing on Joy's cheeks, looking very dark against the grew, waxy skin. His face was composed and rested. The gnawing bitterness was gone from it" (210). This callous act of evaluating Joy's value as spectacle seems reminiscent of something a freak show entrepreneur might do. But here it also emphasizes the metaphoric and performative power of the body. Ultimately, Mac decides to present only the coffin to the men because he believes the memory of his freakish, "gnome-like" body, not his life as a war veteran or Communist, will be more effective for inciting their anger. Joy represents the potential outcome that all these men may face if they accept wage cuts; these conditions, in other words, have the power to deform the men by tearing apart their only tools for survival—their bodies.

Two other bodies (Burke's and Jim's) get displayed in similar ways—as a tactic for sustaining communal, as opposed to individual, action against oppression. Like the marginalized bodies in *Of Mice and Men*, Steinbeck sees isolation as a deforming force, and he captures this through Burke's attempts to fragment the camp. London must fight Burke to retain his leadership, and Burke's damaged body frightens the men into allegiance. After London hits Burke's face with his fist, "his head hung over the edge of the platform, broken jaw torn sideways, shattered teeth hanging loosely between his lips. A thin stream of blood flowed from his mouth, beside his nose and eye, and disappeared into his hair" (320). Burke's body is draped on the platform, in effect taking the place of Joy's. While Joy was used to represent the danger of inaction (the reluctance of the men to organize and strike), Burke's damaged body warns of the dangers of sedition. In both cases, the bodies function performatively to suggest the need for community. Both are placed on a stage for the men to stare at. Unlike a freak exhibit, however, the intention in these examples is to collapse the distance between viewer and spectacle. Mac wants the men to see how close they are to becoming spectacles—casualties of the Depression—themselves.

The novel culminates with the display of Jim's faceless body on the same stage. When Mac and Jim are ambushed, Jim is shot in the face with a shotgun; immediately Mac decides to use Jim's body again to incite the men into violent action. "He leaned over and picked Jim up and slung him over his shoulder, like a sack; and the dripping head hung down behind. . . . He deposited the figure under the hand-rail and leaped to the stand. He dragged Jim across the boards and leaned him against the corner post, and steadied him when he slipped sideways" (349). Jim's facelessness symbolizes the dehumanizing impact of the abusive conditions facing the working class, and his presentation on stage reinforces Steinbeck's interest in reading bodies as indicators of both suffering and the need for action. The labor conditions depicted in this novel are isolating men from one another; they have merely become the bodies of anonymous workers who can be replaced. In other words, Steinbeck sees the loss of individual identity as an effect of the breakdown of families and communities during the Depression. In *Of Mice and Men*, the damaged body is perceived as a type of albatross that prevents men from achieving a better life. Early in this story about George and Lennie's dream to settle down and own a farm, Lennie's mental retardation is reinforced by descriptions of his ungainly body: "a huge man, shapeless of face, with large, pale eyes, with wide sloping shoulders; and he walked heavily, dragging his feet a little, the way a bear drags his paws . . . [He] drank with long gulps, snorting into the water like a horse" (2, 3). To some extent, his amorphous, animal-like form is a physical manifestation of the disability that George assiduously tries to hide. But Lennie's body is not so unusual that he cannot temporarily pass as normal. George repeatedly reminds him: " 'you jus' stand there and don't say nothing. If he finds out what a crazy bastard you are, we won't get no job, but if he sees ya work before he hears ya talk, we're set' " (6). Not only does his disability need to be masked in front of potential employers, but a story must also be created to disassociate his impairment from manual labor. George's claims that Lennie was "kicked in the head by a horse . . . [as] a kid" (25), therefore, are an attempt to prevent him from being seen as an adverse symbol for contemporary working conditions.

Unlike Lennie's disability, Crooks cannot hide his physical and racial differences from others: "His body was bent over to the left by his crooked spine, and his eyes lay deep in his head, and because of their depth seemed to glitter with intensity. His lean face was lined with deep black wrinkles, and he had thin, pain-tightened lips which were lighter than his face" (74). His damaged body also prevents him from leaving the farm and finding work elsewhere: "Being a stable buck and a cripple, he was more permanent than the other men" (73). When he learns that Lennie, George, and Candy are planning to buy a farm, however, he offers to work for free as a way of mitigating possible assumptions about his body: "I ain't so crippled I can't work like a son-of-a-bitch if I want to" (84). To counter the stigma of disability, in other words, he presents his body as capable and useful, but his hopes for inclusion are quickly undermined by the racism of Curley's wife: " 'Listen Nigger . . . You know what I can do to you if you open your trap?' . . . Crooks had reduced himself to nothing. There was no personality, no ego—nothing to arouse either like or dislike. He said, 'Yes, ma'am,' and his voice was toneless" (88–89). For Crooks, the will to work is not enough. His blackness irrevocably marks him for exclusion and reinforces his sense of physical disability: "Crooks sat on his bunk and looked at the door for a moment, and then he reached for the liniment bottle. He pulled out his shirt in back, poured a little liniment in his pink palm and, reaching around, he fell slowly to rubbing his back" (91). Confronted with insurmountable racial barriers, Crooks abandons his dream to share the farm. His body becomes an image both for his own debilitating isolation and for the impact of racism in America.

The reaction to Candy's dog also represents some of the social attitudes that construct disability as a spectacle and a burden: "A drag-footed sheepdog, gray of muzzle, and with pale, blind old eyes, . . . struggled lamely to the side of the room and lay down, grunting softly to himself and licking his grizzled, moth-eaten coat" (26). Carlson, one of the other workers on the Weed ranch, is repulsed by the deteriorating body of Candy's dog, saying first to Slim: "Whyn't you get Candy to shoot his old dog and give him one of the pups to raise up? I can smell that dog a mile away. Got no teeth, damn near blind, can't eat." (39). For the reader, his obsession with killing the dog seems inexplicable until he remarks: "I wisht somebody shoot me if I get old an' a cripple" (50). The men in this novel live in a world where survival is predicated on an able body, and Carlson fears the possibility of becoming "a cripple." By killing and burying the dog, however, he removes this symbol of physical decay. The tacit acceptance of these acts by the other men also suggests that they share his anxieties about disability, making Candy perceive his own body as a liability: "I ain't much good with on'y one hand. I lost my hand right here on this ranch. That's why they give me a job swampin'. An' they give me two hundred dollars, 'cause I los' my hand" (65). In relation to everyone else, Candy's damaged body makes him feel obsolete, so he dreams of living in a place that would allow him to be defined by something other than his body.[9]

In *The Grapes of Wrath* (1939), Steinbeck specifically evokes freak shows as an image for the physical and psychological deterioration of migrant workers during the Dust Bowl. A combination of drought and over-plowed farmlands in the Dakotas, Montana, western Kansas, eastern Colorado, northern Texas, and Oklahoma destroyed millions of acres of arable land by 1934, forcing thousands of families to flee their homes. Steinbeck's account of these massive migrations to California centers around the Joad family, whose encounters with freakish bodies reinforce their anxieties about displacement and disability. From the outset of the novel, Steinbeck describes bodies marked by illness, abnormal features, and disproportionate clothes. Tom Joad's "coat was too big, the trousers too short, for he was a tall man" (9), and his friend Casey, the former preacher, had "a long head, bony, tight of skin, and set on a neck as stingy and muscular as a celery stalk. His eyeballs were heavy and protruding; the lids stretched to cover them, and the lids were raw and red. . . . It was an abnormally high forehead, lined with delicate blue veins at the temples. Fully half of the face was above the eyes" (25–26). But only the disabled Noah, Tom's eldest brother, is described as physically abnormal: "Noah moved slowly, spoke seldom, and then so slowly that people who did not know him often thought him stupid. . . . Although an observer could not have told why, Noah left the impression of being misshapen, his head or his body or his legs or his mind; but no misshapen member could be recalled" (106). Noah's disability is perceived entirely in abstract, physical terms, suggesting underlying fears about the bodily dangers facing this community. Most of these men and women depend on their bodies as tools for survival, and this makes disability a threatening prospect. So even though Tom's and Casey's bodies may appear strange, their ability to work for the good of the family distinguishes them from Noah. As the bodies around them become increasingly damaged, however, the distinction between work-worn bodies and disabled bodies blurs, and both become freakish as families fragment and lose hope.

Specific references to carnivals and sideshows link freakishness with the social forces uprooting working-class communities: "Every night a world created, complete with furniture—friends made and enemies established; a world complete with braggarts and with cowards, with quiet men, with humble men, with kindly men. Every night relationships that make a world, established; and every morning the world torn down like a circus" (265). The itinerant nature of the circus makes it an effective metaphor for the dispossessed farmers who rush to California. They don't have a stable community, nor are they accepted anywhere else; this transitory, marginal status makes them akin to circus hands and freaks. Rose of Sharon, for example, feels ashamed after her husband Connie Rivers abandons her, worrying that this broken family will somehow transform her child into a freak: " 'What chance that baby got to get born right? I know—gonna be a freak—a freak! I never done no dancin. . . . I don't care. I'll have a freak!' " (537). Freakishness is not defined here by physical deformity, but by being an outcast—having a child without a father. Like a circus troupe, this community is tolerated only while they perform a service (picking fruit), and when the job is finished, they must pack up and move on.

An earlier reference to Jenny Lind[10] also suggests working-class fears about freakishness. Lind, a virtuoso opera singer in the nineteenth century, first toured the United States under the management of P. T. Barnum in 1850.[11] Though he hoped that this business arrangement would give him a new degree of respectability, Barnum never escaped his legacy as a freak show entrepreneur. Steinbeck taps into this famous link between Lind and Barnum through the character Sairy, whom the Joads befriend on their journey west. Sairy hopes to escape her physical deterioration and connection with freakishness through Lind:

> When I was a little girl I use' ta sing. Folks roun' about use' ta say I sung as nice as Jenny Lind. Folks use' ta come an' listen when I sung.
>
> An'—when they stood—an' me a-singin'; why, me an' them was together more'n you could ever know. I was thankful. . . . Thought maybe I'd sing in theaters, but I never done it. An' I'm glad. They wasn't nothin' got in between me an' them. An'—that's why I wanted you to pray. I wanted to feel that clostness, oncet more. It's the same thing, singin' an' prayin', jus' the same thing. (298)

Lind becomes an image for the ways that singing, like prayer, can transcend the body, and Sairy finds comfort in forms of expression that emphasize spirituality, not the physical. Ultimately, song/prayer enables her to "escape" her debilitating body—"a face wrinkled as a dried leaf and eyes that seemed to flame in her face, black eyes that seemed to look out of a well of horror. She was . . . a skeleton with wrinkled skin" (183). Poverty and illness have isolated her and her husband from others, and this final prayer, like her childhood songs, momentarily renews her sense of community with others.

In order not to see images of physical deterioration as a threat to his own well-being, Tom Joad rejects the notion of disability as limiting. After the family truck first breaks down, he describes the embittered junkyard attendant as "a specter of a man [who] came through the dark shed. Thin, dirty, oily skin tight against stringy muscles. One eye was gone, and the raw, uncovered socket squirmed with eye muscles when his good eye moved. His jeans and shirt were thick and shiny with old grease, and his hands cracked and lined and cut. His heavy, pouting underlip hung out sullenly" (242).[12] In a somewhat Barnumesque fashion, Tom tells him to reconstruct his image, explaining that self-pity is more of a problem than deformity:

> You got that eye wide open. An' ya dirty, ya stink. . . . Course ya can't
> get no woman with that empty eye flapping aroun. . . . Why, I knowed
> a one-legged whore one time. Think she was takin' two-bits in a alley?
> No, by God! She's getting' half a dollar extra. She says, "How many
> one-legged women you slep' with? None!" she says. "O.K.," she says.
> "You got somepin pretty special here, an' it's gonna cos' ya a half a
> buck extry." . . . An' I knowed a hump-back in—in a place I was. Make
> his whole livin' lettin' folks rub his hump for luck. Jesus Christ, an' all
> you got is one eye gone. . . . You ain't no cripple. (244–245).

This passage deconstructs assumptions about the damaged body and
argues that disability is about interpretation. In all of Tom's examples,
disability can be viewed either positively or negatively, and his distinction between damaged and "crippled" bodies—associating the later
with people who see themselves as victims—suggests that being a
"cripple" is a state of mind.

He constructs this view, in part, to diminish the danger of disability for himself and his family. Tom wants to believe that people are not
victims of their environment, and that an empowering concept of self
can overcome social hardships. But the novel suggests otherwise.
Even though Tom momentarily restores the attendant's sense of self-
worth, his damaged body undermines it: "The one-eyed man watched
them go, and then he went through the iron shed to his shack behind.
It was dark inside. He felt his way to the mattress on the floor, and he
stretched out and cried in his bed, and the cars whizzing by on
the highway only strengthened the walls of his loneliness" (247). The
attendant still blames his body for this isolation. For him, like so many
struggling to find work, the injured body persists as a frightening
image for personal loss and psychological suffering.

Images of freakishness haunt the injured and ill characters in both *Of
Mice and Men* and *The Grapes of Wrath*. As men struggle to find work,
they encounter disabled bodies that remind them of their own physical
limitations and mortality. One of the ways they disassociate themselves
from these images is by linking disability with freakishness. People who
do not (or cannot) mask their differences are perceived as spectacles,
imposing a new and less threatening metaphoric meaning to these bodies. At the same time, specific allusions to freak shows in *The Grapes of
Wrath* suggest that many of these people could not escape the debilitating isolation and deforming impact of the Depression. They were
victims of an environment that was tearing apart their bodies.

The Body in Black and White: The Photography of Dorothea Lange and Margaret Bourke-White

In 1936, John Steinbeck wrote a series of articles for the *San Francisco News* that was published two years later as the pamphlet "*Their Blood Is Strong*": *A Factual Story of the Migratory Agricultural Workers in California*. This collection includes anecdotes, statistics, and facts about the abysmal living conditions facing these workers, and it is accompanied by several photographs of Dorothea Lange. Both Lange and Steinbeck used their art to fight for political and social change, and not surprisingly, many similarities can be seen in their 1930s work.[13] Like Steinbeck's California novels, Lange's photography captured vivid, first-hand images of working-class life in Depression America, often presenting body parts as a reflection of individual hardships and strengths. While Lange's images of hands, feet, and backs suggest some of the ways that landowners and corporations were reducing individuals to tools for labor, these fragmented bodies also communicate strength and agency. They represent a universal determination in America to overcome adverse conditions—a characteristic that distinguishes her work from many contemporaries, such as Margaret Bourke-White, whose more contrived images attempt to evoke pity by equating disability and illness with victimization.

Born in Hoboken, New Jersey, Lange first studied photography with Clarence White at Columbia University from 1917 to 1918 and then moved to San Francisco to work as a photofinisher and freelance photographer for several years. In 1935, the Historical Section of the Farm Security Administration, an agency started under Franklin Roosevelt's New Deal, hired Lange, Arthur Rothstein, Walker Evans, Carl Mydans, and Ben Shahn to photograph every aspect of American rural life in the hopes of generating public and political support for social legislation. The government also wanted a visual record of the rehabilitation work being accomplished by New Deal programs.

Like most FSA photography, Lange's work does not show deformed and disabled bodies; instead, as James Guimond argues in *American Photography and the American Dream*, "FSA photographers seemed to have avoided photographing people who looked noticeably strange or grotesque. . . . The photographers' subjects may look very poor—the men wear overalls, the women sometimes wear sack dresses, and the children may be dirty and half-naked—but at least they look like human beings" (120). But this characteristic in Lange's work can also be attributed to her personal experiences with disability. At the age of seven, she suffered a bout with polio that permanently impaired her right leg from the knee down, a condition that had a vital impact on her art:

> No one who hasn't lived the life of a semi-cripple knows how much that means. I think it was perhaps the most important thing that happened to me. [It] formed me, guided me, instructed me, helped me, and humiliated me. All those things at once. I've never gotten over it and I am aware of the force and power of it.[14]

She also used her disability to win the trust and confidence of others. "Being disabled gave me an immense advantage," Lange once explained. "People are kinder to you."[15] Though she avoided photographing disabled people, her focus on the body suggests an interest in its metaphoric possibilities. In "Peculiar Grace: Dorothea Lange and the Testimony of the Body," Sally Stein argues that Lange's emphasis on bodies was a reaction to the ways that Roosevelt masked his disability: "[She viewed] the trials of the Great Depression as something registered and grappled with first and foremost in the body. . . . She resolutely looked to the body for a truth that [Roosevelt] was inclined to conceal, dress up, or belittle. . . . She looked down . . . offering the viewer the solace of a body disclosed and vulnerable" (73). Just as Lange's images tell the stories of human suffering, they also embody hopefulness. Refusing to let her own disability limit her, she could recognize the power, capability, and beauty of her subject's bodies. "Former Texas Tenant Farmers Displaced by Power Farming," for example, shows a row of five men without homes, presumably waiting for work (figure 3.2).[16] Their bodies are standing and poised for action, suggesting a certain confidence in their ability to work. Hope rests in their physical strength, and in this respect, I disagree with Stein's reading of the "grotesquely foreshortened shapes" in some of Lange's pictures (95). Lange was not trying to depict grotesque bodies at all; instead, she recognized the ways they were strong and weak at the same time.

The second image in *An American Exodus: A Record of Human Erosion* (1939), a book Dorothea Lange compiled with her husband Paul Taylor, reinforces this type of dual message through a body part. "Hoe Culture, Alabama, 1937"[17] shows dark, worn, strong hands holding the end of a hoe (figure 3.3). We don't see the blade or the field, just a man's forearms, fingers, tattered shirt, and patched pants, suggesting an individual fragmented by the relentless need to work. To some degree, these working conditions have taken away his

Figure 3.2 "Former Texas Tenant Farmers Displaced by Power Farming" (North Texas, June 1937). Photograph by Dorothea Lange. All of the men here appear ready and eager for work. Though no action is taking place, none of the poses suggest stasis. The man on the far left pushes out his abdomen. The two men to his left fidget with their hands impatiently. And the men with crossed arms standing on flagstones appear taller and out in front of the others. Courtesy of the Library of Congress. FSA-OWI Collection.

individuality, reducing him to a tool or part, but this reduction does not completely define him. His hands imply a whole that is strong and resilient, showing his body to be a site for physical strain and survival. Similarly, in "Alabama Plow Girl," the woman's body and plow seem indistinguishable (figure 3.4)—her angled feet and thin legs parallel the mechanism of the plow. She has become a tool, trying to cultivate a dry, barren land, but her ongoing effort implies a tremendous will. Other images (within and outside of this text) also feature able bodies trying to cope with the working conditions of the Depression. "Back, 1938" shows a man who has his hands clasped behind his head; the dirty fingernails, torn sleeve, and darkened wrists identify him as a field laborer who has worked recently and is now waiting.[18] In "Back, 1935," a man has placed his arms against his lower back while nervously clenching his fingers, and "Spring Plowing, Cauliflower Fields, Guadalupe, California, 1937" shows the strong naked back of a field laborer (figure 3.5). Lange remarkably captures a range of experiences

Figure 3.3 "Hoe Culture" (Alabama, June 1936/1937?). Photograph by Dorothea Lange. In this tightly cropped shot, the hoe seems to be an integral part of the man's body. The handle is both swallowed by his hands, and it extends from him like another limb. Courtesy of the Library of Congress. FSA-OWI Collection.

among the laboring class through these backs—waiting, anxiety, and work. These faceless bodies illustrate the type of synecdoche that Lange regularly uses to represent the American working class. As with so many of her photographs, she seems to privilege bodies over faces because body parts are more ambiguous; they can be both worn and strong at the same time.

While Lange and other FSA photographers avoided grotesque bodies, Margaret Bourke-White embraced them. After studying with Clarence White at Columbia University, she pursued photography as a full-time career. In 1935, she traveled to the South with her husband Erskine Caldwell to document the living conditions of tenant farmers. Their subsequent book *You Have Seen Their Faces* (1937) not only set the stage for documentary photography,[19] but its commercial success also made her one of the best-known photographers of the 1930s. This collection of images and essays presents the South as a "retarded

Figure 3.4   "Alabama Plow Girl" (July 1936/1937?). Photograph by Dorothea Lange. Lange highlights the symmetry between the girl's feet and the plow, suggesting the ways in which her body is also a tool. Courtesy of the Library of Congress. FSA-OWI Collection.

and thwarted civilization" (1) through images of flood victims, tenant farmers, sharecroppers, and chain gangs. Like Lange, Bourke-White suggests that bodies have become tools for labor, but her emphasis on deformity offers no hope for improvement. Tired, hungry, and wizened, these workers have become debilitated by labor, and after their bodies fail, America abandons them.

Unlike Lange's *An American Exodus*, the bodies in *You Have Seen Their Faces* become increasingly deformed as the text progresses. Without the captions, which detail the subject's location and affliction, the opening montage could represent any working-class individual or family in America—a happy boy messily eats a watermelon, a mother from Ocelot tenderly holds her sleeping baby, and a near-toothless grandmother grins. By the end of the collection, Bourke-White and Caldwell conclude with a series of deformed bodies that illustrate the devastating physical impact of rural living conditions in the South: an elderly couple with missing teeth and lined faces think the government needs to consider the poor; a mother with a pain-distorted face

Figure 3.5 "Spring Plowing" (Guadalupe California, 1937). Photograph by Dorothea Lange. Lange sets up a parallel between the back of this muscular worker and the horse. Notice how both are connected by rope. Courtesy of the Library of Congress. FSA-OWI Collection.

complains about a toothache; a woman with a huge growth on the left side of her face watches her half-naked grandson sitting on a porch; and a dirty mother with a misshapen face sits on top of her tattered bed holding her child. The bodies in these photographs mirror the tattered homes and cracked, barren fields depicted throughout the text.

But these images are highly sentimental, featuring the spectacle of these bodies as a means for soliciting empathy. In the final image mentioned above, the mother and child from Happy Hallow Georgia are presented like an exhibit, clearly posed as they look up and out at viewers. Her position suggests passivity, showing her seated and helplessly waiting. She seems to lack the agency of Lange's subjects. As James Guimond explains in *American Photography and the American Dream*, "[Bourke-White] . . . made extreme close-ups of many of her subjects, particularly when they had grotesque or misshapen features, to heighten the emotional impact of her images" (117). He goes on to criticize the ways that the book's captions could easily be used to reinforce attacks on the poor. Underneath the image of an Okefenokee woman, for example, the text reads: "Every month the relief office gives them four cans of beef, a can of dried peas and five dollars, and the old lady generally spends a dollar and a half of it for snuff." This statement suggests that the poor deserve to be poor. Like the image of the passive mother, this language implies that the poor were not always working to change their circumstances.

Both Lange and Bourke-White read the struggles of the Depression through bodies. For Bourke-White, many men and women had become grotesque spectacles—victims of abusive working conditions. Defined entirely by their environment, they are not seen as able to help themselves. For Lange, field laborers and sharecroppers often provided the necessary body parts to pick cotton or plow a field. But her photographs of bodies also suggest that these men and women defied such reductions. On some level, they possess the strength to endure, and this characteristic was visible on the body—a mark of pride and strength, not failure and deformity.

A DIFFERENT STAGE: NATHANAEL WEST AND URBAN AMERICA

The subject of Nathanael West's work is also 1930s America, but instead of focusing on the lagging hopes of dispossessed farmers and coal miners, he uses freak shows as an image for modern, urban malaise. *The Day of the Locust* (1939) specifically juxtaposes sideshow freaks with the display of beautiful bodies in Hollywood—bodies that seem freakish in their ability to remain untouched by the Depression. In this urban setting, the dignity of physical labor, which many of Steinbeck's characters and Lange's subjects find in farming, is absent; healthy bodies are destroyed by violence, alcohol, and lust. West ultimately uses freak shows to suggest that the film industry carries on the traditions of this nineteenth-century entertainment by reducing bodies to spectacles.[20]

In *The Day of the Locust*, strange, freakish bodies populate the city of Los Angeles. The central character Tod Hackett, who has recently started working as a set and costume designer in Los Angeles, immediately encounters the disgusting and truculent Abe Kusich—an obnoxious dwarf with a "slightly hydrocephalic head" (63). In a Barnumesque fashion, Kusich prints "Honest Abe" on his business cards, evoking the characteristics of Abraham Lincoln. The juxtaposition of the tall, slender Lincoln with the small Kusich is typical of freak show advertising and humor, but this Abe, who organizes cockfights and incites brawls, is neither honest, friendly, nor compassionate. He is a figure we dislike and turn from. West thus inverts the original strategy behind this type of freak show advertising, which alludes to an important figure in American history, to suggest that urban life has mutated the ideals embodied by Lincoln into something grotesque and violent.[21]

Through Harry Greener's association with traveling stage performances, West specifically implies that the film industry constructs bodies in a similar fashion. For over forty years, Harry worked as a clown in vaudeville and burlesque shows, and his most successful role was in an act that damaged his body on stage. As a review of his performance explains: "By the time [the Flying] Lings, four muscular Orientals, finish with him, however, he is plenty bedraggled. He is tattered and bloody" (77). This act used staged bodily injuries, in which Harry was kicked and thrown around, as its primary vehicle for humor: "When he stands up, the audience, which failed to laugh at his joke, laughs at his limp, so he continues lame for the rest of the act" (78). The reviewer, however, suggests that his pain would not be funny if it were real: "The pain that almost, not quite, thank God, crumples his stiff little figure would be unbearable if it were not obviously make-believe" (78). It is not simply the artifice of pain that appeals to these audiences—but the tension between illusion ("make-believe" pain) and reality (his "tattered and bloody" body). This play between reality and verisimilitude was an integral part of sideshow and vaudeville entertainment. And West presents Hollywood as offering a more glamorous and ornate version of such performances.[22]

Life in Los Angeles seems to transform people into grotesque caricatures of the roles they play in their professional lives. Faye Greener, who wants to be an actress, does limited work as an extra, and her roles have the effect of making her look ridiculous. Tod's one picture of her—"In it, she was wearing a harem costume, full Turkish trousers, breastplates and a monkey jacket" (67)—shows an outfit that was designed to make her alluring in a film; instead, it only incites his frustration and anger. Throughout the novel, Tod cannot distance his acquaintances from the roles they have assumed in Hollywood—Faye remains (and literally becomes) a prostitute whom he repeatedly thinks about raping; Earle is a cowboy both in actuality and in his job as a live advertisement for a saddlery store on Sunset; and "Honest" Abe exploits his image as a dwarf to advertise himself. Even though Abe is not the stereotypical dwarf from fables and fairy tales (which are continually being recycled by the film industry in works like Victor Fleming's *The Wizard of Oz* [1939]), Tod cannot see him in any other way: his hat "was the proper green color and had a high, conical crown. . . . Instead of shoes with long points and a leather apron, he wore a blue, double-breasted suit. . . . Instead of a crooked thorn stick, he carried a rolled copy of the *Daily Running Horse*" (64). Tod essentially imposes a new "costume" onto this stereotypical image of dwarfishness.

Not surprisingly, Tod's artwork presents Abe and the others as sideshow-like performers. "Despite the sincere indignation that Abe's grotesque depravity aroused in him, . . . the little man excited him and in that way made him feel certain of his need to paint" (62). Abe as well as Faye and Homer have become grotesque muses for his art, relentlessly "performing" a particular image of themselves in front of others throughout the novel: Homer the martyr, Faye the actress, Abe the jerk, and so on. And Tod's lithograph "The Dancers" depicts each of them gyrating violently onstage: ". . . The group of uneasy people who formed their audience remained the same. They stood staring at the performers in just the way that they stared at the masqueraders on Vine Street. It was their stare that drove Abe and the others to spin crazily and leap into the air with twisted backs like hooked trout" (62). The performative quality of their lives inspires them to maintain their staged behaviors: Faye enjoys having men stare at her body; Abe's truculence is affected ("Later, when he got to know him better, he discovered that Abe's pugnacity was often a joke." [66]); and Homer (a refugee from the Depression) performs a kind of sanctimonious martyrdom—at least Todd and Faye interpret his facial expressions and body language in this way. Ultimately, working in and around the film industry makes people unable to distinguish their identity from the images they have created and accepted for their bodies.[23]

Whether one was a film actor or field laborer, life in the 1930s changed the way people looked at damaged and disabled bodies. Just as many Americans needed Roosevelt to mask his disability, they also wanted to avoid reminders of damaged bodies in their everyday lives. Anxieties about disability were augmented by the fact that the working class relied on physical labor for survival. Like the families in Steinbeck's fiction and Lange's photography, injury and illness threatened one's ability to work, making the damaged body a metaphor for unbearable loss—a tangible sign for the eroding impact of unrelenting poverty, hunger, and unemployment. Contemporary literature often alluded to freak shows as a way of suggesting the physical and psychological devastation of the Depression. This presence of freakishness also captured underlying fears about the self. In a society where survival depended on healthy bodies and community, the freak was an image for those who had lost both. As Rose of Sharon fears, a fatherless child, her child, is "gonna be a freak—a freak!" Perhaps West's novel can be seen as the culmination of these darkest fears, for his characters have been completely deformed by their environment. They dream of achieving fame and fortune not through hard work, but through physical beauty and gambling. Los Angeles, a place without compassion and community, inevitably transforms those who live there into grotesque caricatures. Like changing attitudes about blackness and war-injured bodies in the 1920s, new associations with disability during the Depression contributed to the erosion of freak shows as a popular form of entertainment and helped forge stigmas that would persist into the twenty-first century.

* * *

Connecting Flights

As he squeezed into the seat next to mine, I could smell wine and peanuts on his breath.

It was ten o'clock in the morning.

I shifted in my seat, and he turned to me. Sweat was beading on his upper lip, and his dress shirt clung too tightly to his body. He smiled. It was one of those well-practiced smiles that salesmen and flight attendants wear like an old coat.

"I'm not much of an athlete," he said sarcastically and smiled.

That was the only encouragement he needed to keep talking—about his travels as a computer consultant, missing an early-morning flight, our current delay, and then, a woman.

"I remember waiting five hours for a connection in Dallas-Fortworth last Christmas. Most of the flights had been cancelled because of an ice storm, but mine was still scheduled to leave.

"We must have lost our minds. All the passengers rushed onto that plane, as if our will to go would somehow get us out of there. When I stepped in the cabin, there was still plenty of room, so I grabbed the first aisle seat I could find. Someone was sitting by the window. An empty seat separated us.

"She must have been in her early twenties. She was small with brown, shoulder-length hair. Nice face. I introduced myself.

"Don't misunderstand me. Usually, I'm not one of those plane-talkers—the kind that make safety-cards compelling reading and walk-mans one of the greatest invention in the twentieth century. But after the pilot announced a thirty-minute delay, which turned into two hours, I was more than eager to chat. We started with the usual—weather, horrendous in-flight movies, crying babies, delays. She was worried about missing her connecting flight to Australia once we reached Los Angeles, and the thought of another sixteen hours on a plane made me cringe.

"Then she pulled out a deck of cards.

'Want to play?' she asked.

'Sure.'

"She was a magician with the deck, shuffling the cards with the cut-throat grace of a Vegas dealer. Each finger seemed to move independently, and she had this sky-blue fingernail polish that sparkled. We used the tray table between us as a surface.

"Game after game, I learned about her trip to Australia, the parents who recently moved there, a brother who had suffered from a 'rage control problem' as a child, and her family's annual tradition of smoking pot on Christmas Eve. I couldn't imagine sharing a Yuletide joint with my parents—let alone telling all of this to a stranger—but I liked her honesty.

"During our third game of seven-card stud, she rang the call button and asked for a drink. The flight attendant brought us some wine, and my card-dealing neighbor took a bottle of pills from her purse.

"I drew two more cards.

"Only in an industry as masochistic as air travel would the simple act of doing one's job seem like a Christmas miracle, but that was what it felt like when we finally de-iced and took off. Our conversation continued, energized by the prospect of getting out of Dallas. We only stopped playing when the dry turkey sandwiches and additional bottles of white wine arrived.

"She told me about the old men who came into the bar where she works. 'You're as purdy as a speckled trout,' one of them told her.

'The fish?' I asked.

'He wasn't so bad, but I was still with my boyfriend then. We're not together now.'

"With our fourth glass of wine, I untied my shoes. She had turned off the overhead light, and I did the same. Then, something strange happened. We started holding hands.

"It was like something out of a nineteenth-century romance novel. Honestly, I'm not sure how it happened, but there we were—touching each other. She rubbed the top of my hand with her thumb, and I occasionally caressed her arm as we talked. We both forgot about the trout, the number of pills she had taken, and the long flight. We sat like this for almost an hour.

"There is tremendous freedom at 35,000 feet. With strangers, you can seem more daring, more charming, more open-minded than you actually are. I knew this was a momentary thing, but that's what made it so great, so easy.

"At one point, she noticed some constellations through the window. I leaned over until our cheeks touched and our noses were pressed against the plastic portal. I could smell her perfume. It reminded me of lilacs and orange blossoms.

"I turned to say something, maybe even to kiss her. That's when I saw the braces on both of her legs, the metal clamps surrounding each ankle. They must have run up both legs, hidden under the loose material of her

dress. I looked up at her face and realized she was watching me watching her. Something changed in her expression. Her smile flattened.

"Suddenly, the seatbelt warning rang, and the captain's voice blared through the intercom. It was time to land. The flight attendants were collecting empty cups and dirty napkins. My neighbor and I started to fasten our belts. She searched through her purse for her ticket, concerned once again about the connecting flight to Australia that should have left an hour ago. I closed my eyes. I didn't know what to say.

"We were silent during the landing, and I began thinking about our lives outside the 757, about the mystery of her body and her ex-boyfriend, about the pills in her purse. I began thinking about the fact that we would never see each other again. But, I didn't say anything. I just took her hand in mine one-last time as the wheels touched the ground and the lights went on.

"She let me hold it, but as soon as the plane began to roll along the bumpy surface of the runway, she let go.

'Do you need any help?' I cleared my throat. 'I can grab your bag or—'

'No, thanks.'

'Really, I don't mind. The international terminal is pretty far away, and I—'

'No. Thank you,' she said. 'I'm fine.'

"We sat in silence for another moment as the plane parked at the gate, and the lights came on in the cabin. The rest of the passengers sprung up from their seats, but she didn't move.

'Don't feel sorry for me.'

'Excuse me,' I asked.

'Don't feel sorry for me,' she said. 'Don't treat me like someone who needs to be taken care of.'

'I'm not,' I told her, but I knew I was lying.

"She started digging through the contents of her purse again.

"That was the last time I saw her face. She kept it down as I grabbed my overhead bag and started down the aisle. Even as I looked back one last time before leaving, I could only see the top of her head, the long chestnut hair that fell down both sides of her face.

"Inside the terminal, I found myself hurrying past the other passengers toward baggage claim. I wasn't trying to catch another flight or make an airport shuttle. My feet were just moving faster and faster. It was like body needed to run,

The man paused, or at least I thought he was pausing. Instead, he closed his eyes. The story was over. Our flight was already thousands of feet above the clouds, pushing through the cold, thin air. Fight attendants shuffled along the aisles. People shifted in their seats uncomfortably. I looked down at my legs.

I pictured the young woman of his story serving drinks in some Texas bar with hands as smooth and crystalline as ice. Customers laughing and flirting with her. Music blaring. Alcohol spilling on the bar. And a smoky *haze over everything in the room—every table and chair, every body and face.*

I just wondered how she felt about the men who came in week after week to look at the top half of her body, to drink, and to forget about their own problems.

The man sitting next to me began to snore. He slept through the rest of the flight, and I imagine that he dreamed of her hands.

* * *

"Some Unheard-of Thing": Freaks, Families, and Coming of Age in Carson McCullers and Truman Capote

Even though sexually ambiguous freaks played with questions of authenticity ("Is it a man or a woman?"), they never explicitly challenged accepted gender roles. Bearded ladies were presented as the embodiment of Victorian womanhood, dressing elegantly and claiming to be devoted wives (figure 4.1). Hermaphrodites, or half-and-halfs, appeared to be divided in two (with a male right side and a female left side), clearly displaying characteristics of each gender. Like most freak exhibits, bearded ladies and hermaphrodites reinforced the idea that difference was visible, that ambiguity could not go undetected.

As homosexuality became a more visible part of American culture in the early twentieth century, however, these bizarre images of "aberrant" sexuality became less popular. Many people started to see homosexuality as a threat to both the family and democracy, making these types of exhibits a dangerous validation of nonheterosexual desire and behavior. Even though these performers were being cast as freaks, they were undermining tenuous binaries between male and female, heterosexual and homosexual, and right and wrong. They were suggesting possibilities that mainstream America wanted to suppress.

Like wounded World War I veterans and injured workers during the Depression, queer bodies in the 1940s and 1950s suggested that something had gone wrong in America. Many assumed that homosexuality could be seen on the body, relying on "signs" such as male effeminacy, cross-dressing, and tomboyish behavior in women to reinforce prejudices. But just as African Americans could pass as whites, homosexuals could pass as heterosexuals. The body was rarely a reliable

Figure 4.1   Bearded lady (Madame Myers) and husband (1880). Photograph by Bogardus. As with the image of Charles Tripp (figure I.1), the carved furniture and formal dress reinforce both the freak's desire for the trappings of upper-class society and the visible ways in which s/he does not fit. Courtesy of the Becker Collection, Special Collections Research Center, Syracuse University Library.

indicator of sexual preference, and this ambiguity only intensified efforts to see same-sex desire as freakish. Freak shows may have occupied the margins of popular culture by the 1940s, but for more than a hundred years, this entertainment had given people a language for seemingly deviant behaviors and bodies. Sideshows, in other words, had helped make the idea of homosexuality and/or bisexuality freakish. Writers Carson McCullers and Truman Capote explore the implications of this connection by using the freak show as a central metaphor in their coming-of-age fiction. For adult characters, freaks represent the social marginalization that comes with a nonheterosexual lifestyle, but sexually conflicted teenagers feel an affinity for these performers. Freaks possess a freedom that they don't.

This chapter focuses on the ways that Carson McCullers's play *The Member of the Wedding* (1950) and Truman Capote's novel *Other Voices, Other Rooms* (1948) use freakishness to criticize homophobia. On the threshold of young adulthood and faced with making choices about their own sexual desires, protagonists Frankie Addams and Joel Knox associate their conflicted feelings about heterosexual norms with sexually ambiguous freaks. Scholarship has recently begun exploring the intersections between freak discourse and queer theory,[1] and I would like to apply these methodologies to McCullers's dramatic adaptation of *The Member of the Wedding*, arguing that significant differences between the play and the novel enhance her thematic use of freak shows. In many respects, the theater allows McCullers to stage a kind of freak show—putting the unusual bodies of her characters on display and challenging audiences (who are already participating in a viewer/performer dynamic) to reevaluate social attitudes about normality. Capote goes even farther than McCullers in presenting homosexuality as a viable option, and he makes a more explicit critique of marriage and compulsory heterosexuality. For both authors, freakishness not only reflects contemporary anxieties about sexuality and marriage, but it also provides a tool for condemning social imperatives that try to enforce desire. By linking freak shows with the repressive sexual climate in America, McCullers and Capote capture some of the more destructive aspects of intolerance and ultimately suggest the need for alternatives.

Homosexuality and the American Family

The freak is not merely the despised Other—but the Other without community, without family. Given the increased visibility of homosexuality by the late 1940s, sexually ambiguous freaks were an unwelcome, visible threat to compulsory heterosexuality. They challenged the idealized place of marriage and the family in American society, not by offering a more positive alternative (few would want to trade places with those onstage) but by suggesting other sexual possibilities.

Although poverty during the Great Depression brought many families together, increasing the number of two- and three-generation families under one roof,[2] this dependence on extended family, as well as unemployment, also emasculated many men. George Chauncey explains in *Gay New York: Gender, Urban Culture, and the Making of the Gay Male World, 1840–1940* that "as many men lost their jobs, their status as breadwinners, and their sense of mastery of their own futures, the central tenets undergirding their gender status were threatened. . . . [As a result] lesbians and gay men began to seem more dangerous in this context" (353–354). This threat inspired greater restrictions on public expressions of homosexuality; in New York, for example, the repeal of Prohibition became a tool for an increased surveillance of and crackdown on homosexuality.[3] These efforts to criminalize homosexuality—based on stereotypes about "gay" behavior—certainly reflected anxieties about sexual passing.[4] But this persecution would be stalled by the military and social demands of U.S. involvement in the war.

World War II destabilized the family—separating large numbers of men who either volunteered or were conscripted and women who worked as part of the labor force for the war effort: "It uprooted tens of millions of American men and women, many of them young, and deposited them in a variety of non-familial, often sex-segregated environments" (D'Emilio, *Sexual Politics*, 23). This separation of families not only gave women new levels of economic and social freedom, but same-sex working environments also opened up greater possibilities for expressing and experiencing homosexuality. "The unusual conditions of a mobilized society allowed homosexual desire to be expressed more easily in action. For many gay Americans, World War II created something of a nationwide coming out experience" (24). These increased opportunities to explore sexuality did not last long after the war, however, and a new, more insidious assault on homosexuality began.

The social instability of the war years sparked efforts to define stability and security more closely through the family. By the 1950s the heterosexual family—with its implicit whiteness and stabilized gender roles—embodied the financial and social successes of postwar America.[5] After Alfred Kinsey published his reports on American sexuality in 1948 and 1953, however, homosexuality was perceived as much more pervasive and dangerous than previously thought. Kinsey's best-selling study, which was based on individual interviews with over 10,000 white Americans, revealed data that "disputed the common assumption that all adults were permanently and exclusively either homosexual or heterosexual and revealed instead a fluidity that belied medical theories about fixed orientations" (D'Emilio, *Sexual Politics*, 35). Not surprisingly, this report intensified anti-homosexual sentiment and helped establish homophobia as part of McCarthy's anticommunist persecution in the 1950s. More specifically, since heterosexuality was integral to America's image of itself, marriage was viewed as evidence that one was not a communist: "Anticommunists linked deviant family or sexual behavior to sedition. The FBI and other government agencies instituted unprecedented state intrusion into private life under the guise of investigating subversives. . . . Some men and women entered loveless marriages in order to forestall attacks about real or suspected homosexuality or lesbianism" (Coontz 33). The family had become a much-needed symbol for political and social conformity.

This brief overview of anti-homosexual policy and social attitudes about the family in America can help us understand representations of "freakish" sexuality in popular forms of entertainment. Hollywood films in the 1930s, for example, followed a production code that prohibited references to homosexuality.[6] This type of injunction may also explain, in part, the popular decline of freak shows that featured sexually ambiguous exhibits. While Hollywood adapted to the social pressures of homophobia, freak shows continued to play with gender boundaries, showcasing bearded ladies and hermaphrodites who held a traditional place in these troupes. The incompatibility of these exhibits with contemporary sentiment (particularly attitudes that equated homosexuality with effeminate behavior and lesbianism with masculine behavior) made these performers particularly off putting— giving many people another reason to stay away from the sideshow.

MEMBERS OF THE FREAK SHOW IN CARSON MCCULLERS

By 1950 Carson McCullers successfully adapted her 1946 novel, *The Member of the Wedding*, for the theater.[7] An immensely popular and critical success, this play opened in New York on January 5, 1950 and closed the following year after 501 performances. In addition to grossing $1,112,000, *The Member of the Wedding* was also awarded the New York Drama Critic's Award and the Theater Club's gold medal for best American play that year, and many contemporary critics believed that McCullers would have won the Pulitzer if the work had not been an adaptation.[8] I want to argue that in adapting this work McCullers made significant changes between novel and play to capitalize on the ways a staged production could enact the dynamics of a freak show. This is not entirely surprising given McCullers's fascination with freak shows as a young girl:

> "Let's skip the cotton candy and hot dogs and save our dimes for the Rubber man and all the freak shows this year. The Pin Head, the Cigarette Man, the Lady with the Lizard Skin."... Lula Carson Smith viewed once more with terror and fascination the midway freaks. . . . The child craved eye contact with these strange withdrawn creatures who sometimes stared at her sullenly or smiled and crooked a finger beckoningly. Yet she dared only to steal oblique glances, fearful of a mesmeric union. (Carr, *The Lonely Hunter*, 1)

Many years later McCullers would revisit these images in her writing, and her play, *The Member of the Wedding*, would specifically use freak shows to present the nuclear family as a questionable antidote for unconventional behaviors and desires.

The marriage at the heart of *The Member of the Wedding* both defines and shapes twelve-year-old Frankie Addams' struggles to reconcile her conflicted sexual desires with her idealized notions about the family. Impatient with long summer afternoons filled with card games in the dilapidated kitchen of her father's house, Frankie wants to escape the smallness of this world. In Act I, she meets Jarvis's fiancée, Janice, and decides to run away with them after the wedding: "I know that the bride and my brother are the 'we' of me. So I'm going with them, joining with the wedding" (52). Her hopes that their marriage will somehow give her a sense of belonging begin to break down in Act II. Before the wedding, Frankie gets an orange dress for the ceremony and begins telling people in the town that she will be leaving—as if leaving will provide an escape from her tall, lanky body (which Janice assures her is not too big). Frankie's behavior worries Berenice, the family cook and surrogate mother-figure who decides to tell Frankie about her own obsession with marriage. After a happy, five-year marriage to Ludie Freeman, whose most distinguishing physical characteristic was a mangled and grotesque thumb, she married a series of abusive and unreliable men (Jamie Beale and Henry Johnson) in an attempt to recapture her first love[9]: "What I did was marry off little pieces of Ludie whenever I come across them. It was just my misfortune they all turned out to be the wrong pieces. My intention was to repeat me and Ludie" (79). Berenice uses this story to warn Frankie against doing the same thing with marriage—not to fall in love with an ideal or "some unheard-of thing" (80). Because Frankie feels alienated from her family (her mother died during child-birth, her father is aloof and mostly absent, and her brother has been stationed in Alaska for the war), she fantasizes about the possibilities that marriage offers for companionship, beauty, stability, and family.

Act III begins when the wedding has just finished, and Frankie tries to leave with her brother and sister-in-law. When the couple refuse to let her come, she storms out of the house with a suitcase and her father's pistol. She gets only as far as the alley behind her father's store (where she briefly contemplates suicide) before returning home. Four months pass between Scenes Two and Three. John Henry has died from spinal meningitis; Honey, Berenice's foster-brother, has hanged himself after his arrest; Mr. Addams and Frankie are moving to the suburbs to live with John Henry's parents; and Frankie has become friends with Mary Littlejohn. This relationship, like her friendship with Evelyn Owen before the play begins, temporarily assuages her desire to find belonging through marriage.

In many ways, the staging of the play enacts a type of sanitized freak show—one in which the audience is insulated from the anxiety of looking. Since theatergoers remain in the dark, a safe distance from the gaze of the performer, the drama effectively removes one of the increasingly unpopular dimensions of freak shows—the reciprocated gaze. The fixed setting, the Addams' "ugly" kitchen, also enhances the freakishness of the characters by preventing the audience from seeing an actual freak show; they only hear descriptions of one from Frankie. As a result, the audience is invited to see those on stage as standing in for the freaks who are repeatedly invoked through language. Just as freak shows relied on the juxtaposition of extremes to construct a per-former as freakish, *The Member of the Wedding* relies on this conven-tion to make the bodies of Frankie, Berenice, and John Henry seem more extraordinary.

When juxtaposed with John Henry's smallness (Frankie literally calls him a "midget") and Berenice's stout black body, Frankie's height, pale-white skin, boyish clothes, and short haircut accentuate her physical freakishness—to the point where she fears becoming a freak: "I am so worried about being so tall. . . . If I keep on growing like this until I'm twenty-one, I figure I will be nearly ten feet tall. . . . Do you think I will grow into a freak?" (28, 30). There is also a performative dimension to Frankie's freakishness. She makes her body appear disproportional by twisting and wrapping her legs around a small kitchen chair to get comfortable, and she acts out her frustration through verbal and physical abuse, yelling at John Henry and Berenice, and "[banging] her forehead on the table. Her fists are clenched and she is sobbing" (40). Her explosive behavior, however, is not over; she immediately threatens to throw a knife in front of Berenice: *"Frankie aims the knife carefully at the closed door to the bedroom and throws it. The knife does not stick into the wall"* (41). Like a failed magic trick, the knife falls to the ground; it is no longer a threatening symbol, nor an impressive act.

The spectacle preceding this moment taps into several traditional freak show conventions as well. After rummaging through Berenice's purse early in Act I, John Henry pulls out her blue glass eye, and she proceeds to place it into her socket—a scene that is absent from the novel (24–25). The stage directions indicate that: "[*Berenice takes off her patch, turns away, and inserts the glass eye*]" (25). Removing the patch draws attention to her damaged body, and turning away to insert it plays with the audience's curiosity to "see" more. Given McCullers's fascination with freak shows, this stage direction is more than a practical solution for the actor playing Berenice, who could have simply worn a patch throughout the play. Instead, McCullers uses the type of game-playing typical of freak shows to generate dramatic tension and momentum and, most likely, to allay criticisms that her novel lacked "a sense of drama."[10] This scene with Berenice's eye is both disturbing and compelling to watch, and like most freak show acts, it invites questions that remain unanswered—most obviously, how did she lose her eye? Furthermore, its blue color, which Frankie feels is out of place on an African-American woman, alludes to the types of ploys that sideshows used to exoticize race.[11]

McCullers's theatrical version does not engage with questions of race as convincingly as does her novel;[12] instead, it primarily focuses on questions of belonging and alienation as they relate to family and sexuality. The strange ensemble on stage—the tall, boyish Frankie, cousin John Henry's sickly small body, and the disabled Berenice—represent a kind of anti-American family (one without the white parents and siblings). Together, these unusual bodies and their abusive interactions suggest that Frankie's confusion stems from not having a more traditional home. She is preoccupied, for example, with her father's aloofness and her brother's disinterest in her: "I wrote you so many letters, Jarvis, and you never, never would answer me" (5). The image of this trio clearly contrasts Jarvis's marriage as well, which symbolizes all of the beauty and potential of the nuclear family to be: "They are so beautiful. . . . They were the prettiest people I ever saw" (12, 13).

Frankie's body and age (being two years younger than the local girls who don't select her as a member of their club) exclude her from feeling accepted by those around her, and she worries that her unusual body will also prevent her from ever getting married—from achieving the social ideal ("some unheard-of thing") of the American family. Berenice explains to her that "the whole idea of a club is that there are members who are included and the non-members who are not included" (22)—a truth that alludes to her own social standing as an African-American woman. The play makes it clear that those who belong are white and heterosexual. And marriage can provide a greater degree of social acceptance for those who fit into these categories.

Because Berenice equates marriage with comfort and sexual certainty, she uses sexually ambiguous figures, such as Lily Mae Jenkins, a local man who "turned into a girl" because he fell in love with another man (57), to reinforce heterosexual imperatives for Frankie. Interestingly, Berenice's racial marginalization has not made her bitter and resentful like her foster-brother Honey. Her own disenfranchisement as an African American only seems to heighten her desire to protect Frankie from being stigmatized for being different. As a white girl, Frankie has access to freedom and power that Berenice and Honey do not, but Berenice warns her that rejecting heterosexuality will jeopardize the social acceptance that marriage and family offer.[13]

Several scholars have recently argued that McCullers internalized contemporary attitudes about sexual inversion, believing herself to be a "sexual invert."[14] Along the same lines, we can interpret her remarriage to ex-husband James Reeves McCullers in 1945 as another example of her acceptance of certain social norms about marriage. Consider the autobiographical elements of her only other play, *The Square Root of Wonderful* (1957), in which the characters continually struggle (but fail) to achieve the ideal American family. The protagonist, Mollie Lovejoy, is torn between her love for her ex-husband Phillip (whom she has married twice) and her new tenant John Tucker. Despite her painful past with Phillip and his suicide in Act III, she associates "family" with happiness and love, as do her son and John, who declares: "I am going to marry your mother! . . . And I am going to build that house, I told you about" (156). The house, which they dream about throughout the play, symbolizes their ongoing quest to achieve some version of the nuclear family. This powerful drive for marriage and family also appears in *The Member of the Wedding* as a force that restricts the possibilities of homosexual and bisexual desire. Still naive about sex, Frankie links her romanticized notion of marriage to a sense of belonging, not sexual behavior; as a matter of fact, the idea of sex frightens and repulses her: "[Other girls] were telling nasty lies about married people" (22). She also reacts vehemently when Berenice suggests that she "make out" with a boy:

> BERENICE: Yep, I have come to the conclusion that what you ought to be thinking about is a beau. A nice little white beau.
> FRANKIE: I don't want any beau. What would I do with one? . . .
> BERENICE: . . . How 'bout that little old Barney next door?
> FRANKIE: Barney MacKean! That nasty Barney!
> BERENICE: Certainly! You could make out with him until somebody better comes along. He would do. . . .
> FRANKIE: Yonder's Barney now with Helen Fletcher. They are going to the alley behind the Wests' garage. They do something bad back there. I don't know what it is.
> BERENICE: If you don't know what it is, how do you know it is bad?
> FRANKIE: I just know it. I think maybe they look at each other and peepee or something. They don't let anybody watch them.
> (58–59)

For Berenice, making out with a boy is not about love and romance but social acceptance, and she believes that Frankie's aversion to heterosexual behavior can be overcome by going through the motions with Barney.

Torn between her refusal to accept this option and her hope that marriage will provide some sense of belonging, however, Frankie recalls her feelings of alienation at freak shows. Though she fears heterosexual behavior, she is more frightened of the possibility that her body may exclude her from the type of community and sense of belonging embodied in marriage: "I doubt if they ever get married or go to a wedding. Those freaks. . . . at the fair" (28–29); "Do you think I will grow into a freak?" (30). Though the novel further magnifies Frankie's isolation by revealing her odd sense of community with these freaks—"She was afraid of all the Freaks, for it seemed to her that they had looked at her in a secret way and tried to connect their eyes with hers, as though to say: we know you" (17)—both Frankie *and* Berenice share their experiences with freak shows in the play. While the novel has Frankie describe the hermaphrodite, the play relies on Berenice to interpret sexual ambiguity. This narrative shift situates Berenice as the authority figure on sexuality—a guardian of heterosexual imperatives who teaches her "children" how to respond to such images: "That little old squeezed-looking midget in them little trick evening clothes. And that giant with the hang-jaw face and them huge loose hands. And that morphidite! Half man-half woman. With that tiger skin on one side and that spangled skirt on the other" (29). Though Berenice says that the freaks "give [her] the creeps" (29), she never points to the act of looking as a problem; it is only the image of the hermaphrodite that disturbs her. Berenice's response, therefore, reinforces the link between freakishness and nonheterosexual expression.

Despite this adult-sanctioned perspective on sexuality, Frankie's relationships with girls are her only source of contentment. The play is framed by her friendships with two girls—Evelyn Owen (32), who has moved away before the play begins, and Mary Littlejohn, whom she befriends at the end of the narrative. Mary's clear heterosexual desires do not offer Frankie much opportunity to experience alternate forms of sexual expression. Instead, she imitates Mary's desires in contradiction to her previous attitudes about Barney. Unlike her earlier reference to him as "that nasty Barney!" (58), she tells Berenice in Act III that "Barney puts me in mind of a Greek god. . . . Mary remarked that Barney reminded her of a Greek god" (116). Though many critics have seen hope in Frankie's friendship at the end of the story, little has changed for her. The only townspeople who have broken with heterosexual norms have been marginalized; they are made invisible both on stage and outside the context of the play. And even though Frankie is shocked that she has never seen Lily Mae, Berenice isn't. She understands that the town has kept her hidden from the children. Like the sexual exhibits of freak shows, the implications of her visibility are too dangerous for pubescent children on the verge of making choices about their own sexual identity: Normative behavior and desires were at stake; the American family was at stake.[15]

OTHER CHOICES: TRUMAN CAPOTE AND SAME-SEX DESIRE

While Frankie still clings to marriage as an ideal, as something to aspire to, Joel in Truman Capote's *Other Voices, Other Rooms* has no models for heterosexual happiness. Families don't seem to work—parents separate, couples stay in loveless marriages, and children want to run away. But the failure of marriage does not make his burgeoning homosexuality an unproblematic choice. Even though Capote presents same-sex desire as the "right" lifestyle for some (an option McCullers remains equivocal about), a powerful nostalgia for the traditional family still grips the narrator, making homosexuality a problematic choice. The strange setting of the novel—populated by unusual bodies and the deformed casualties of heterosexual love—suggests that homosexuality is only possible in such a place. In this way, Capote's narrative struggles to balance its critique of heterosexual imperatives and its ambivalence about the place of homosexuality in contemporary America.

By his teenage years, Truman Capote claims to have accepted his sexuality: "I always had a marked homosexual preference, and I never had any guilt about it at all. As time goes on, you finally settle down on one side or another, homosexual or heterosexual. And I was homosexual" (qtd. in Clarke 63). Homosexuality, however, does not explicitly appear in his later fiction. As Peter Christensen argues, works like *In Cold Blood* and "A Diamond Guitar" do not present homosexuality as a positive alternative: "Capote is unable at a later date to imagine a story in which the love of two adult men would lead to mutual salvation or even help" (63). He may have been untroubled by his own sexuality, but his fiction suggests that he was ambivalent about its place in art. Though recent queer scholarship reads the role of homosexuality in *Other Voices, Other Rooms* positively,[16] the central metaphor of freakishness captures some of these tensions about homosexuality in this early work,[17] linking them to the narrator's idealizations about family and masculinity.

Other Voices, Other Rooms is the coming-of-age story of thirteen-year-old Joel Harrison Knox. After his mother dies, Joel comes to live with his estranged father at his stepmother's dilapidated mansion in Skully's Landing. After passing through Noon City, a town filled with an array of deformed people, he finally arrives and meets his stepmother Amy and effeminate cousin Randolph. Like Frankie, Joel wants to belong and to feel loved. But ultimately it is his encounter with freakishness that helps him accept his own sexual desires. The novel culminates in his decision to be with the reclusive, gay Randolph, and the ongoing association between homosexuality and freak shows in the text presents queer desire as a distorted form of the new American family.

Capote frames the novel with two freak shows that feature both extraordinary bodies and sexually ambiguous figures, reinforcing the narrator's initial interpretation of homosexuality as freakish. By seeing Noon City and Skully's Landing in terms of a freak show, Joel mimics mainstream social attitudes about homosexuality and hints at his own struggles with desire. When he first meets Idabel Thompkins, for example, she is described as a wild, feisty troublemaker whose tomboyish behavior makes her a freak in the eyes of the town: "Well, it wasn't no revelation to me cause I always knew she was a freak, no ma'am, never saw that Idabel Thompkins in a dress yet" (21). Not only does her resistance to social expectations about female identity make her freakish, but her body is also somewhat grotesque. In an attempt to ridicule her, Florabel, her twin sister, tells Joel that "her thumbnail won't grow the least bit: it's all lumpy and black. . . . Now me, I couldn't stand to have such a nasty old . . . show him your hand, sister. . . . It don't pay to treat Idabel like she was a human being" (34). At first Joel sees Idabel and the other people in the community as strange because he wants to feel normal—to "go away to a school where everybody was like everybody else" (110–111). Still afraid of his homosexuality, he worries that deviating from the norm will make him freakish like those who live around his father's house. He later uses his relationship with Idabel as a testing ground for his own masculinity and conflicted desires. When he tries to kiss her, she wrestles him to the ground, and on their journey to Cloud City, she must kill the snake that terrifies him. Like Frankie Addams, Joel fails to fit into expected gender roles and desires. He is only going through the motions.

Idabel's masculine traits make her a type of freak, explicitly linking her with other sexually ambiguous figures in the text. Zoo, the grand-daughter of Jesus Fever who works at the Sansom mansion, tells him the story of Randolph's mother Angela Lee: "Honey, a mighty peculiar thing happened to that old lady, happen just before she die: she grew a beard; it just commence pouring out her face, real sure enough hair; a yeller color, it was, and strong as wire. Me, I used to shave her, and her paralyzed from head to toe, her skin like a dead man's" (124). Her inadvertent transformation into a bearded lady becomes an image for aberrant sexuality, suggesting that Randolph's flamboyant homosexuality was somehow being manifested on his mother's aging body. Randolph is not merely gay; he cross-dresses, becoming a "queer lady" who gazes out an upstairs window and wears hair like "a wig of a character from history: a towering pale pompadour with fat dribbling curls" (67). His homosexuality, like Idabel's, is visible on the body, which makes it less threatening to people like the shopkeeper Miss Roberta, the town barber, and society more broadly. Being able to "see" homosexuality leaves the categories of normal/abnormal and self/freak intact, enabling the townspeople to see their own damaged bodies (like the "bandy-legged, little one-armed man glowering at him from the doorway of a barbershop" and Miss Roberta's dark-fuzzy arms, hairy wart, dirty fingernails, and enormous breasts) as normal.[18]

In order to perceive himself as normal (i.e., heterosexual), Joel sees Skully's Landing and its inhabitants as a type of carnival sideshow. Amy and Randolph, for example, "were fused like Siamese twins: they seemed a kind of freak animal, half-man half-woman" (120). And Jesus Fever has a face "like a withered apple, and almost destroyed; his polished forehead shone as though a purple light gleamed under the skin; his sickle-curved posture made him look as though his back were broken: a sad little brokeback dwarf crippled with age" (29). As a matter of fact, the bodies of almost every character in the novel are marked and deformed in some way—with one notable exception, Joel. Throughout this *bildungsroman*, Joel actually sees his own body transform into something freakish. When he first looks into the mirrors at his father's house, he sees a distorted version of himself: "The stairs sloped down to the circular chamber he remembered from the night, and here a full-length mirror caught his reflection bluely; it was like the comedy mirrors in carnival houses; he swayed shapelessly in its distorted depth" (50). Later, before Joel sees Randolph dressed as a woman for the first time, his reflected image is linked with sexual identity; at this moment, he is frightened, as if facing something he is not yet ready to see:

> He swished the lavender curtains apart, and moved into the bleak light filling the barren, polished chamber towards his image floating on the watery-surfaced looking glass; his formless reflected face was wide-lipped and one-eyed, as if it were a heat-softened wax effigy; the lips were a gauzy line, the eyes a glaring bubble. "Miss Amy . . . anybody" (63–64).

Still wanting to define himself as normal in terms of heterosexual masculinity, Joel realizes that this freakish reflection and Randolph's effeminacy challenge his notions of gender identity and sexuality.

Anxiously waiting to see his father, Joel hopes he will be a model for heterosexual manhood, fantasizing about rebuilding some sort of "normal" family with him. But he fears that his own effeminate body ("He was too pretty, too delicate and fair-skinned; . . . and a girlish tenderness softened his eyes" [4]) will disappoint his father: "And his father thought: that runt is an imposter; my son would be taller and stronger and handsomer and smarter-looking. Suppose he'd told Miss Amy: give the little faker something to eat and send him on his way" (51–52). He assumes his father will be a strong, manly figure; instead, Ed Sansom is paralyzed and completely dependent on others: "The eyes were a teary grey; they watched Joel with a kind of dumb glitter, and soon, as if to acknowledge him, they closed in a solemn double wink, and turned . . . so that he saw them only as part of a head, a shaved head lying with invalid looseness on unsanitary pillows" (121). Sansom had already failed as a father, abandoning Joel and his mother thirteen years earlier, and now he fails as a model for masculinity. "If only he'd never seen Mr. Sansom! Then he could have gone on pic-turing him as looking this and that wonderful way, as talking in a kind of strong voice, as being really his father. Certainly this Mr. Sansom was not his father" (171). Just as the town associates homosexuality with freakishness, Joel equates disability with weakness, femininity, and even his own conflicted sexual desires. No longer able to see his father as a model for what a man "should" be, he rejects any familial connection with him.

Though this failed image of masculinity brings Joel closer to accepting his own homosexuality, it is ultimately Randolph's and Idabel's ability to find love by rejecting traditional heterosexual rela-tionships that offers Joel another model for happiness. Before meeting Pepe, Randolph's marriage to Dolores was strained by her repeated fantasies about killing him. She keeps a dream book/diary, in which she writes about Randolph "fleeing before her, or hiding in the shadow," and "she'd murdered in Madrid a lover she called L., and [Randolph] knew . . . that when she found R. . . . she would kill him, too" (144). Ironically, her affair with a bullfighter, Pepe Alvarez, kills their marriage, for it awakens Randolph's homosexuality. Randolph's passionate sexual relationship with Pepe is his first experience with true love. As he recalls to Joel, "Strange how long it takes us to discover ourselves; . . . The brain may take advice, but not the heart, and love, having no geography, knows no boundaries: weight and sink it deep, no matter, it will rise and find the surface: and why not? Any love is natural and beautiful that lies within a person's nature; only hypocrites would hold a man responsible for what he loves" (147). Randolph and Dolores' relationship with Pepe forges a new family— "always now they were together, Dolores, Pepe, Ed, and I. . . . Grotesque quadruplets" (149). This grotesque family doesn't last either—Pepe and Dolores run off together, Randolph shoots Ed in a delusional rage, and his cousin Amy—to feel needed—marries the invalid Ed. In the end, Randolph is left sending letters for Pepe around the world, care of the postmaster: "Oh, I know that I will never have an answer. But it gives me something to believe in. And that is peace" (154).[19] Peace, however, is what Randolph hopes to offer Joel, giving him a model for accepting his own sexuality regardless of what others say. But Randolph's effeminacy and reclusiveness continue to make Joel uncomfortable, and it is only through his relationship to Idabel that he sees same-sex desire as a viable option for himself.

Idabel not only rejects stereotypically feminine behavior, but she also finds happiness in her infatuation for another woman, a sideshow performer. Frustrated with the ways the town labels her a freak, Idabel convinces Joel to run away with the traveling circus, and there she meets Miss Wisteria: "At the 10 cents Tent, they saw [her.] . . . They did not quite believe she was a midget, though Miss Wisteria herself claimed to be twenty-five years old" (191). Idabel's excited interest in Miss Wisteria gradually becomes clear to Joel: "Then a queer thing happened: Idabel, borrowing the lipstick, painted an awkward clownish line across her mouth, and Miss Wisteria, clapping her little hands, shrieked with a kind of sassy pleasure. . . . But as she continued to fawn over tiny yellow-haired Miss Wisteria it came to him that Idabel was in love" (192–193). Ironically, Miss Wisteria attributes Idabel's behavior to freakishness: " 'Poor child, is it that she believes she is a freak, too?' " (195). But Idabel's happiness opens Joel up to the possibility of same-sex love. In the last lines of the novel, he goes to Randolph who, dressed as a woman, beckons him to his room. Looking at Randolph, he gains a new sense of self: "I am Joel, we are the same people" (227). As these words suggests, Capote validates homosexual desires in ways that McCullers does not, but we are still left wondering to what extent Joel has come into his own. A teenager being seduced by an older man is far from ideal, and this choice does not seem better than the family life he had with Aunt Ellen. However, this experience has enabled Joel to shake off the specter of the American family and the heterosexual imperatives it reinforces, suggesting that the freakish is preferable to the normal as long as it allows people to love and desire whom they want.

Closing the Curtain: Love Without Boundaries

Perhaps Randolph best articulates the message of these texts when he tells Joel that love is without boundaries: "Any love is natural and beautiful that lies within a person's nature; only hypocrites would hold a man responsible for what he loves" (147). It is the hypocrisy of political and social practices that promote exclusion based on sexual identity that fuels *Other Voices, Other Rooms* and arguably *The Member of the Wedding*. In the 1940s and 1950s, the American Dream was so closely linked with images of the nuclear family that homosexuality was considered dangerous. Gay culture threatened society by challenging many of the ideas it held sacred—particularly the importance of raising children in a heterosexual environment. The queer body, therefore, had to be vilified. It had to be seen as a kind of freakish spectacle—an unattractive alternative to heterosexual life. Capote and McCullers use this intersection between freakishness and same-sex desire as central metaphors in their coming-of-age fiction to criticize the debilitating impact of heterosexual imperatives on everyone, regardless of sexual preferences. By choosing young adults poised to make their own choices about sexuality, heterosexual imperatives have an insidious overtone. They make sexuality an issue of social control, a way of preserving white, middle-class hierarchies.

This tradition would continue in the following decade in stories such as Flannery O' Connor's "A Temple of the Holy Ghost," which uses a sexually ambiguous freak as a catalyst for the protagonist's sexual awakening. The narrator's cousins Susan and Joanne enjoy seeing all the freaks except "the you-know-what" (92). This unspeakable exhibit is a hermaphrodite whose tent was "divided in two parts by a black curtain, one side for men and one for women. The freak went from one side to the other, talking first to the men and then to the women, but everyone could hear" (92). While listening to this description, the young narrator "felt every muscle strained as if she were hearing the answer to a riddle that was more puzzling than the riddle itself" (93). Susan quickly explains that "it was a man and woman both." O'Connor does not explicitly deal with same-sex desire in this story, but she does attack social repression in the form of religion. Organized religion forces the girls to conform and wear identical uniforms at the convent. She juxtaposes this practice with the freak who claims "this is the way [God] wanted me to be" (96). In this setting, conformity is clearly freakish, for it promotes an artificial purity. Since difference threatens the control that religion has over these young children, local preachers have the freak show closed: "Some preachers from town gone out and inspected it and got the police to shut it down" (96). Like McCullers's and Capote's freaks, this exhibit offers an outlet for thinking about sex and sexual desire— desire the Church wants to regulate under the banner of morality.

In all of these works, the freak violates sexual norms that seem to threaten society. It represents possibilities that are dangerous and exciting, restricting and freeing. But its place in the sideshow is an image for the costs of difference, for the costs of not being like everyone else. Though Capote most explicitly presents homosexuality as a viable choice for young adults, the freakishness in his novel, like McCullers's work, speaks to the power of the social prejudices. These writings portray America as a place with clearly defined boundaries, a place willing to marginalize its own from some unheard-of thing.

Breakfast at Brian's

My friend Brian's move to San Francisco coincided with his desire to live openly as a gay man, and a few months after starting his new life there, he invited me to visit:

"You've got to see my new place," Brian tells me over the phone. "It's fabulous."

He doesn't say the word "fabulous" like a character from Will and Grace; *he says it like Brian always says things—with an easy-going smile in his voice. His apartment, I soon discover, is just around the corner from The Faerie Queen Chocolate Shop and a burger joint called Hot 'n' Hunky. After finding a parking spot, I grab my bag from the trunk and start to climb up the street. The hills make everything feel unsteady, as if one is walking on the deck of a ship. The muscles in my legs burn by the time I get to his place.*

The front door is partway open, and I can see Brian serving drinks to several people. As soon as I step inside, he introduces me to the group. Randy, who is lounging on the couch, lives next door, and his apartment, he proudly informs me, adheres to the principles of Feng Shui. Brad, the hair stylist, believes in color psychology, and his neon orange shirt puts any construction sign to shame. And then there is Michelle, formerly Michael, who sits in the chair beside them. She rattles off statistics about the American Presidents like some people talk baseball.

At first, Michelle—with her long blond hair, red lipstick, and black stockings—looks like a woman. Maybe, I wouldn't have second-guessed this, but now, looking closer, everything about her body seems slightly off—her wide shoulders, the thick-knuckled fingers around her Champagne flute, and the way her hair doesn't quite hide the squareness of her chin.

Brian's pet turtle, Pit Stop, watches all of this from a safe distance across the room—under the potted ficus.

For hours, we drink and snack on chips and hummus. Dance music pulses in the background, and the group grows. Colleagues from Brian's job, other neighbors, and even some friends from college gradually fill the small living room. It's too crowded to move around, so I stay on the couch near Randy, Brad, and Michelle. In truth, I want to figure out Michelle's body, like some strange puzzle. I want to see which part of her is still a man.

I'm not sure what time it is when the music stops, and Brian announces that it's time to go. He is standing on a barstool near the kitchen—a margarita in one hand and a sombrero on his head.

"Where?" I ask.

"The Pendulum."

I quickly learn that The Pendulum is the first in a long list of gay dance clubs that we would gyrate through that night. Detour. Midnight

Sun. Badlands. Each place shakes with a mixture of techno music, Donna Summer, and Madonna. Each place seems to have a topless policy for men.

With my shirt on and a drink in hand, I linger near the bar. Brian is easy to spot on the dance floor. He is sandwiched between two white men—dancing, laughing, and balancing a drink at the same time.

I turn to one of the women standing next to me at the bar—or at least I'm fairly sure that she's a woman—but I doubt that she can hear me through the din. I ask how she is doing. She smiles politely.

Randy suddenly slaps me on the shoulder. "Stop being so straight!"

Before I can respond, Michelle steps between us: "Did you know that Teddy Roosevelt was shot before giving a speech in 1912?"

"Teddy Roosevelt wasn't assassinated," I say.

"No one cares, baby," Randy blurts.

"No, it was only a surface wound," Michelle adds quickly, tossing her hair to the side and turning her back on Randy. "But he insisted on finishing the speech before going to the hospital."

"Always the Rough Rider," I mutter.

The three of us stand in silence for a moment. Michelle looks at me with a smile as we wait for our drinks.

"Did it hurt?" I ask.

"What?"

"Becoming a woman."

"I've always been a woman. This"—she looks down at her body—"is just a shell."

I nod without conviction. "But did it hurt?"

"Change always hurts."

Suddenly, Randy grabs one of Michelle's hands and then one of mine. "We're going to dance," he calls over his shoulder as he drags us onto the floor. "And I promise it won't hurt at all!"

Men and women surround us—surround Michelle. Her eyes brighten as she dances inside the tight circle. Everyone cheers her on. She moves naturally with the music.

The next morning, Brian is already awake and reading the Chronicle when I get up. My body feels stiff from sleeping on the couch. My feet ache from dancing. And my head hurts from the margaritas.

Brian tells me that there is a great brunch place nearby. "We're supposed to meet Michelle there in ten minutes. Let me grab Pit Stop."

With Pit Stop tucked in Brian's satchel, we stumble out into the cool San Francisco sun. The Castro looks different in the morning. It still bustles with men and women. Parked cars crowd the streets. But somehow everything feels more sedate, as if the entire city is waiting for its first cup of coffee.

When we turn the corner, I notice a young woman walking toward us. She has a slender, elegant frame, and her amber hair highlights the rich brown color of her skin. As she gets closer, my heart quickens. She passes without noticing me at all.

My heart slows, and my bruised ego shifts my attention to the scrambled eggs that I plan to order as soon as we get to the restaurant.

When Brian and I finally get to the restaurant, I look around the room. It's mostly filled with men. Couples sitting at tables, sipping coffee, and chatting softly. Couples waking up on a slow Sunday morning.

I see Michelle before Brian does. She is sitting in the far corner, waiting for us. Alone. I suddenly realize that I've been looking at her body all weekend without seeing her at all.

After we sit down, Michelle asks Brian if she can hold Pit Stop. Brian lifts him out of his bag, and she takes him carefully. Pit Stop, whose head has been hidden all morning, emerges slowly. We all watch him for a moment, in silence, before the waiter comes over and takes our order.

Epilogue

Until a few years ago, I had never been to a fair, much less to a freak show, and I can't say that I ever had the desire to go. They reminded me of ocean-side boardwalks with rust-colored roller coasters, arcades, and sun-burnt tricksters who ran games no one could ever win. At least I never could. But after working on this manuscript, I went to the annual state fair in Raleigh, North Carolina, to see what, if anything, remained of the freak show's legacy. I wanted to know what it would *feel* like to buy tickets for an exhibit featuring the Lobster Boy or Khan, the World's Tallest Man.

Libraries can be cold, lonely places. Motivated by the excitement and wonder of new ideas, we often get buried behind stacks of books, losing track of what brought us to these topics in the first place—a deeper understanding of ourselves, the culture around us, and our place in it. Perhaps that is why I needed to go to a freak show. After examining freakishness in early-twentieth-century material culture, I had pieced together a narrative about difference in America that freak shows, as both a form of entertainment and an artistic tool, helped define and shape. But this "discovery" of their artistic, social, and historical value made me question my own role as a spectator. Did freak shows still have any emotive power? Would seeing one enhance or change my understanding of this project?

On the fairgrounds, the cacophony of bells, sirens, pop music, and voices was deafening. As I wandered past game booths and food stands, the hot, sunny afternoon seemed too bright for displaying freaks. Individual exhibits featuring extraordinary animals littered the fairgrounds: the world's smallest horse, the largest pig, and the longest alligator. But human curiosities were hard to find. Eventually, I saw a large tent with banners featuring the world's fattest lady, the Skeleton Man, Siamese twins, the Fiji Mermaid, and Johnny the Legless Wonder. Near the entryway, local newspaper articles, which had been enlarged and placed on poster board, described the freak show as an artifact of American entertainment history. It was a place to see the past, not the spectacular and unusual of the present.

I walked through the flaps after handing a dollar to a barker who didn't speak—a prerecorded spiel blared over the loudspeakers instead: "Come see . . . the Fattest Woman in the World. She will astound . . . and amaze."

There were no fat ladies, skeleton men, or live performers of any kind, only a hodgepodge of rundown displays against the tent walls: a desiccated version of Barnum's Fiji Mermaid, some plastic shrunken heads, a stuffed six-legged cow, and the body of an alien baby recovered from a UFO crash site. Interspersed among these exhibits were photographs of famous nineteenth- and early-twentieth-century freaks. These images seemed to be both a haphazard testament to freak show history and a meager way to justify the banners outside. The show clearly relied on human curiosities to entice audiences, but these simulacra were a far cry from the real thing. Instead of laughing at the absurdity of these exhibits, most of the people I observed left quickly, disappointed by the deception. In truth, I was too.

In a booth not far from the tent, the Snake Lady—a woman surrounded by a very plastic snake's body—was having a miserable time between the Slam-Dunk basketball game and the Titanic Waterslide. I imagined Barnum's frustration with such a half-hearted display. Like the tent, this exhibit didn't play with the tensions between truth and humbug. It was all humbug, making almost no pretense of truth. As I walked off the Snake Lady's platform, two high school students with baggy clothing asked me:

> "Is it real?"
> "No," I replied.
> "What does it look like?"
> "Plastic."
> They glanced at each other, clearly impatient with my lack of detail.
> "Is it *worth* it?" One of them asked.
> "Worth it?"
> They held out their tickets.
> "No," I said.

After a brief pause, they handed their tickets to the barker, who smiled at me, and then they walked up to see the Snake Lady for themselves. I couldn't really blame them. Like freak show audiences since the 1840s, we had all come to do the same thing—to see for ourselves.

While looking for an exit from the fairgrounds, I saw a sign advertising the "Smallest Woman in the World." It hung above the Disneyland-like façade of a miniature, sky blue Victorian house. To the side of the ticket booth, an image of a tiny African-American woman with a bright, engaging smile had been painted on some plywood. She stood behind a white picket fence, patting a dog with one hand and waving with the other. Above her head, someone had painted the words: "The Smallest Woman Alive! Only 2 feet tall! A mother with two sons in college!" A prerecorded spiel repeated: "Talk to her and she'll talk back. The smallest woman in the world. Only 48 inches." I handed over my last tickets.

On the other side of the façade, an African-American woman was actually sitting there. She was perched on a ragged couch with one foot tucked under her body and the other stretched out in front of her, barely reaching the edge of the cushion. The platform was filthy and disheveled. A precarious end table leaned against the armrest of her couch, and an old black-and-white television had been placed on top of a miniature refrigerator. On a torn piece of cardboard in front of the couch, she had written: "I'll stand for $1." "Take your picture with me for $1."

Something about the sign moved me—the uneven, smudged writing in black magic marker, the random shift between cursive and print. But when I looked up from the sign, I saw something I didn't expect. Disgust. She looked at me with such intense loathing and anger. Within a matter of seconds, I had passed by the platform and was outside again, never standing still to look. I hurried back to the car as a hazy twilight settled over the growing crowds. Carnival lights were flashing feverishly, and the smoke from grills and frying pans made it difficult to see. But I found relief in this, being lost in the crowds and the haze for the moment.

I didn't want to be seen.

*   *   *

In many ways, the Smallest Woman in the World was a "perfect" freak exhibit. Through juxtaposition, she invoked and validated a certain ideal about the American family—having a house with a white picket fence, two children, and dog. Not only was her race and size anachronistic in this pseudo-Victorian setting, but the distorted, filthy "living room" also demonstrated her failed attempt to find some place, some type of belonging in middle-class society. Like Barnum's exhibits, this woman does not fit into American class and social paradigms; she serves as a foil for what the audience presumably has—community, social acceptance, and normality. The sign referencing her children also taps into one of the most popular tropes of freak exhibits—sexuality. For audiences, the claim that she has successfully raised children invites questions about the father, the height and appearance of her children, and her capacity as wife and mother. All of these ploys make her a successful exhibit by nineteenth-century standards, but my discomfort while looking speaks to some of the changes discussed in this study.

Just as science began providing a new language for the damaged body and technology broadened the possibilities for popular entertainment, each decade in the early twentieth century offered new social challenges to the freak show as well. Exotic displays of non-whites reinforced prejudices that further intensified anxieties about racial difference and growing immigrant populations. Bodies injured by war and debilitated by economic depression changed public perceptions about disability, making the damaged body an unwanted symbol for social and political discord. And visible signs of homosexual desire—public displays of same-sex affection and cross-dressing—threatened certain ideals about the American family. As images of blackness, disability, and sexual ambiguity posed an increasing threat to white middle-class hierarchies and values, the desire to suppress and persecute visible difference intensified. The changes being brought on by modernity were making the boundaries between self and other—white/black, male/female, able/disabled, heterosexual/homosexual—more and more tenuous, and the freak show was no longer a successful outlet for assuaging these social anxieties. Gradually, the crowds stopped coming.

Many of the writers and artists in the early twentieth century went to carnivals and freak shows as children, and thus it isn't surprising that this entertainment plays a significant role in the modern artistic imagination. They use the viewer-spectacle dynamic of freak shows as a disturbing image for American attitudes about difference. After Dan Moore sees a boxing match between two dwarfs in Jean Toomer's "Box Seat," for example, he finally recognizes his own status as a spectacle; as a Southern black man in urban Chicago, he feels alienated from everyone around him except the freak performers on stage. He has learned, like Irene in Nella Larsen's *Passing* and the narrator in both Richard Wright's *Black Boy* and Ralph Ellison's *Invisible Man*, that race is socially constructed. It is a tool, similar to the ritualized presentation of racially exotic freaks, for reinforcing social and economic hierarchies that privilege whites.

As discussed in chapter 1, photographic images of lynching victims and freak performers also contributed to the politics of visible difference in America. These pictures were collected in family albums and became an integral part of popular entertainment in the Victorian era.

They provided unusual and titillating images that one could share with neighbors, visitors, and family friends. In this context, the spectacle of the black body served another social function as well. Its juxtaposition with elegant portraits of white families reinforced the cultural superiority of whites. The photo album, in other words, functioned as a kind of home-constructed freak show—displaying degrading images of African Americans for amusement.

The scientific theories of eugenics deepened racial divisions in the early twentieth century. They fueled growing concerns about miscegenation and immigration, and they provided "evidence" for the superiority of the Anglo-Saxon race—giving people a new language for fear and hatred. Fictional characters like Tom Buchanan in *The Great Gatsby* echo this type of paranoia ("It's up to us, who are the dominant race, to watch out or these other races will have control of things" [13].), and writers such as F. Scott Fitzgerald, Willa Cather, William Faulkner, and Eudora Welty explore some of these anxieties about miscegenation to portray the ugliness and cruelty of social practices based on visible difference. Like the role of passing in *Light in August* and Larsen's *Passing*, all of these works expose the hypocrisy of a social system that judges people on the basis of skin color.

Some of the same techniques used in freak show exhibits appear in World War I propaganda posters as well. Both H. R. Hopps's "Destroy This Mad Brute!" and Ellsworth Young's "Remember Belgium: Buy Bonds Fourth Liberty Loan" transform the enemy into a dark, monstrous beast. Hopps specifically racializes the German soldier in order to cast the threat in ethnic terms. Nonwhites were already considered dangerous in America, and the depiction of Germans with dark, exaggerated bodies provided further evidence that the United States needed to join the war effort. This tendency to demonize difference (physical as well as racial), however, would have complex ramifications for injured soldiers by the end of war. As veterans returned home, many Americans started to view the damaged body as a symbol for postwar disillusionment, for the ugliness of war and its devastating physical costs.

Many writers in the 1920s explore this problem of interpretation, in part, by examining the wounded body. Cather, Hemingway, Faulkner, and Dos Passos portray soldiers who are being seen as symbols, rather than individuals. For many, their injuries signify a world disassembled by years of fighting, but as these authors suggest, it is the soldier's individuality and humanity that are being sacrificed by a society trying to distance itself from the memory of World War I. As the experiences of Donald Mahon in *Soldiers' Pay* and the convalescent soldiers in Hemingway's "In Another Country" demonstrate, the prejudices surrounding disability—the need to interpret the damaged body—were far too pervasive for veterans to reintegrate into mainstream society. The government recognized this problem as well, and even though many propagandists were producing posters that characterized disability as noble and strong, these works could not offset the marginalization experienced by many injured veterans.

Writers and photographers during the Depression explored the impact of deteriorating social conditions on attitudes about physical difference and disability as well. Since the physical costs of unemployment, illness, and hunger could often be seen on the body, the sideshow performer was often an unwanted reminder of everyday hardships and physical vulnerability. It suggested that anyone could become a "freak" in these debilitating economic conditions. Freakishness also became an image for the alienation, displacement, and loss of community that many people experienced in the 1930s. As discussed in chapter 3, Rose of Sharon in *The Grapes of Wrath* fears that her baby is going to be "a freak" because she has neither a husband nor enough food. This deterioration of family threatens both her and her child's humanity. The dangers of isolation permeate Steinbeck's and Nathanael West's works. Without some kind of community, characters like the deformed junkyard attendant in *The Grapes of Wrath* and the debilitating loneliness of Homer Simpson in *The Day of the Locust* become freakish. They turn to self-destructive behavior.

Dorothea Lange's photography, like most of the work done by FSA photographers, tried to counter fears about the devastating effects of the Depression. Though her snapshots capture some of the hardships, suffering, and worry at the time, they also display the body as a source of tremendous strength and hope. Her photography holds up the working-class body as an image for America's determination to overcome adverse conditions. Her contemporary, Margaret Bourke-White, chose more graphic and grotesque images of the body for her book, *Your Have Seen Their Faces.* Here she captures—and presents—the damaged body as a spectacle, an image for the abusive and debilitating working conditions of the 1930s. Though more sensational than Lange, both photographers understand the ways in which the body was often seen and read as a symbol.

In post-1930s fiction, freak shows also became an effective tool for exploring homophobia in the United States. Sexuality and sexual ambiguity had always been staples of freak show entertainment, but as social and political tensions regarding homosexuality intensified during this period, freaks, such as bearded ladies and hermaphrodites, were seen as visible threats to heterosexuality and the nuclear family. Like racial passing and injured soldiers, the queer body had become an image for something that had gone wrong in America—the breakdown of binaries held sacred by the white middle class. As discussed in chapter 4, Carson McCullers and Truman Capote both used freak shows to critique mainstream heterosexual imperatives. McCullers, who was fascinated with freak shows as a child, enacts one in her dramatic adaptation of *The Member of the Wedding* to expose some of the social prejudices surrounding difference. Bernice's glass eye and Frankie's awkward body not only play with sideshow conventions, but as characters they also represent groups that are marginalized in American culture—African Americans and homosexuals. Although McCullers doesn't ultimately present a positive alternative for same-sex desire (the figure of Lily Mae Jenkins, a transsexual, remains on the margins of the story), she does use Frankie's plight to suggest possibilities for finding happiness outside the paradigm of the nuclear family.

Truman Capote's *Other Voices, Other Rooms* goes one step farther and presents homosexuality as a positive alternative. Surrounded by relatives and a town that resemble a freak show troupe, the protagonist, Joel, struggles with his own sexual identity throughout the novel—trying to mimic heterosexual behavior in his relationship with Idabel and to see his father as an ideal for stereotypical masculinity. When these relationships fail to do this, Joel ultimately chooses to be with the cross-dressing Randolph, who articulates the importance of being true to one's own desires. Though this option is less than ideal, Capote does create a setting in which homosexuality is a viable way to find and experience love.

In many ways, the social changes occurring in the early twentieth century made the spectacle of difference too dangerous and offensive for most audiences. Even when the public turned away and tried to suppress these images of difference, underlying prejudices remained; in fact, they intensified and sometimes even reached a boiling point, as, for example, in the civil rights movement. Despite the ways that many modern artists explored the social and historical forces affecting the freak show's popularity, neither these works nor the freak show itself galvanized significant social change. By their very nature, freak shows, which had always featured exotics, dwarfs, giants, and legless wonders, could not adapt to early twentieth-century anxieties about the body and still be considered "freak shows." Their decline, in other words, was precipitated by their inability to change, yet the public did not condemn these ongoing, increasingly distasteful exhibitions. They simply stopped going.

By the 1940s, freak shows had failed to inspire significant social protest because they primarily evoked feelings of guilt, not under-standing. In Eudora Welty's "Keela, the Outcast Indian Maiden" (1941), for example, Max, who had worked as a sideshow barker, seeks forgiveness for having helped enfreak Little Lee Roy many years ago. His guilt, however, inspires a flawed empathy—one that does not ultimately change his perception of Lee Roy. Instead, when Max finally confronts him, he can only think of giving Lee Roy money to go away. As this story illustrates, guilt does not have the power to bring about personal and social change. It is a feeling that makes us recognize and acknowledge our own faults—things that we don't like to confront or think about ourselves. So we seek atonement, hurriedly put away our pardons, and, as the closing words of the story suggest, "hush up."

This may explain some of my reaction to the Smallest Woman in the World. Her gaze made me feel guilty, and I didn't want to think about that. None of my reasons for being there, as a researcher and a writer, would have made any difference to her anyway.

I had bought a ticket. I had gone to stare at her.

NOTES

INTRODUCTION

1. For more on the history of freak shows in American culture, see Robert Bogdan's *Freak Show: Presenting Human Oddities for Amusement and Profit*, Rosemarie Garland Thomson's *Extraordinary Bodies: Figuring Physical Disability in American Culture and Literature*, the essay collection *Freakery: Cultural Spectacles of the Extraordinary Body*, Rachel Adams's *Sideshow U.S.A.: Freaks and the American Cultural Imagination*, Leslie Fiedler's *Freaks: Myths and Images of the Secret Self*, Daniel Mannix's *Freaks: We Who Are Not As Others*, and Frederick Drimmer's *Very Special People*.

2. According to the Bible, the disfigurement of Cain is not only a mark of shame and marginalization, but it is also a sign of God's will:

> What hast thou done? The voice of thy brother's blood crieth unto me from the ground. And now art thou cursed from the earth, which hath opened her mouth to receive thy brother's blood from thy hand; When thou tillest the ground, it shall not henceforth yield unto thee her strength; a fugitive and a vagabond shalt thou be in the earth. And Cain said unto the LORD, My punishment [is] greater than I can bear. Behold, thou hast driven me out this day from the face of the earth; and from thy face shall I be hid; and I shall be a fugitive and a vagabond in the earth; and it shall come to pass, that every one that findeth me shall slay me. And the LORD said unto him, Therefore whoever so slayeth Cain, vengeance shall be taken on him sevenfold. And the Lord set a mark upon Cain, lest any finding him should kill him. (Genesis 4:10–15)

To prevent Cain from being killed, God visibly scars him. Cain's body, in other words, becomes something that people could use to interpret God's will. They could read the damaged body as a symbol for Cain's wickedness.

For more studies of monstrosity in the ancient world, see Marie-Hélène Huet's *Monstrous Imagination*, Dudley Wilson's *Signs and Portents*, Geoffrey Galt Harpham's *On the Grotesque*, C. J. S. Thompson's *The Mystery and Lore of Monsters*, and George Gould and Walter Pyle's *Anomalies and Curiosities of Medicine*.

3. For more on the rise of entertainment in nineteenth-century American culture, see Lawrence Levine's *Highbrow/Lowbrow*, Andrea Dennett's *Weird and Wonderful*, Robert Allen's *Horrible Prettiness*, and David Nasaw's *Going Out*.

4. To further advertise his ventures, Barnum cultivated relationships with famous individuals, such as Mark Twain and Oliver Wendell Holmes, in the hopes of associating them with his exhibits. Holmes was one of the doctors who certified that Captain Costentenus was the most remarkable tattooed man that he had ever seen. Not surprisingly, Barnum sent letters and season passes to Holmes throughout his professional career. Consider this letter dated April 22, 1878 (from the Oliver Wendell Homes Collection at Harvard University):

> My Dear Dr. Holmes,
> On the 27th of May I shall come down on Boston like an Avalanche.
> My horses beat the record—and I want you to share in the enjoyment which they give to all lovers of these noble animals. Tattoo and the "Dedo" are still on hand.
> Very truly yours,
> P.T. Barnum
> With enclosed ticket for two reserved seats to 1878 Barnum's Greatest Show on Earth.

5. Robert Bogdan describes the different types of freak in the introduction to *Freak Show: Presenting Human Oddities for Amusement and Profit*.

6. Tom Thumb, born Charles Sherwood Stratton in 1838, was one of Barnum's most famous and financially successful exhibits. Barnum initially offered the impoverished Stratton family $3 a week to display Charles at the American Museum. Soon afterward, they toured throughout the United States and Europe. (In 1844, for example, Queen Victoria invited him to the palace twice.) Barnum advertised Tom Thumb as a twelve-year-old dwarf; though he exaggerated his age, Thumb was apparently twenty-five inches and fifteen pounds when Barnum first met him in 1842. He most likely had ateliotic dwarfism—"his diminutiveness resulted from a deficiency of the growth hormone that is normally produced by the pituitary gland" (Saxon, *P.T. Barnum: The Legend and the Man*, 124).

7. Born in 1811 in Siam, Chang and Eng Bunker were joined together at birth "at the xiphoid [the lowest portion of the sternum] by a band of tissue just a few inches long" (Alexander, 66). As Robert Bogdan explains, "Chang and Eng were the vanguard of joined twins. They were the first put on display in this country, and it is to them we can attribute the term *Siamese Twins*" (201). In fact, Barnum first gave Chang and Eng the label "Siamese Twins," and this term has been synonymous with conjoined twins ever since.

One night, at the age of sixty, Chang died in bed, and his brother, legend has it, died several hours later of "fright." In a recent article for the *North Carolina Medical Journal*, Dr. Eben Alexander, Jr. argues that Chang and Eng actually died of exsanguination: "The vascular connection between the two may not have been very large, but we know that Eng's heart was still beating after Chang's had stopped, and the connection was sufficient to let Eng's blood drain away over the two to four hours it took him to die. It seems clear: Eng died of blood loss" (67).

8. See chapter 3, note 16, for more on Joice Heth.

9. Quoted from A. H. Saxon's *P. T. Barnum: The Legend and the Man*, 122. The italics here are mine.

10. This letter is part of the collected papers of Townsend Walsh—who was also a circus/sideshow producer. These materials are housed in Special Collections at the main branch of the New York Public Library. "The Billboard" printed the following biography of Walsh on June 21, 1930:

> Townsend Walsh has been a trouper 34 years. Graduated from Harvard in 1895, he cubbed [*sic*] for a while on the "New York World," then went on the road with Mrs. Fiske, continuing with that star 4 years. Subsequent engagements were with Montgomery and Stone 4 years, 8 years with Charles Frohman's most prominent stars, next with Winthrop Ames and then for a year dramatic editor of the "Boston Traveller." He rejoined Fred Stone for a Coast tour with "Tip-Top," then spent four years with the Ringling Bros.' Press department. He is the author of "The Career of Dion Boucicault," and now has in preparation a book, "Love of the Circus." He is a confirmed globe trotter, and knows Paris better than his home town, Albany, N.Y.

11. See Ann Douglas, *Terrible Honesty: Mongrel Manhattan in the 1920s*, 187–188.

12. See John Kasson's *Amusing the Millions: Coney Island at the Turn of the Century*.

13. Scholars debate the exact dates of the Harlem Renaissance, but I find Ann Douglas's frame in *Terrible Honesty: Mongrel Manhattan in the 1920s* to be the most persuasive. She considers the Silent Protest Parade on July 28, 1917 (a powerful image of communal solidarity) the start of this movement and the 1935 race riot (which symbolized the ideological failure of Harlem Renaissance goals) the end: "The real end of the Harlem Renaissance came, not with the onset of the Depression, but five and a half years later, on March 19, 1935, when thousands of blacks, protesting the brutalization of a young Puerto Rican shoplifter named Lino Rivera at the hands of white policemen, took to the streets and destroyed $2 million of white property. Effectively deployed or otherwise, this full-scale violence gave the lie

to the dream of racial collaboration on which the Harlem Renaissance was founded" (322).

For more on the Harlem Renaissance, see George Hutchinson's *The Harlem Renaissance in Black and White* and the collection *Temples for Tomorrow: Looking Back at the Harlem Renaissance* (ed. Michel Feith and Genevieve Fabre).

CHAPTER 1   "HELPLESS MEANNESS": CONSTRUCTING THE BLACK BODY AS FREAKISH SPECTACLE

1. As William Welling explains in *Photography in America: The Formative Years 1839–1900*, Queen Victoria had albums designed for her photographs that "sparked yet another new vogue; people everywhere began putting *cartes de visite* not only of their family and friends but also of celebrities into what became known as the 'family album' " (143).

2. In *Reading American Photographs*, Alan Trachtenberg discusses J. T. Zealy's daguerreotypes of African-born slaves on South Carolina plantations. Hired by Louis Agassiz, a natural scientist at Harvard, Zealy took pictures that "would supplement [Agassiz's] anthropometric evidence with visible proof of 'natural' difference in size of limbs and configuration of muscles, establishing once and for all that blacks and whites did not derive 'from a common center' " (53). Though these were not mass produced images, Zealy's pictures offer an early example of the ways that photographic images of blacks were used to reinforce prejudices.

3. See William M. Tuttle's *Race Riot: Chicago in the Red Summer of 1919*.

4. In *Exorcising Blackness: Historical and Literary Lynching and Burning Rituals*, Trudier Harris describes this ritual as having several components. Lynching is a communal event that includes "burning, mutilation, gathering trophies, and initiating children" (2).

5. Bogdan discusses the tremendous popularity of freak *cartes de visite* in the introduction to *Freak Show*: "Although the cabinet photo eventually replaced the *carte de visite*, enough of the smaller images remained in circulation in the 1880s to warrant at least a few pages in contemporary photography albums. In the last three decades of the nineteenth century, freak shows and photographers flourished. . . . In some cases, thousands of reproductions would be ordered at one time" (12–13).

6. Will James was accused of killing Anne Pelly, "the seven-year-old daughter of Mr. Boren, who found the murdered [girl] in an alley she was crossing on the way to her grandmother's house; the 'course the hounds took'; the trains the mob took over to reach Belknap, Illinois,

where James was apprehended, and to return him to Cairo for a public execution. The rope from which James was hanged broke before he died. His body was then 'riddled with bullets,' dragged by rope for a mile to the alleged scene of the crime, and burned in the presence of ten thousand spectators. According to the *New York Times*, "five hundred 'women were in the crowd and some helped to hang the negro and to drag the body' " (exhibit notes by Allen).

7. Bogdan explains in *Freak Show* that African Americans with this condition were often "cast as 'missing links' or as atavistic specimens of an extinct race" (112). Also see his section on William Henry Johnson, 134–142.

8. Throughout his career, Barnum also had to shift his "stories" about Joice Heth in response to shifting anxieties about race (see Benjamin Reiss "P. T. Barnum"). To offer one early example, Adams's *E Pluribus Barnum: The Great Showman and the Making of U.S. Popular Culture* discusses the ways Barnum juxtaposed his racial freak exhibits with some of the more controversial dramas appearing in his Lecture Room. The display of "What Is It?" between acts of Boucicault's *The Octoroon* essentially made this play "safe for even the most anti-abolitionist of patrons" (163).

9. See Sollors, "Immigrants and Other Americans," 569–570, and John Higham, *Strangers in the Land*, 267.

10. See Daniel J. Kevles's *In the Name of Eugenics: Genetics and the Uses of Heredity*.

11. As Robert Rydell explains, "[B]y 1916 eugenicists had joined anthropologists in applying hierarchical ideas about race and culture to selected white populations, thereby laying the intellectual foundation for mass support of immigration restriction" (3). See also Christina Cogdell's discussion of eugenics in "The Futurama Recontextualized: Norman Bel Geddes's' Eugenic 'World of Tomorrow.' " She explains that "during the 1920s and 1930s, eugenic thinking in the U.S. and abroad undergirded key legislation, hotly debated social issues, basic high school health education, and various facets of popular culture. . . . Some passively adopted it as a sound scientific principle for the betterment of humanity while others used its accepted scientific validity as a springboard for (well-intentioned or not) racist policies that erupted internationally in the early 1940s in World War II" (205).

12. Expanding on some of Madison Grant's theories in *The Passing of the Great Race*, Stoddard's *The Rising Tide of Color* argues, in part, that the purity of the Anglo-Saxon race was being destroyed by other ethnic groups through miscegenation.

13. Of course, Madison Grant does not limit this solution to miscegenation. In chapter 4 ("The Competition of Races"), he applies these theories to the disabled, criminals, and the insane. For Grant, all of these

groups present a genetic threat to the Nordic races. The danger is allowing these threats to go unchecked:

> Where altruism, philanthropy, or sentimentalism intervene with the noblest purpose, and forbid nature to penalize the unfortunate victims of reckless breeding, the multiplication of inferior types is encouraged and fostered. Indiscriminate efforts to preserve babies among the lower classes often result in serious injury to the race. . . . Mistaken regard for what are believed to be divine laws and a sentimental belief in the sanctity of human life, tend to prevent both the elimination of defective infants and the sterilization of such adults as are themselves of no value to the community. The laws of nature require the obliteration of the unfit, and human life is valuable only when it is of use to the community or race. (48–49)

Grant's underlying concern here is class. Since he sees the lower classes as literally breeding genetic and social problems, he criticizes philanthropy that reaches out to them. These efforts, Grant contends, only preserve "defective infants" and people who have no communal value. They impede the right of any society—a natural right—to eliminate the unfit. He elaborates as follows:

> Those who read these pages will feel that there is little hope for humanity, but the remedy has been found, and can be quickly and mercifully applied. A rigid system of selection through the elimination of those who are weak or unfit—in other words, social failures—would solve the whole question in one hundred years, as well as enable us to get rid of the undesirables who crowd our jails, hospitals, and insane asylums. The individual himself can be nourished, educated, and protected by the community during his lifetime, but the state through sterilization must see to it that his line stops with him, or else future generations will be cursed with an ever increasing load of victims of misguided sentimentalism. This is a practical, merciful, and inevitable solution of the whole problem, and can be applied to an ever widening circle of social discards, beginning always with the criminal, the diseased, and the insane, and extending gradually to types which may be called weaklings rather than defectives, and perhaps ultimately to worthless race types. (50–51)

Social factors are irrelevant to Grant. One becomes a criminal, in other words, because s/he is genetically predisposed to do so. It is not entirely surprising, therefore, that he equates all kinds of "deviant" groups—the ill/diseased, the insane, criminals, and "worthless race types" (i.e., nonwhites); they all threaten white America.

14. Similar ideas were promoted by Nativism and Nordicism at the time. In "Gatsby's Pristine Dream," Jeffery Louis Decker discusses Nordicism and the anxieties of immigration in Fitzgerald's *The Great*

Gatsby. Specifically, he sees *Gatsby* as "a story of entrepreneurial corruption, accented by the language of nativism, [that] competes with and ultimately foils the traditional narrative of virtuous American uplift" (52). Gatsby's association with immigrant gangsters suggests that this novel links whiteness with national identity. In other words, "Gatsby's association with immigrant crime, particularly in the form of bootlegging, jeopardizes both the purity of his white identity and the ethics of his entrepreneurial uplift" (60).

15. See chapter 4 of Kevles's *In the Name of Eugenics*.
16. This scene has been interpreted in a number of ways by various scholars. Henry B. Wonham, for example, has recently argued that "Jim's impersonation of a 'Sick Arab' has more in common with late-nineteenth-century caricature than with the minstrel show's ambiguous racial inversions. . . . . Instead of complicating notions of self and authenticity, the extravagance of Jim's racial disguise merely conceals—one could say absorbs—the identity of the caricatured subject. At this point, *Huckleberry Finn* becomes a study in coon caricature, and its echoes of minstrel performance fade into an irretrievable pastoral background" (144). Wonham, however, completely ignores the explicit connection between Jim's disguise and freak shows in his reading. In another example, Sander L. Gilman's *Difference and Pathology: Stereotypes of Sexuality, Race, and Madness* discusses Jim's disguise as "[giving] him the protective coloration of both death and insanity"—because of blue's historical association with madness. He goes on to argue that "Twain is also pointing at the traditional Western confusion between the Arab and the black embodied in the ambiguous use of the word *Moor* in English. . . . Jim becomes the mythic black in order to escape the realities of blackness" (135). Given that the Duke and Dauphin were consummate con-artists/entertainers and that Twain showed considerable interest in Barnum and his museum, it is more likely that Twain was drawing on this type of racial ambiguity as it was presented in freak shows.

In fact, Twain and Barnum became friends in the 1870s. Twain admired Barnum's 1869 autobiography, and he even referenced the showman in one of his satirical pieces for the *New York Herald* in 1874. At one point in their correspondence, Barnum told Twain about the "bushels" of letters that he received from people all over the country—asking for jobs, offering to sell him curiosities, and so on. Barnum eventually sent some of these letters to Twain, whose response was quite enthusiastic: " 'Headless mice, four-legged hens, human-handed sacred bulls, 'professional' Gypsies, ditto 'Sacasians,' deformed human beings anxious to trade on their horrors, school-teachers who can't spell—it is a perfect feast of queer literature! Again I beseech you, don't burn a single specimen, but remember that *all* are wanted & possess value in the eyes of your friend' " (qtd. in Saxon, *P. T. Barnum*, 259). As biographer A. H. Saxon explains, Barnum happily "complied with the request and continued to send Twain batches of letters of the next several years, all the while encouraging him in his publication plans" (259). In the end, Twain never published anything about the letters. For more on Twain's relationship with Barnum, see Saxon's *P. T. Barnum*, 257–261.

17. In *The Incorporation of America*, Alan Trachtenberg explains that blacks were excluded from the "White City" at the Chicago World's Columbian Fair in 1893: "American blacks stood beyond the gates, petitions for an exhibition, a building, or a separate department all rejected. They were denied participation in the Fair, in its administration on the National Commission, even on the construction force and ground crews (except as menials). . . . [As a result] prominent blacks organized an independent 'Jubilee' or 'Colored People's Day,' at which the distinguished Frederick Douglas renamed White City 'a whited sepulcher' " (220).

Inside the fairgrounds, anthropological exhibits allowed white spectators to see representations of people and customs from around the world. These displays began with the most primitive black tribes and ended with the white middle-class family, a progression designed to reinforce white cultural and ethnic superiority. As Robert Rydell has argued, these exhibits "provided visitors with ethnological, scientific sanction for the American view of the nonwhite world as barbaric and childlike and gave a scientific basis to the racial blueprint for building a utopia" (43). This racial blueprint also helped erode long-standing political and popular resistance to America's increasing role in international expansion.

18. When Barnum first tried the "What Is It?" exhibit in England (1846), he hired an actor, Harvey Leech, who was known as the "Gnome-Fly" (Bogdan, *Freak Show*, 135). He was recognized on the first day and the exhibit failed (Saxon, *Letters of P. T. Barnum*, n. 36).

19. In *E Pluribus Barnum*, Bluford Adams explains that "the laziness and intemperance of blacks, Indians, and Irish were popular themes in both the Museum and Lecture Room. In the case of the Irish, however, the Museum was forced into a twofold strategy: while Irish peasants were mocked as preindustrial primitives, assimilated Irish Americans were invited to take their place among the Museum's loyalists. Barnum's split response speaks to his reliance upon the Irish as both subjects and objects of his entrepreneurial rhetoric. In his years as manager, Barnum witnessed the transformation of New York's working class from native-born to immigrant, and the Irish were easily the largest group of immigrants" (95–96). We might also add to this argument that it was much easier and more socially acceptable for Barnum to accommodate white immigrants over black patrons.

20. In other aspects of *Black Boy*, Wright also describes the disenfranchisement of African Americans by white society in terms of disability. For example, his next door neighbor, who had become an insurance agent, is described as being "handicapped by illiteracy" (159).

21. "In present teenage vernacular, 'geek' means a strange person, a person who does not have the proper social graces. In the amusement world, a 'gloaming geek' was a wild man who, as part of his presentation, would bite the heads off of rats, chickens, and snakes" (Bogdan, *Freak Show*, 262).
22. Joice Heth, for example, was Barnum's first exhibit as a showman. Her previous owner claimed that she was 161 years old and had been George Washington's nurse. Barnum purchased the rights to display her in 1835. When controversy erupted about her age, Barnum claimed that she was an automaton (among other things), which only made people want to see her again. See also Benjamin Reiss's *The Showman and the Slave*.
23. Susan V. Donaldson's "Making a Spectacle: Welty, Faulkner, and Southern Gothic" argues that Welty's *A Curtain of Green* invites the reader into a voyeuristic role. As a result, s/he is responsible in part for making a spectacle of women's bodies: "But we are also urged to consider those who do the scrutinizing and the act of scrutiny itself. As a result, reading [this collection] is roughly akin to looking at an exhibit and being vaguely uneasy about the possibility of being an exhibit oneself" (574). Although Donaldson applies this only to grotesque women's bodies, suggesting that they are sites of resistance (blurring boundaries between viewer and subject), she does not examine disabled bodies and the role of freak shows in constructing the spectacle of race and difference.
24. See Woodress 291.
25. These are fears that Fitzgerald arguably shared. In a November 1921 letter to Edmund Wilson, Fitzgerald laments the impact of miscegenation on both race and art:

> God damn the continent of Europe. . . . The negroid streak creeps northward to defile the Nordic race . . . . Already the Italians have the souls of blackamoors. Raise the bars of immigration and permit only Scandinavians, Teutons, Anglo-Saxons and Celts to enter. . . . My reactions were all philistine, anti-socialistic, provincial and racially snobbish. I believe at last in the white man's burden. We are as far above the modern French man as he is above the Negro. Even in art! (*Letters* 326)

Miscegenation—"[t]he negroid streak"—is not only a burden in social and political terms; it also threatens art. As the closing of this letter suggests, Fitzgerald reads art as a measure of the achievements of any race or culture, and he makes an association between racial purity and the value of art. Using France as an example, he sees European art as compromised by nonwhite influences and racial hybridity. Ultimately, he fears that ethnic difference will have the same detrimental effect in America.

26. Felipe Smith discusses the sexual connotation of this scene as well in "Figure on the Bed: Difference and American Destiny in *Tender Is the Night*" from *French Connections: Hemingway and Fitzgerald Abroad* (1998). See also Bryan Washington's discussion of African Americans in Fitzgerald, *The Politics of Exile: Ideology in Henry James, F. Scott Fitzgerald, and James Baldwin* (1995).

27. In *The Politics of Exile: Ideology in Henry James, F. Scott Fitzgerald, and James Baldwin*, Bryan R. Washington explains: "The extent to which blacks, Afro-American and Afro-European, threaten the white exile's idea of order in France is central to the novel. . . . Black exiles in *Tender is the Night* are caricatures. Jules Peterson manufactures shoe polish—a clear reference to blackface" (64).

28. In the essay "Change the Joke and Slip the Yoke," Ralph Ellison argues that the primary anxiety underlying white men's use of blackface was a fear of becoming the other: "He is not simply miming a person-ification of his disorder and chaos but that he will become in fact that which he intends only to symbolize" (53). At the same time, we could infer that minstrelsy raised questions about the other becoming white. If one could "act white," in other words, one could *be* white, and this is one of the central fears that eugenics, anthropology, sociology, and nativism were trying to assuage in the 1920s. Thus, as Eric Lott explains, the act of blackface "combined fear of and fascination with the black male, cast a strange dread of miscegenation over the minstrel show" (25). Even though the minstrel figure traditionally enacted a "safe" version of racial passing, he implied a much greater danger to Anglo-Saxon culture, and by the twentieth century, white literature often fused this ridiculed spectacle with the freak to reinforce these dangers.

29. The reference to Native Americans here also links this scene to the novel's preoccupation with imperialism. *Tender Is the Night* begins by describing the Divers' French Riviera home as a colonial settlement that forcefully makes a space for itself in the established surroundings. Their garden "stood in the ancient hill village of Tarmes. The villa and its grounds were made out of a row of peasant dwellings that abutted on the cliff—five small houses had been combined to make the house and four destroyed to make the garden. The exterior walls were untouched so that from the road far below it was indistinguishable from the violet gray mass of the town" (25). America seems to be invoked in this description as a new force (their home) that tears down and replaces the old (an ancient village). Even though the Divers destroyed nine existing homes to build their house, that structure is indistinguishable from the town at a distance, and this fusion becomes an image for the contradictory impulses of colonialism. On one level, colonialism distinguishes between self/other by creating categories such as civilized/savage, white/black, and right/wrong to help justify its political, economic, and cultural agenda. At the same time,

colonizing nations need to integrate into native surroundings to establish control, but this mixture of cultures inevitably threatens the notion of racial and cultural purity upheld by the colonizer.

Throughout *Tender Is the Night*, Fitzgerald presents empire as this kind of threat to America. Tommy Barban, for example, is associated with both the dangers of racial integration and capitalism. He is an exotic, cultural hybrid (being half American, half French) and has "worn the uniforms of eight countries" (29). And Nicole is sexually attracted to his racial Otherness: "His handsome face was so dark as to have lost the pleasantness of deep tan, without attaining the blue beauty of negroes—it was just worn leather. The foreignness of his depigmentation by unknown suns, his nourishment by strange soils, his tongue awkward with the curl of many dialects . . . these things fascinated and rested [*sic*] Nicole" (266). Her attraction to Tommy's foreignness points to the narrative's underlying concerns about the appeal of racial and ethnic differences for women. When Tommy confronts Dick about his affair with Nicole, the narrator explains that "Tommy was moved by an irresistible *racial* tendency to chisel for an advantage" (308; my emphasis). This description suggests that Dick's downfall culminates with both Nicole's desire for a divorce and her impending marriage to a non-Anglo. Whenever Tommy appears throughout the novel, his ethnicity, either through physical descriptions or the fact that he often chooses to speak French, is always foregrounded, and the only issue that rattles Dick's composure in his confrontation with Barban involves his ethnic difference. "Tommy returned to Dick. 'Elle doit avoir plus avec moi qu'avec vous?' 'Speak English! What do you mean "doit avoir?" ' " (307). Confronted with Nicole's love for Tommy, Dick's personal empire has been destroyed by this interracial relationship. Arguably, Dick's demise, losing his wife to a racial other, reflects larger fears in white America about the extinction of Anglo-Saxon purity and culture through exotic appeal and racial hybridity.

30. Many critics have commented on the connection between the character of Abe North and Abraham Lincoln. In *The International Theme of F. Scott Fitzgerald's Literature*, Elizabeth Weston explains that "Abe's launching of the 'small race riot' and the black man's, Freeman's, struggle to escape injustice are ironic allusions to the Civil War and to Lincoln's role as the Great Emancipator" (102). No scholarship has yet examined the connection between African Americans and Native Americans. Washington does devote one sentence to this idea: "[Blacks] are like stereotypical nineteenth-century 'Injuns': murderers, thieves, rapists" (68). But his analysis focuses on the treatment of women and the Afro-American/Afro-European and doesn't explore this idea further.

31. Dick's failure with the women around him—many of whom become infatuated with foreign men and the exotic—also reinforces his inability

to remove racial otherness from his world: Nicole's affair with the dark-skinned Barban; Mary North's marriage to a "ruler-owner of manganese deposits in southwestern Asia. He was not quite light enough to travel in a pullman south of Mason-Dixon; he was of the Kyble-Berber-Sabaean-Hindu strain" (256). Even Rosemary, a typical American traveler, becomes bored with southern France rather quickly because "no stimuli worked upon [her] . . . no fragments of [her] own thoughts came suddenly from the minds of others, and missing the *clamor of Empire* [she] felt that life was not continuing here" (11–12; my emphasis). Since American vitality is associated with the clamor of Empire, imperial growth, and development, Rosemary feels that French life is sterile; it only recalls "whispering of old kings come here to dine or die, or rajahs tossing Buddah's eyes to English ballerinas, or Russian princes turning the weeks into Baltic twilights in the lost caviare days" (13). Although her sense of an imperial power (like Dick's) is highly romanticized and associated with the superficial trappings of empire, she is willing to see the exotic interchange between different cultures as a source of vitality and can envision a multiethnic empire, a vision which Dick cannot share.

32. Deborah McDowell also reads "passing" as functioning on the level of sexuality. See *"The Changing Same": Black Women's Literature, Criticism, and Theory*. See also Judith Butler's chapter on Larsen in *Bodies That Matter*. For an overview of this book, see my review in *African-American Review* 33.3 (1999).

33. Gertrude Stein uses the language of freakishness similarly in "The Good Anna" to undermine heterosexist norms. See my article "Iteration as a Form of Narrative Control in Gertrude Stein's 'The Good Anna.' "

CHAPTER 2 WAR-INJURED BODIES: FALLEN SOLDIERS IN AMERICAN PROPAGANDA AND THE WORKS OF JOHN DOS PASSOS, WILLA CATHER, ERNEST HEMINGWAY, AND WILLIAM FAULKNER

1. When a German submarine sank the British liner *Lusitania* on May 7, 1915, 1,195 people died, including 124 Americans. This event fueled Wilson's aggressive stance toward Germany and his support of Britain's hunger blockade of the North Sea, which violated international law. Woodrow Wilson's speech to Congress can be found in *The Papers of Woodrow Wilson, January 24-April 6, 1917* (525–527). Wilson's Secretary of State, William Jennings Bryan, resigned in June of 1915 because he believed that the administration was headed for

war. Between 1915 and 1919, the national debt grew from $1 billion to $25 billion. And the Espionage Act of 1917 was used to suppress and arrest those who criticized the war effort. It also targeted socialists and citizens of German descent. For more on these details, see Ralph Raico's "World War I: The Turning Point."

2. For more on the role of propaganda in fostering antiforeign sentiment, see chapter 1 of Brett Gary's *The Nervous Liberals: Propaganda Anxieties from World War I to the Cold War*, and Stewart Halsey Ross's *Propaganda for War: How the United States Was Conditioned to Fight the Great War of 1914–1918*.

3. Brett Gary's *The Nervous Liberals* also discusses the ways that propaganda contributed to American fears about national security.

4. Ernest Hemingway explores this issue in the short story "Soldier's Home." Krebs's sense of isolation induces him to lie about his experiences in the war, and subsequently he creates exaggerated and spectacular stories to get people to listen to him: "His town had heard too many atrocity stories to be thrilled by actualities. Krebs found that to be listened to at all he had to lie, and after he had done this twice he, too, had a reaction against the war and against talking about it" (111). Krebs shares this antiwar sentiment and eventually loses his desire to find a place within the community. Abandoning this need to sell himself, he accepts his otherness after he discovers that "even his lies were not sensational at the pool room. His acquaintances . . . were not thrilled by his stories" (112). Just as his hometown cannot find a place for him, he realizes that the values and ideals of rural America are incompatible with his experiences as a soldier.

5. Similar tactics appeared in European posters as well. In Jules Abel Faivre's famous 1916 poster, "On les Aura!," a youthful soldier raises his open hand in a gesture that suggests he is ready to seize immanent victory. The angle of his body, gun, and arm portray quick, forward motion; he represents a country ready to act. Battle-ready and strong, this soldier—a leader who calls out to his comrades with wide-eyed hope—appears unstoppable. He is also feminized through his lashes, arched eyebrows, and shining eyes, which are highlighted over his surrounding features. Through these details, the artist tries to make the soldier beautiful—an image of someone the viewer wouldn't want to see killed.

Two years later, however, the front-line French soldier in Maurice Neumont's 1918 "On Ne Passe Pas!" has become a monster. There is no image of motion in this poster, only deathly silence and stasis. The landscape lies in smoldering ruins as flames engulf the horizon and debris (barbed wire, guns, helmets, and gas cans) litters the foreground. Unlike the distinct facial portrait in Faivre, this soldier has no face. His eyes and mouth are covered; his body and garments decimated. Without a face, he has become a steadfast fighting machine—strong in determination but without compassion or humanity. His legs literally merge with ruins. As Peter Paret explains in *Persuasive Images: Posters of War and Revolution from the Hoover Institution*, "The poilu, who has again stopped the Germans on the Marne as he had in 1914, is by now an almost inhuman figure. He has become a part of the debris of war around his feet and of the French soil out of which he grows and to which he my return at any moment" (48). In the two years between these posters, a significant shift had occurred in the way the war effort was portrayed. Faivre's vision of war as heroic and the soldier as someone to be admired and envied (a true symbol of patriotism) was replaced by an image of deformity. Freakishness had become one of the costs of war. It was the irrevocable loss of humanity as a result of battle.

6. Colonialism had played an integral role in both forming the United States (which annexed a continent from British, French, Mexican, and Native American control) and defining it in terms of whiteness. In the last few years of the nineteenth century, the United States also started to justify the acquisition of foreign territories as an economic necessity, annexing Hawaii (to protect international trade with the East) and demanding the Philippines from Spain after the Spanish-American War. International colonialism was becoming part of American national identity, and world's fairs and freak shows continued to make this an active component of ethnological exhibits.

On the freak show stage, exotic exhibits were often presented as imperial conquests to demonstrate the colonizer's ethnic and cultural superiority. The St. Louis World's Fair in 1904, for example, actually featured displays from the first colonial possessions of the United States—members from six Philippine villages. As Christopher Vaughan explains in "Ogling Igorots: The Politics and Commerce of Exhibiting Cultural Otherness, 1898–1913," this exposition "was a critical forum for the promulgation of a new imperial agenda" (221). Advertised as dog-eating barbarians and dressed in native outfits, the Bontoc Igorot tribe was such a popular display that it was eventually leased to the traveling sideshow circuit. As this example illustrates, imperialism helped encourage the spectacle of racial and ethnic difference and inadvertently popularized exotic representations of nonwhites as exhibits in traveling freak shows.

For more on the importance of examining American culture through the lens of imperialism, see Gesa Mackenthun's "State of the Art: Adding Empire to the Study of American Culture," Amy Kaplan's " 'Left Alone With America': The Absence of Empire in the Study of American Culture," and Edward Said's *Culture and Imperialism*. Said, for example, argues the "obsessive concern in Cooper, Twain, Melville, and others with United Sates expansion westward, along with the wholesale colonization and destruction of native American life . . . [reveals] an imperial motif . . . [which] rivals the European one" (63).

7. I am borrowing the term "enfreakment" from David Hevey's *The Creatures Time Forgot: Photography and Disability Imagery.* In Chapter Five, he examines photographic images of disabled people with a particular emphasis on the works of Diane Arbus. Hevey notes that disabled people are largely absent in "photographic genres," but when they do appear, they "are represented almost exclusively as symbols of 'otherness' placed within equations which have no engagement to them and which take their non-integration as a natural by-product of their impairment" (54). He goes on to blame Arbus— and the critical validation of her work by Sontag, Bosworth, and others—for labeling disabled people as "freaks." "Although Arbus's work can never be 'reclaimed,' it has to be noted that her work, and the use of 'enfreakment as message and metaphor, is far more complicated than either her defenders or critics acknowledge. . . . In terms of disability . . . Arbus read the bodily impairment of her disabled subject as a sign of disorder, even chaos; that is, as a physical manifestation of *her* chaos, *her* horror" (58).

8. Though biographical information is very scarce, Hopps may have been a German American name. Regardless, several of the poster's sponsors (Schmidt Lithograph, O. E. Olsen Lithograph, and Traung Label and Lithograph) are clearly German American, and this group, the largest ethnic population in the United States before World War I, had a definite stake in distinguishing themselves from European Germans. It is not surprising, therefore, that they would take such a visible role in America's anti-German campaign.

9. The background of this poster also seems reminiscent of nineteenth-century romantic paintings such as Caspar David Friedrich's *Abbey in the Oakwood* (1810) and *The Ruins of Eldena* (1806). German romantics were fascinated by ruins because they equated them with the culmination of civilized culture—a notion that clearly distinguished them from the newness of American culture.

10. In U.S. propaganda, this move can also be interpreted as a reaction to certain German propaganda. As Thomas Britten explains, "German troops apparently feared fighting black troops as much as fighting Native Americans. Consequently, German propagandists aimed their tracts at fomenting disloyalty among African American units. . . . German propaganda worked to undermine African American loyalty on the Western Front by stressing the racial inequities that blacks endured in the United States. German propaganda placed particular emphasis on lynchings in the South and promised African American troops that they would receive much better treatment if they crossed over to the German lines" (121).

11. Germany's attack on Belgium was a regular subject in British propaganda as well. British papers reported "German troops [mutilating] babies during their occupation of Belgium. . . . 'Babies not only had their hands cut off, but they were impaled on bayonets, and in one

case nailed to a door' " (Gordon 303). By presenting children as victims of German atrocities, this fabricated story, used to encourage American involvement in the war, incited indignation and even retributive rage, but the image of dismemberment is also a significant part of the horrors being evoked here. Implicit in this account is the image of the decimated body as one of the potential costs of war.

Another infamous example of this type of propaganda is the "corpse factory" story. As Gilbert Carr recounts in his essay "The 'Body Economic': In Contemporary Critiques of First World War Propaganda," the British, Dutch, and Belgium press claimed in April of 1917 that " 'train-loads of the stripped bodies of German soldiers, wired into bundles' were being 'simmered down in cauldrons' to produce stearine and refined oil—or, according to other versions, 'for munitions and pig and poultry food' or 'glycerine.' Were it not a forgery, the 'corpse factory' might appear as a macabre foretaste of the Third Reich. . . . When the "corpse factory" scare drove a Westminster M. P. to express concern on behalf of bereaved British parents that their sons' bodies might be put to such use as 'reported,' at least the prejudice that alleged abuse was committed in 'barbaric' Germany might have been a last reassurance that such a nightmare could not happen on the Allied side" (373).

12. To encourage support for its war effort, Axis propaganda often presented blackness and the ethnic diversity of America as a serious threat to European culture. In a particularly striking example, one Italian poster issued later in the war depicted American troops as black destroyers of Christianity. A black soldier, who is wearing a WWI helmet, crouches over some looted valuables in a decimated church. Like the gorilla from Hopps's cartoon-like image, this soldier's hunched back, large lips, and wicked grin—"primitive" features often associated with Africans and African Americans—make him look apish. His crooked face and lopsided eyes also contrast the balance and symmetry expected in more idealizing portraits. This figure lacks symmetry of face and body, thereby establishing his otherness. His blackness is also starkly contrasted with the white body of Christ on the cross above—a body that is marked and scarred with suffering. Underneath the broken cross, the soldier's gun forms a cross with a candlestick beneath the fallen Christ, suggesting a new religion defined by violence and thievery. And Christ's right hand, which now clenches nothing, is juxtaposed with the black soldier's claw-like fist clutching a bag full of church valuables. These two fists become metaphors for the cost of war—Europe is gradually left in ruins while America loots its riches by partaking in its destruction. In much of this propaganda, we see an overall tendency to cast the enemy as black, whether American or European. Thus racial otherness became a powerful way to generate support for the war effort because it tapped into pervasive social fears about racial difference and miscegenation. This poster can be found in Zbynec

Zeman's *Selling the War: Art and Propaganda in World War II* (115). As far as I know, this book is out of print, and the publisher no longer exists. Unfortunately, the author does not cite the exact source of the poster.

13. In fact, most of the other characters see Claude as a misfit (Leonard later remarks "he don't seem to fit in right" [116]), and Claude realizes this. Even though he thinks about changing his life, his gradual acquiescence to every value of his community (going to a denominational college, leaving school to work the family farm, and marrying), leaves him disgusted with himself for being unable to stand up to his father and make independent decisions. As Maureen Ryan points out in "No Woman's Land: Gender in Willa Cather's *One of Ours*": "Claude's problem is not that he is so different from his family and his community, but that he is so much like them. Despite his impatience with his parochial family, . . . he accepts the traditional values of his society" (68). This tension is captured, in part, by the sense of freakishness he feels throughout the first half of the novel. In addition to being described as a "block-head," he gets into a disfiguring farming accident during his courtship with Enid. His mules "carried him right along, swinging in the air, and finally ran him into the barb-wire fence and cut his face and neck up" (115). After this event, Claude felt "disgusting to himself; when he touched the welts on his forehead and under his hair, he felt unclean and abject. At night, when his fever ran high, and the pain began to tighten in his head and neck, it wrought him to a distressing pitch of excitement. He fought with it as one bull-dog fights with another. His mind prowled about among dark legends of torture—everything he had ever read about the Inquisition, the rack and the wheel" (118–119).

Claude feels that the welts on his head have transformed him into something grotesque, and his inability to get out of bed puts him on display to his family and Enid, who forces her way into his room to see him. Even though her visits help him "forget the humiliation of his poisoned and disfigured face" (118), he sees himself as a victim of torture. The reference to the Inquisition, whose tribunals often tortured people publicly as a deterrent to heretical beliefs, also suggests Claude's guilt about his dislike for Brother Weldon and his unwillingness to share Enid's commitment to U.S. missionary imperialism. (She later leaves him to become a missionary.) His detachment from religion, in other words, makes him a nonbeliever, a type of heretic in this community. This reference also reveals some of the changes in twentieth-century attitudes about pain. In contrast to Victorian beliefs that pain and suffering were ennobling and a part of the moral and spiritual growth of an individual, Claude, like many other post-Victorian Americans, sees suffering as unjust and pointless. Nevertheless, for Claude the humiliation of these injuries stems not only from his disfigurement, but also from the recognition that his marked body signifies his failures as both a farmhand and a prospective husband. Like Al's injuries in *Three Soldiers*, Claude's wounds, which transform him into a spectacle, become a mark of his cowardice and inability to live up to the expectations of those around him.

14. James Woodress points to Bayliss's "desiccated body" as one of the ways Cather transforms him into a "caricature of the self-made businessman" (328).

15. While writing *One of Ours*, Cather "took a break from her novel and wrote a long story just for fun, an uncharacteristic act but one that turned out well. The story was 'Coming, Aphrodite!' (Woodress 309). Given the presence of the carnival in the novel, it is not surprising that one of the central scenes in "Coming, Aphrodite!" takes place at a carnival where Eden tries Molly's act as a balloonist in front of a crowd standing around the tents. "She's coming down on the bar. I advised her to cut that out, but you see she does it first-rate. And she got rid of the skirt, too. Those black tights show off her legs well. She keeps her feet together like I told her, and makes a good line along the back. See the light on those silver slippers" (85). In this scene, Eden puts her own body on display, which works with Don's voyeurism through a peep-hole earlier in the story.

16. After researching the war in preparation for *One of Ours*, Cather's attitude about imperialism changed considerably. Critic Elizabeth Ammons recently examined the tension between Cather's "love of empire" and multiculturalism in her works. She specifically offers a postcolonial reading of "The Old Beauty" to highlight Cather's support of empire, suggesting that the character Gabrielle "represents the colonial trophy, the living symbol of European power around the world" (261). For Ammons, Cather's romanticization of empire minimizes the problems of a multiracial society in America by either keeping other races on the periphery of her works or reducing them to stereotypes. Although these dimensions are evident in her works, some of Cather's fiction in the 1920s recognizes the often violent consequences of white America's expansionist projects. In *Death Comes for the Archbishop* (1927), for example, the story of Friar Baltazar Montoya, who is killed by the people of Ácoma as an act of retaliation, foreshadows the potential violence resulting from colonization in the Western United States. Cather also explicitly confronts the topic of ethnicity in this novel without depicting Native Americans and Mexicans stereotypically. Even though she was troubled and ambivalent about race, often exoticizing racial characters as a way of confronting these anxieties, I believe the war gave her an understanding about the dangers of American imperialism that mitigated some of her own racism. Both "Tom Outland's Story" from *The Professor's House* (1925) and *One of Ours* offer useful examples for broadening our understanding of empire in Cather, enabling us to recognize both her sympathetic portraits of racial difference and her problematic ones.

In "Tom Outland's Story," Cather's characters view the remains of the Mesa Verde tribe as exotic objects for display, and their attempts to "preserve" them reflect the problematic fetishization of Native American culture by anthropologists in the mid-twentieth century. Tom's desire to give anthropologists these artifacts, including an Indian woman's desiccated body, for display in museums suggests an America fascinated by its own history as an imperial power. Through the narrator's description of her tortured body, we discover that he values only the "secrets" scientists can learn from it: "We thought she had been murdered; there was a wound in her side, the ribs stuck out through the dried flesh. Her mouth was open as if she were screaming, and her face, through all those years, had kept a look of terrible agony. Part of the nose was gone, but she had plenty of teeth" (440–441). Here, grotesque bodies and race come together in the image of an Indian woman, transforming her body into a "text" for white men to read and interpret. Whether these bodies (freaks or Native Americans) are displayed in such pseudo scientific settings, like expositions and museums, or in sideshows, they occupy a safe space for white Americans—that of the exoticized and interpretable other.

Like Claude in *One of Ours*, Tom (who later goes off to fight and die in World War I) clearly aligns himself with colonial attitudes about the "savage" other, assuming "they were probably wiped out, utterly exterminated, by some roving Indian tribe without culture or domestic virtues, some horde that fell upon them in their summer camp and destroyed them for their hides and clothing and weapons, or from mere love of slaughter" (444). He also believes that preserving this culture is the right thing to do because it offers white America a common heritage: "[The artifacts] belonged to this country, to the State, and to all the people. They belonged to boys like you and me, that have no other ancestors to inherit from" (457). Tom does not see the parallel between his appropriation of these items and America's role as an empire during westward expansion. But Cather does. In part, during the postwar years when she felt the world "broke in two," Cather's ideals about America's empire began to rupture as she learned of the deplorable treatment of American veterans—particularly after her cousin G. P. Cather was killed in action and she began interviewing veterans.

17. As Leuchtenburg explains, "[from] 1914–1932 . . . the supremacy of rural, small-town America was being challenged by the rise of the city to the dominant position in American life. . . . Most of all the older America was alarmed by the mores of the metropolis. The city represented everything—Europe, Wall Street, religious skepticism, political radicalism, sophistication, intellectual arrogance—which prewar America most feared" (7–8).

18. See Joseph Blotner's *Faulkner: A Biography*, 200–233. In "Fictional Facts and Factual Fiction: William Faulkner and World War I,"

Duane J. MacMillan uses Faulkner's fictional claims about his own military service as a way to read the tension between fact and fiction throughout *Soldiers' Pay*. See also Donald M. Kartiganer's " 'So I, Who Never Had a War . . .': William Faulkner, War, and the Modern Imagination."

CHAPTER 3   WORN, DAMAGED BODIES IN THE GREAT DEPRESSION: FSA PHOTOGRAPHY AND THE FICTION OF JOHN STEINBECK, TILLIE OLSEN, AND NATHANAEL WEST

1. See John Gunther's *Roosevelt in Retrospect*, 239.
2. For more on the debates surrounding this addition, see Benjamin Forgey's "Wheelchair Dispute Rolls on," *The Washington Post*, May 19, 2000, C01 and Rosemarie Garland Thomson's editorial, "Imaging FDR: Separate Still" (Raged Edge Online). In this piece, Thomson discusses the room added to the memorial in 2001. Designers asked scholars from the field of disability studies to recommend a quotation for the room, and after much debate, they decided on the following statement by FDR: "We know that equality of individual ability has never existed and never will, but we do insist that equality of opportunity still must be sought." Instead, the designers chose to use the words of Eleanor Roosevelt: "Franklin's illness gave him strength and courage he had not had before. He had to think out the fundamentals of living and learn the greatest of all lessons—infinite patience and never-ending persistence." According to Thomson, disability scholars were disappointed and frustrated with the choice for two reasons. First, it doesn't allow Franklin Roosevelt to speak for himself. Second, Eleanor Roosevelt's words make disability a private, not a political issue. As Thomson explains, "it tells the stereotypical, apolitical story of disability as an individual catastrophe, psychological adjustment, and moral chastening: Impairment is a private problem that an individual must overcome, not a public problem of environmental and attitudinal barriers."
3. See Sandy Grady's "Let's not put FDR's heroism in a wheelchair just to be PC," *Milwaukee Journal Sentinel*, April 27, 1997.
4. Quoted from Martin Kettle's "Roosevelt's wheelchair comes out of the closet," *The Guardian (London)*, July 3, 1998.
5. The formation of the National Foundation for Infantile Paralysis in 1937 led to the March of Dimes and eventually a vaccine for polio (Gould 72–76). For more see Chapter 4 of Tony Gould's *A Summer Plague: Polio and Its Survivors* and Chapter 5 and 6 of Gallagher's *FDR's Splendid Deception.*

6. Quoted from Kettle's "Roosevelt's wheelchair comes out of the closet."
7. In addition to this body, almost all of the male characters in the text have been injured (Mac's broken arm, Burke's shattered jaw, Dan's broken hip, Jim's faceless body, etc.) or transformed into a bizarre spectacle (i.e., London and Dakin are described in terms of animals [59, 136, 191] and Doc is feminized [129, 132, 206]). At the outset of the novel, for example, Jim meets a recruiter for the Communist party (Harry Nilson) through whose body he reads the experiences of the group: "His thick hair was combed straight down on each side from the top in a vain attempt to cover a white scar half an inch wide that lay horizontally over the right ear. . . . his face bore heavy parenthetical lines of resistance to attack. His hands were as nervous as his eyes, large hands, almost too big for his body, long fingers with spatulate ends and flay, exploring hands of a blind man, feeling the edges of paper, following the corner of the desk, touching in turn each button on his vest" (12). His body, like most of the bodies in the novel, becomes a text or visual testament to the suffering caused either by abusive working conditions or attempts to reform this abuse.
8. In *Rabelais and His World*, Mikhail Bakhtin describes the grotesque in terms of materiality, a "bodily element" that is universal (19). Images of the body are therefore linked with degradation, irregularity, copulation, carnality, defecation, mortality, and renewal. Like the masks and disguises of carnivals, the grotesque, degraded body can be both threatening and terrifying, but only temporarily. Bakhtin points out that the social critiques of the grotesque and carnivalesque are mitigated and, in effect, transformed by laughter. This balance between physical degradation and humor drives Mark Fearnow's study of the Depression in *The American Stage and the Great Depression: A Cultural History of the Grotesque*.

Fearnow argues that theater, film, and journalism in the 1930s tapped into a pervasive sense of the grotesque in American culture. The grotesque, more specifically, was often expressed through images that evoked unresolved contradictions in contemporary society, but these tensions were quickly mitigated, to some degree, by humor:

> The word "grotesque" refers to one's apprehension of an unresolved contradiction among two or more elements in an object. . . . The grotesque object thus operates as part of a social "machine" that transforms vague anxieties and discordant fears of a culture into forms in which they are represented and mingled with comic elements. Thus reified, these cultural "nightmares" are rendered less frightening but remain troubling and disruptive of an easy acceptance of "reality." (12)

The grotesque, in other words, offers a type of containment. It does not dismiss the problems underlying the social contradictions it raises; it keeps them temporarily at bay. Many Americans in the 1930s were torn between a seemingly incongruous past—idealizations and hopes about an American way of life that would help them survive the struggles of the present—and the radical solutions being posed by the New Deal. For Fearnow, this contradiction is the primary source of the grotesque in the 1930s, and successful plays and films of the period combined these tensions with touches of humor. (In fact, plays that did not incorporate humor into the grotesque often failed at the box office. And Hollywood was acutely aware of this as well. The film version of Nathanael West's *Miss Lonelyhearts* (1933), for example, became a comedy [33].)

The grotesque may have been mitigated by humor but not when freaks were concerned. Humor was both less effective and, very often, not present when freaks and freak shows were employed in works of this period. As Steinbeck's and Olsen's novels suggest, the freak was a terrifying possibility, embodying the ultimate physical costs of the Depression. Although the freak figure is often subsumed in discussions of the grotesque, these and many other contemporary works suggest the need to understand the freakish as having its own distinct conventions. It has a darker edge than the grotesque—one that cannot be contained so easily by humor.

Humor, of course, is not entirely absent from all of these examples, but freaks and freak shows primarily appear as disturbing images, suggesting that the boundaries between self/other (audience/freak) were dangerously fluid. Anyone could become a freak. At street fairs, for example, masks allowing bodies to assume the grotesque are temporary; they are only momentarily applied to protest social and class hierarchies. But the mask can be put away. As Bakhtin says, "carnival is not spectacle seen by the people; they live it, and everyone participates because its very idea embraces all the people. While carnival lasts, there is no other life outside it" (7). Because the carnival is a "temporary suspension" of hierarchies, participants do not remain spectacles afterwards; the freak, however, is always a spectacle. Once an individual's damaged body has been constructed as freakish, it carries a much more lasting and insidious stigma.

9. Paul K. Longmore has argued that *Of Mice and Men* "reflects continuing views of people with cognitive disabilities. . . . Given that historical context and that the central focus of the story is the relationship between Lenny and George, I cannot agree that the main subject is the situation of workers. I would argue that the main subject is the social danger created by the presence of someone like Lenny. The story dramatically represents the contemporaneous eugenic argument that people with disabilities, particularly people with what we now call developmental disabilities, were a source of social disorder and a drain on scarce social resources. They burdened those closest to them and the entire society. Steinbeck pits Lenny against the other men and their dreams. Lenny's disability, which is to say, his inability to control himself, destroys the dream of the farm they all hope to share. Throughout the

story, Lenny is an albatross around George's neck. When George euthanizes Lenny, he eliminates the burden and danger, the socially destructive force, that is Lenny. All of this is consistent with the contemporaneous agenda of advocates of eugenics and euthanasia. "[Steinbeck] is repeating a frequent and vicious stereotype: the big, strong, violent, uncontrollable mentally retarded adult male, who in eugenic propaganda was presented as a sexual predator. I would argue that in this story Lenny is implicitly a sexual predator because Steinbeck has him break the neck of a beautiful, highly sexual woman. In addition, Steinbeck also portrays Lenny as animalistic. It is not just that the mercy killing of the impaired dog foreshadows George's 'mercy killing' of Lenny. Steinbeck describes George and Lenny as drinking water from the stream in ways that mark them as human and animal. George cups the water in his hands. Lenny puts his face in the water.

"In closing I would just add that George's attitude toward Lenny is far from simple. In the opening scene, he verbally abuses Lenny. I have never regarded George in the way that Steinbeck seems to want the reader to view him: as Lenny's overburdened protector and merciful euthanizer. To the contrary, Steinbeck repeatedly has George show a great deal of hostility toward Lenny." Longmore wrote this as part of an ongoing discussion about Steinbeck on the DS-HUM listserv (February 24, 2005). I think that Steinbeck's portrait of Crooks and Candy, however, suggests a more sympathetic understanding of disability than Longmore gives the author credit for.

10. Jenny Lind, also known as "The Swedish Nightingale," was a famous nineteenth-century soprano and well-known philanthropist; she was considered one of the greatest singers of her day. In his quest for respectability, P. T. Barnum managed her first tour in the United States. He decided to market her for American audiences based not on her reputation (he had never heard her sing before paying her enormous expenses to come to the United States), but on his ability to advertise her. Her tour was not only a financial success, but it also reinforced his belief in the working classes' willingness to embrace art of all types.

11. Neil Harris explains that "her life story was made to order for American adulation. Her biography could have been written by Samuel Smiles (or Horatio Alger) and subtitled: 'A Struggle Against Difficulties' " (113–114).

12. Images of damaged cars appear throughout *The Grapes of Wrath*, suggesting that many migrants will end up like the cars wrecked at the side of the road or in junkyards—their wounded, broken-down bodies pushing West to find work: "Cars limping along 66 like wounded things, panting and struggling. Too hot, loose connections, loose bearings, tattling bodies. . . . Fifty thousand old cars—wounded, steaming. Wrecks along the road, abandoned. Well, what happened to

them? What happened to the folks in that car? Did they walk? Where are they? Where does the courage come from? Where does the terrible faith come from?" (165). Cars are not only metaphors for damaged bodies, but they stand for isolation and the loss of community. These people become lost, displaced, and, in some cases, their isolation from one another is linked to deformity: " 'We seen a wreck this mornin.' . . . Must a been doin' ninety. Steerin' wheel went right on through the guy an' lef' him a-wigglin' like a frog on a hook. Peach of a car. A honey. You can have her for peanuts now. Drivin' alone, the guy was" (215). This observation implies that isolation is both part of the tragedy and partially responsible for it. By associating this isolation with the accident, Steinbeck reinforces the importance of community for survival throughout these novels.

13. Robert Coles, for example, describes her "pictures of Tom Collins, the camp manager who was the model for the manager in John Steinbeck's *The Grapes of Wrath*" (20). Lange also took several photographs of a billboard advertising the film version of *The Grapes of Wrath* in 1939. See the Lange collection at the Oakland Museum of California (image numbers: LNG 35003.1 and LNG 35003.2).

14. Quoted in Milton Meltzer's *Dorothea Lange: A Photographer's Life*, 6.

15. Ibid.

16. In *An American Exodus: A Record of Human Erosion* (1939), Lange reprinted this photograph in the section entitled "Plains." Paul Taylor's caption for this image, which is labeled "North Texas, June 1937," reads: "All Displaced Tenant Farmers. The Oldest 33."

17. This photo was originally taken for the FSA, and the Library of Congress lists it as "Hoe Culture" (Alabama, June 1936). Lange dates the photograph from 1937.

18. Both "Back, 1938" and "Back, 1935" can be found in Robert Coles's *Dorothea Lange: Photographs of a Lifetime*.

19. In *The Real Thing: Imitation and Authenticity in American Culture, 1880–1940*, Miles Orvell refers to this text as "a prototype of documentary photojournalism during the 1930s. . . . With the new orientation toward society that resulted after the Depression, the rhetorical power of photography to expose the present state of things and thus point toward the need for action, was rediscovered" (227).

20. West uses bodies in a similar way in his novel *Miss Lonelyhearts* (1933). Set in New York, this book uses the disabled body as a metaphor for both the loss of spirituality in modern America and the meaninglessness of suffering. The narrator, a newspaperman who writes an advice column for forlorn lovers, begins to see the letters that he receives as "humble pleas for moral and spiritual guidance" (32). It is not the isolating, alienating nature of the city that motivates the narrator's compassion; it is the body damaged by life in the 1930s: "Crowds of people moved through the street with a dream-like

violence. As he looked at their broken hands and torn mouths, he was overwhelmed by the desire to help them" (38–39). In fact, many of the people who write to him attribute their emotional and spiritual pain to physical disability: Desperate (a suicidal teenage girl with no nose), Gracie (a rape victim who is deaf and dumb), a paralyzed boy (who wants a violin), and Fay Doyle, who blames the miseries in her life on her crippled husband, has "legs like Indian clubs, breasts like balloons and a brow like a pigeon . . . [with] massive hams . . . like two enormous grindstones" (27–28). Even Peter Doyle, who wants to find meaning in the suffering and pain that he feels because of his leg, "used a cane and dragged one of his feet behind him in a box-shaped shoe with four-inch sole. As he hobbled along, he made many waste motions, like those of a partially destroyed insect. . . . The cripple had a very strange face. His eyes failed to balance; his mouth was not under his nose; his forehead was square and bony; and his round chin was like a forehead in miniature" (44–45). In this description, the narrator views Peter as a kind of spectacle, and later he reads his own spiritual void through Peter's damaged body: "He would embrace the cripple and the cripple would be made whole again, even as he, a spiritual cripple, had been made whole" (57). But the narrator's attempts to reach out to Peter and his wife don't help anyone. They only lead to his own death.

21. Barnum frequently "Americanized" many of his freak exhibits in order to sell them to the public. He billed Joice Heth as the 161-year-old nurse of George Washington; he gave one of his midgets the name George Washington Morrison Nutt ("Commodore"); he repeatedly used aggrandized labels for freaks, such as "general," "major," and "admiral"; and it was the rags-to-riches story of Jenny Lind that helped make her such a phenomenal success. Like exotic backgrounds for racial others, Barnum used American iconography to appeal to an audience's sense of patriotism, but to achieve this, he needed to distance the patriotic allusion from the freak body evoking it. Freaks, in other words, could represent what was best about America—posing as great presidents, reenacting important battles, and showing, as in the case of Tom Thumb, that wealth and fame were possible even for the most disadvantaged individual.

So Barnum brought difference out into the open, throwing parades and orchestrating spectacular events that suggested a startling, somewhat appealing quality to difference. As A. H. Saxon points out, Barnum's exhibits, such as Tom Thumb, "were invariably conducted with decorum, were attractive to all classes of society, and generally followed some carefully thought out structure" (74). In this way, Barnum introduced a celebratory dimension to the freak. With his first managed exhibit, Joice Heth in 1835, for example, Barnum did this by associating her with Revolutionary America. Of course,

Barnum still describes her in terms of a freak exhibit (which was part of her appeal):

> Her lower limbs could not be straightened; her left arm lay across her breast and she could not remove it; the fingers of her left hand were drawn down so as nearly to close it, and were fixed; the nails on that hand were almost four inches long and extended above the wrist; the nails on her toes had grown to the thickness of a quarter of an inch; her head was covered with a thick bush of grey hair; but she was toothless and totally blind and her eyes had sunk so deeply in the sockets as to have disappeared altogether. (74)

Barnum wanted to capitalize on the deformities of her supposedly 161-year-old body, but he also wanted her to create the greatest possible sensation. In order to distinguish her from other freak exhibits, he adds to the above description that this "rare spectacle" was the nurse of George Washington. She supposedly sang him songs, clothed him, and raised him. Barnum's invocation of Washington, the popular embodiment of American independence, leadership, and heroism, offered people a way to see the dignified in this freakish artifact of American history. Barnum was also careful not to tap into antebellum anxieties about slavery and the Union. By emphasizing her status as a free woman, he defused some of the political and social tensions surrounding slavery. If she had lived long enough to be exhibited in the South under Barnum's management, this advertising strategy would have undoubtedly been altered. Joice Heth, like Tom Thumb, was constructed to appeal to all classes of Americans.

Heth's exhibit established a precedent of Americanizing exhibits that continued throughout the nineteenth century and into the twentieth. Much later in his career, Barnum still relied on the invocation of patriotism to celebrate his exhibits. In a letter to Mark Twain in 1876, Barnum describes the Americanizing strategy behind his traveling circus:

> I invest it with such patriotic features as will enable me to give a real old-fashioned Yankee-Doodle, Hail-Columbia Fourth-of-July celebration every day. . . . The procession will abound in American flags, a chariot will be mounted with a group of living characters in the costumes of the Revolution. . . . While singing "The Star Spangled Banner," *cannon* will be fired by electricity & the Goddess of Liberty will wave the Stars & Stripes. (Saxon, *Letters*, 197)

The use of military imagery was essential to this process because America historically defined its independence and power through military prowess. And this was all part of the pageantry that made Barnum's marketing strategies so appealing and successful.

22. Tod sees a similar dichotomy between real and staged pain in the film industry. During the filming of "Waterloo," for example:

> [i]n the center of the plain, the battle was going ahead briskly. Things looked tough for the British and their allies. . . . When the front rank of Milhaud's heavy division started up the slope of Mont St. Jean, the hill collapsed. The noise was terrific. Nails screamed with agony as they pulled out of joists. . . . The whole hill folded like an enormous umbrella and covered Napoleon's army with painted cloth. . . . The armies of England and her allies were too deep in scenery to flee. They had to wait for carpenters and ambulances to come up. (133–135)

This disastrous reenactment of Waterloo (with collapsing mountains, wounded actors, and queasy insurance companies) makes the history that the film attempts to capture something laughable and ridiculous. In the studio, it becomes a battle without glory, honor, and meaning; for the actors/soldiers, injuries mean financial compensation that is preferable to work: "One of the infantrymen had a broken leg, the other extras were only scratched and bruised. They were quite happy about their wounds. They were certain to receive an extra day's pay, and the man with the broken leg thought he might get as much as five hundred dollars" (135). These superficial injuries are immediately evaluated in terms of financial gain as the men turn their damaged bodies into mechanisms for profit. Film, in other words, has become a medium where the injuries during production replace war injuries; greed and self-interest replace valor and sacrifice.

23. As these examples suggest, the film industry (through the illusory dreams it creates) has drained the life and hopes out of those trying to survive in Los Angeles, leaving individuals physically and psychologically abused, exploited, and isolated. In fact, this novel is populated with figures who have no jobs, no integrity, no genuine friendships, and no romantic love; all of the characters and their relationships are superficial, driven by personal gain, lust, anger, and/or greed. Faye, Harry's daughter, believes that she will be actress, in part, because she comes from a family of actors: "Acting is in my blood. We Greeners, you know, were all theater people from away back" (158). Her ambition is selfish, driven by the glamour of stardom that film promises. In effect, movies have become the last frontier, inviting those like Faye and Adore to dream of becoming actors; they offer the most spectacular hope for achieving the American Dream through wealth and fame. But these promises prove hollow in the lives of those involved in the industry. In truth, Faye becomes a drunk and a prostitute; Adore is a cruel, mischievous child; and Homer explodes with uncontrollable violence as he stomps on Adore after the little boy throws a rock at his head. "He saw Homer rise above the mass for a moment, shoved against the sky, his jaw hanging as though he wanted to scream but couldn't. A hand reached up and caught him by his open mouth and pulled him forward and down" (181).

CHAPTER 4   "SOME UNHEARD-OF THING": FREAKS, FAMILIES, AND COMING OF AGE IN CARSON McCULLERS AND TRUMAN CAPOTE

1. Shelly Tremain, editor of a special issue of *DSQ: Disability Studies Quarterly*, discusses the crucial need for scholars to incorporate sexual orientation and sexual identity into the analysis of disability studies. Successfully bringing together these methods, Rachel Adams has done the only substantial reading of McCullers's fiction that links queer theory with the use of freaks. She is interested in the intersection of these concepts with biography (McCullers's bisexuality) and American consumerism in the 1940s. Though she situates her argument in some of the social and economic concerns of the 1940s, she primarily focuses on the cultural implications of McCullers's language, particularly the use of "queer" and "freak"—a fruitful and important way of bringing together the methodologies of queer theory and disability studies. She also sees the use of freak shows in *The Member of the Wedding* and *Clock Without Hands* as an innovative inversion of the audience-freak dynamic in this entertainment. "In McCullers fiction, freak shows fail to cement the distinction between deviance and normality, instead calling the viewers' own normality into question through their identification with the bodies onstage, which remind them of their own lonely, uncomfortable experiences of embodiment" ("A Mixture of Delicious and Freak" 557). Adams does not, however, examine McCullers's dramatic works and does not consider ambiguous sexuality as a force contributing to the decline of freak shows in the 1940s.

2. See Stephanie Coontz, *The Way We Never Were*, 8–22.

3. See Chapter 12 of Chauncey's *Gay New York*.

4. Like the "signs" whites used to identify racial passing, heterosexual society tried to identify homosexuality based on "effeminate looks and behavior." John D'Emilio and Estelle B. Freedman give an example of a World War II naval officer noticing " 'eye contact' that first alerted him to the presence of other gay men in the service" (*Intimate Matters* 289). See also Jonathan Ned Katz's *Gay American History: Lesbians and Gay Men in the U.S.A.*

5. See Stephanie Coontz, *The Way We Never Were*, and Elaine Tyler May, *Homeward Bound: American Families in the Cold War Era*.

6. As Kirstin Ringelberg argues in her essay "His Girl Friday (and Every Day): Brilliant Women Put to Poor Use," the Production Code, which was established by Will Hays in 1930 to circumvent costly lawsuits about indecency, "put a tight leash on behaviors and plots deemed either immoral or amoral, particularly in terms of violence and sexuality. Violent or strongly sexual characters or stories could be shown, but only if the end result was condemned as unacceptable. . . . The

free-wheelingladies of the pre-Code era were explicitly banned, as the Code stated clearly that, 'Out of a regard for the sanctity of marriage and the home, the triangle, that is, the love of a third party for one already married, needs careful handling. The treatment should not throw sympathy against marriage as an institution.' If marriage was to be idealized and the final or constant goal of the characters, then there was little room for the type of freedom real women were experiencing in the 1930s to be shown in film" (93). The same was certainly true for homosexuality. It was perceived as a threat to the sanctity of marriage and, therefore, had no place in Hollywood films. For more information on the Production Code, see Leonard J. Leff's *The Dame in the Kimono: Hollywood, Censorship, and the Production Code.*

7. When the play opened at the Walnut Theater in Philadelphia, it ran for four hours, and cuts were needed before it could be presented to a Broadway audience: "Carson had a great deal to say about the cuts. It was *her* play they were getting ready to operate on, and after her last experience with a script doctor, she was zealous in guarding her off-spring" (V. Carr, *The Lonely Hunter*, 339).

8. See Virginia Spencer Carr's *The Lonely Hunter: A Biography of Carson McCullers*, 330–351.

9. At the end of the novel, she is also planning to marry T. T. Williams, whom she considers an honest and good man.

10. Biographer Virginia Carr points out that McCullers was inspired to write an adaptation, in part, because of "Edmund Wilson's remarks that *The Member of the Wedding* was static and lacked a sense of drama" (274). Visually, this "freakish" behavior certainly intensifies the drama.

11. For more on the role of race in this work, see Thadious M. Davis's "Erasing the 'We of Me' and Rewriting the Racial Script: Carson McCullers's Two *Member[s] of the Wedding*," and Rachel Adams' " 'A Mixture of Delicious and Freak': The Queer Fiction of Carson McCullers."

12. Davis argues that McCullers, for commercial reasons, diluted her treatment of race in this dramatic adaptation by relying on conventional stereotypes in portraying African Americans.

13. A connection between race and homosexuality can be found in many of the works discussed in this study. Consider the presence of lesbianism and race in Nella Larsen's *Passing*, homosexuality in Willa Cather's *One of Ours* (1922) [the sexual overtones of David's and Claude's relationship and the gay German soldiers in the town of Beaufort], and the role of bisexuality, homosexuality, and ethnicity in Hemingway's *Winner Take Nothing* (1933), specifically "The Sea Change" and "The Mother of a Queen."

Fitzgerald also does a similar thing in *Tender Is the Night*, in part, by placing homosexuality and racial difference into the same category of otherness; both represent similar threats to white, heterosexist norms and values. In a note written in the late 1930s, Fitzgerald makes an explicit connection between his anti-Semitism and homophobia: ". . . two of my half dozen best men in History are Jews. But why do they have to be so damned conceited. That minority conceit—*like fairies*. They go ostrich about their faults—magnify their virtues which anyone is willing to grant in the first place" (qtd. in Donaldson 184; my emphasis). This conflation of ethnicity and sexuality doesn't present morality as the primary objection to homosexuality; instead, visibility is the culprit. Jews and homosexuals are too public about their virtues and successes for Fitzgerald. In other words, because difference is not silent, it infringes on white heterosexual culture by offering plausible alternatives.

In "F. Scott Fitzgerald: Homosexuality and the Genesis of *Tender Is the Night*," Angus P. Collins argues that Fitzgerald's attack on homosexuality reflects anxieties about his own same-sex desires: "Fitzgerald in these years appears to have suspected that he himself was the true homosexual in his choice of vocation" (171); as a result, "significant progress on *Tender Is the Night* was possible only when Fitzgerald had mastered any suspicions of himself as emasculate artist and had returned to a view of his art compatible with sexual as well as more self-endorsement" (170). Surprisingly, Collins only reads the scenes involving homosexuality from earlier versions of the novel. He does not discuss these moments in the published text. Similarly, Felipe Smith's "The Figure on the Bed" looks briefly at Fitzgerald's ridicule of homosexuals in the Melarky drafts of *Tender Is the Night* and his anxiety about lesbianism in *The Crack-Up*. Most other scholars have gone no farther than to identify certain characters as gay, and Milton Stern sidesteps the issue of homosexuality by problematically equating male homosexuality with womanhood and praising Fitzgerald's supposedly "antisexist" commentary.

> [Pardo Real's] boy has become a "girl," the "Queen of Chili.". . . Real too calls in the doctors to clean up the mess of a daddy's "girl" he has made. . . . In sum, although Fitzgerald, as a product of his time and place, was trapped within homophobic and sexist stereotypes, he uses those very stereotypes to create a breathtaking multifarious antisexist motif. (*Tender is the Night*, 41).

Cuidad Real, however, is not a woman, and his homosexuality was not created by his father's cruel treatment. Pardo's actions—"I made Francisco strip to the waist and lashed him with a whip" (242)—seem rooted more in concerns about his own sexual identity. Eve Sedgwick's discussion of coming out in *Epistemology in the Closet* can be applied effectively to this scene: "the double-edged scene of gay coming out . . . results partly from the fact that the erotic identity of the person who receives the disclosure is apt also to be implicated in, hence perturbed by it" (81). Pardo's excessive attempts to "cure" his son (beating him, sending him to brothels, giving him medication, and enlisting Dick's help to change him) clearly reflect this type of fear about his own sexual identity.

14. Lori Kenschaft explains that "[Havelock Ellis's] theories of sexual inversion define homoerotic desire as an individual pathological flaw. To the extent that McCullers accepted this model, which she largely did, her vision of the nature of homoeroticism remained that of a soul 'mean of countenance and grotesque in form' " (227). Kenschaft's "Homoerotics and Human Connections: Reading Carson McCullers 'As a Lesbian' " also briefly links her portraits of freakishness to these feelings of sexual inversion.

15. Freak shows were central metaphors throughout McCullers's fiction. Her novella *The Ballade of the Sad Café* (1943), for example, deals with masochistic and transgressive love, linking both desire with dangerous abnormality and freakishness with anxieties about sexuality. It tells the story of Miss Amelia's strange romance with the dwarfish hunchback, Cousin Lymon. Her enormous height (over six feet) links their marriage to staged freak-show pairings. Their seemingly happy relationship is shattered when Amelia's ex-husband, Marvin Macy, returns after being released from prison. Lymon is immediately attracted to Macy, even though he torments him and everyone else in town. As his desire for Macy grows so does his disgust for Amelia. He begins insulting her in public, imitating "her awkward long-legged walk; he crossed his eyes and aped her gestures in a way that made her appear to be a freak" (245). And at the boxing match between Amelia and Macy, Lymon attacks her as soon as she starts choking her opponent: "He landed on the broad strong back of Miss Amelia and clutched at her neck with his clawed little fingers" (250). Unlike Capote's more explicit treatment of homosexual desire in *Other Voices, Other Rooms*, the extent of the intimacy between these men is unclear, and McCullers's text suggests it was probably one-sided. After Lymon and Macy abandon Miss Amelia, for example, "there were rumors that Marvin Macy used him to climb into windows and steal, and other rumors that Marvin Macy had sold him to a side show" (252). Regardless, like McCullers's reluctance to see lesbianism as an option for Frankie, happiness is not found in homosexual relationships (or heterosexual relationships) in this story, and, as we will see, Capote is much more willing to present same-sex desire as fulfilling. It is also interesting to note that Edward Albee adapted this novel for the theater in 1963, suggesting that he too recognized the visible interest audiences would have in images of freakishness.

16. For example, see William White Tison Pugh's "Boundless Hearts in a Nightmare World: Queer Sentimentalism and Southern Gothicism in Truman Capote's *Other Voices, Other Rooms*."

17. Freakishness also seems to be integral to the main characters of *In Cold Blood* (1965). Capote not only suggests a homosexual relationship between the killers Dick and Perry, but he also presents the men as

deformed, using their bodies to reinforce cold-hearted cruelty of this crime throughout the novel. Dick's face, for example, is described as being "composed of mismatching parts. It was as though his head had been halved like an apple, then put together a fraction off center. . . . His eyes [were] not only situated at uneven levels but of uneven size, the left eye truly serpentine, with a venomous, sickly-blue squint" (29). And Perry's body has been damaged in a motorcycle accident, "his chunky, dwarfish legs, broken in five places and pitifully scarred" (30). His skin is also marked by ornate tattoos: "While he had fewer tattoos than his companion, they were more elaborate—not the self-inflicted work of an amateur but epics of the art contrived by Honolulu and Yokohama masters" (30). The freak shows was also part of Capote's fiction before the publication of *Other Voices, Other Rooms*. Specifically, "A Tree of Night" (1945) tells the story of a young college girl who meets two traveling performers who make a living with a sideshow act—"Lazarus: The Man Who Is Buried Alive, A Miracle, See for Yourself, Adults, 25c—Children 10c."

18. Dick Diver in *Tender Is the Night* interprets gender and sexuality in the similar way; he insists that homosexuality can be seen on the body. For Dick, one must be either homosexual or heterosexual because the possibility of bisexuality has the potential to erode existing hierarchies that privilege heterosexuality. When he meets Cuidad Real, for example, Dick suppresses his own attraction to him by interpreting same-sex desire as antithetical to masculinity. Instinctively, Dick appreciates Cuidad's charm, youthful vitality, and physical attractiveness: "The boy . . . was about twenty, handsome, and alert" (242); this attraction is not entirely surprising. As Sedgwick explains in *Epistemology of the Closet*, "it is instead the most natural thing in the world that people of the same gender . . . people whose economic, institutional, emotional, physical needs and knowledges may have so much in common, should bond together also on the axis of sexual desire" (87). Dick, however, rejects this desire because acknowledging it would compromise his identity as a heterosexual. Admitting his attraction to men (as well as women) would be a kind of hybridity, so he subsequently interprets homosexual desire as repugnant: "There was some manliness in the boy, perverted into an active resistance to his father. But he had that typically roguish look in his eyes that homosexuals assume in discussing the subject" (243). Dick must also view Cuidad's desires as a perverse act of youthful rebellion in order to see them as harmful on a social or national level. He tells Cuidad that remaining a homosexual won't leave him the "time or energy for any other decent or social act. If you want to face the world, you'll have to begin by controlling your sensuality—and, first of all, the drinking that provokes it" (243). Dick presents homosexuality here as a force that threatens the moral decency of middle-class society.

Dick's public rejection of homosexuality is an attempt to assert both his heterosexual identity and his hope that the problem of homosexuality and bisexual desire can be remedied in some way. While Dick is talking "pleasantly" with Cuidad, Royal Dumphry, another homosexual character, appears, and Dick thinks, " 'My God, I've stirred up a nest!' " (243–244). Fearing that the appearance of accepting homosexuality will somehow suggest he condones it, Dick "[continues] a crab-like retreat toward the nearest door" (244). Dumphry, however, does get the opportunity to tell him that " 'I've never forgotten that evening in the garden. . . . To me it's one of the finest memories in my life, one of the happiest ones. I've always thought of it as the most civilized gathering of people that I have ever known' " (244). This declaration suggests that Dumphry's sexuality has excluded him from acceptance in most heterosexual communities. Ironically, Dick only tolerated Dumphry's and Campion's sexuality at the garden party because they either masked or repressed it: "Mr. Royal Dumphry, his girl's comeliness less startling in the pleasure world of evening. . . . [And] Campion [managed] somehow to restrain his most blatant effeminacy" (32–33). Dick was willing to "accept" them when the other guests could possibly mistake them for heterosexuals. But Dumphry and Campion only pass in a limited sense. Dick is never unclear about their homosexuality; as a matter of fact, he relies on it to define his sense of self. Their effeminacy is juxtaposed with Dick's masculinity at the party in ways that enhance his sexual appeal for Rosemary. This need for difference, while fearing its power to destroy existing cultural norms, once again highlights the threat of homosexuality and ambiguity in the novel.

19. The ways in which Capote depicts both Randolph's anguish over lost love and his association with freaks has a number of similarities with Djuna Barnes's *Nightwood* (1937). All of the characters in *Nightwood* who fall in love with the bisexual Robin Vote become tragically lost and isolated figures. Not surprisingly, most of them, including Robin herself, are associated with circus and sideshow performers. Before meeting Robin, Felix feels "alone, apart and single" (10). This isolation, as well as his obsession with old European aristocracy, makes him feel a certain kinship with freaks: "Early in life, Felix had insinuated himself into the pageantry of the circus and the theatre. In some way they linked his emotions to the higher and unattainable pageantry of kings and queens. The more amiable actresses of Prague, Vienna, Hungary, Germany, France and Italy, the acrobats and the sword-swallowers, had at one time or another allowed him their dressing rooms—sham salons in which he aped his heart. Here he had neither to be capable nor alien. He became for a little while a part of their splendid and reeking falsification" (11). Felix not only finds community with these performers, but by giving himself the title of "Baron," he participates in the humbug of such performers. Felix doesn't want to distinguish

between fantasy and reality. And the illusory world of the circus makes this possible. Even his friend Frau Mann is described as someone who has fused with her costume: "The stuff of her tights was no longer a covering, it was herself; the span of the tightly stitched crotch was so much her own flesh that she was as unsexed as a doll" (13).

Throughout the novel, Robin continually crosses accepted boundaries: she rejects the traditional expectations of wife and mother, leaving her only child with Felix; she has affairs with women and men; and at the end of the novel, she emulates the behavior of a dog. Her association with freak shows can, therefore, be seen as another example of crossing boundaries—in this case the line between viewer and spectacle, self and other. At the end of the novel, Nora—Robin's second lover in the text and someone who worked with the Denckman circus (53)—has been shattered by Robin's departure. Much like Randolph's heartbreak in *Other Voices, Other Rooms*, Nora's behavior has become self-destructive. In an attempt to console Nora, her father, Dr. O'Connor, literally compares Robin to a freak show performer: "Robin was outside the 'human type'—a wild thing caught in a woman's skin, monstrously alone, monstrously vain; like the paralyzed man in Coney Island (take away a man's conformity and you take away his remedy) who had to lie on his back in a box, but the box was lined with velvet, his fingers jeweled with stones, and suspended over him where he could never take his eyes off, a sky-blue mounted mirror, for he wanted to enjoy his own 'difference' " (146). The doctor sees Robin as too enamored with her own difference to be faithful to anyone. At the same time, this is just one more interpretation of the most illusive character in the text. Barnes, true to her character, doesn't give the reader enough information to really know Robin.

This analysis of Robin's inaccessibility resonates with Robin Blyn's reading of the novel. "Like the circus freaks that people its text, *Nightwood's* surface is a display of language that denies entrace to its readers. As so many critics have noted, the body of *Nightwood* is, like the bodies of Nikka and Frau Mann, impenetrable, a surface composition exorbitant with detail that refuses to explain, a closed body which poses every penetration of its surface as violation" (148). Blyn goes on to read Barnes's use of language and characterization in terms of the freak show spiel and tableau. The narrator's use of language, for example, "blurs its scientific discourse with personal biography and mythological allusion, and it confuses biological and cultural determinism in classic freak show fashion" (150).

BIBLIOGRAPHY

Abrahamson, James L. *The American Home Front: Revolutionary War, Civil War, World War I, and World War II.* Washington, DC: National Defense University Press, 1983.

Adams, Bluford. *E Pluribus Barnum: The Great Showman and the Making of U.S. Popular Culture.* Minneapolis: University of Minnesota Press, 1997.

Adams, Rachel. " 'A Mixture of Delicious and Freak': The Queer Fiction of Carson McCullers." *American Literature* 71.3 (September 1999): 551–583.

———. *Sideshow U.S.A.: Freaks and the American Cultural Imagination.* Chicago: University of Chicago Press, 2001.

Alexander, Eben, Jr. "The Original Siamese Twins: We Know Why Chang Died, But Why Did Eng?" *North Carolina Medical Journal* 63.2 (March/April 2001): 66–68.

Allen, James. *Without Sanctuary: Lynching Photography in America.* New York: Twain Palm Publishers, 2000.

Allen, Robert C. *Horrible Prettiness: Burlesque and American Culture.* Chapel Hill: University of North Carolina Press, 1991.

Altick, Richard D. *The Shows of London.* Cambridge, MA: Belknap Press of Harvard University Press, 1978.

Ammons, Elizabeth. "Cather and the New Canon: 'The Old Beauty' and the Issue of Empire." *Cather Studies.* Ed. Susan J. Rosowski. Lincoln: University of Nebraska Press, 1996. 256–266.

Augustine, Saint, Bishop of Hippo. *The City of God.* Trans. Marcus Dods. New York: Modern Library, 1994.

Baker, Carlos. *Hemingway.* 4th Edition. Princeton, NJ: Princeton University Press, 1972.

Bakhtin, Mikhail. *Rabelais and His World.* Trans. Hélène Iswolsky. Bloomington: Indiana University Press, 1984.

Barnes, Djuna. *Nightwood.* 1937. New York: New Directions, 1961.

Barnum, P. T. *Struggles and Triumphs; or, Forty Years' Recollections of P. T. Barnum, Written by Himself.* Buffalo, NY: Warren, Johnson, and Company, 1872.

Bhabba, Homi. *The Location of Culture.* New York: Routledge, 1994.

Blackmer, Corinne E. "African Masks and the Arts of Passing in Gertrude Stein's 'Melanctha' and Nella Larsen's *Passing.*" *Journal of the History of Sexuality* 4.2 (October 1993): 230–263.

Blotner, Joseph. *Faulkner: A Biography.* New York: Random House, 1974.

Blyn, Robin. "From Stage to Page: Franz Kafka, Djuna Barnes, and Modernism's Freak Fictions." *Narrative* 8.2 (May 2000): 134–160.

Bogdan, Robert. *Freak Show: Presenting Human Oddities for Amusement and Profit.* Chicago: University of Chicago Press, 1988.

Bourke-White, Margaret and Erskine Caldwell. *You Have Seen Their Faces.* New York: Modern Age Books, 1937.

Britten, Thomas A. *American Indians in World War I: At Home and at War.* Albuquerque: University of New Mexico Press, 1997.

Butler, Judith. *Bodies That Matter: On the Discursive Limits of "Sex."* New York: Routledge, 1993.

———. *Gender Trouble: Feminism and the Subversion of Identity.* New York: Routledge, 1990.

Callahan, John F. *The Illusions of a Nation: Myth and History in the Novels of F. Scott Fitzgerald.* Urbana: University of Illinois Press, 1972.

Canguilhem, Georges. *The Normal and the Pathological.* Trans. Carolyn R. Fawcett with Robert S. Cohen. New York: Zone Books, 1989.

Capote, Truman. *In Cold Blood.* 1966. New York: Penguin, 1967.

———. *Other Voices, Other Rooms.* 1948. New York: Vintage International, 1994.

———. *A Tree of Night and Other Stories.* New York: Random House, 1949.

Carlton, Ann. "Beyond Gothic and Grotesque: A Feminist View of Three Female Characters of Carson McCullers." *Pembroke* 20 (1988): 54–68.

Carr, Gilbert J. "The 'Body Economic' in Contemporary Critiques of First World War Propaganda." *Forum for Modern Language Studies* 34.4 (October 1998): 366–379.

Carr, Virginia Spencer. *The Lonely Hunter: A Biography of Carson McCullers.* Garden City, NY: Doubleday, 1975.

———. *Understanding Carson McCullers.* Columbia: University of South Carolina Press, 1990.

Cassuto, Leonard. *The Inhuman Race: The Racial Grotesque in American Literature and Culture.* New York: Columbia University Press, 1997.

Cather, Willa. "Coming, Aphrodite!" 1920. *Collected Stories.* New York: Vintage-Random, 1992.

———. *Death Comes for the Archbishop.* 1927. New York: Vintage, 1990.

———. *My Ántonia.* 1918. Reprint. New York: Vintage Classics, 1994.

———.*One of Ours.* 1922. New York: Vintage, 1991.

———. "Tom Outland's Story." 1925. *Collected Stories.* New York: Vintage-Random, 1992.

Chauncey, George. *Gay New York: Gender, Urban Culture, and the Making of the Gay Male World, 1890–1940.* New York: Basic Books, 1994.

———. "From Sexual Inversion to Homosexuality: Medicine and the Changing Conceptualization of Female Deviance." *Salmaguandi.* 58–59 (Fall 1982–Winter 1983): 114–145.

Chesnutt, Charles Waddell. *The House Behind the Cedars.* 1900. Reprint. Athens: University of Georgia Press, 1988.

Christensen, Peter G. "Capote As Gay American Author." *The Critical Response to Truman Capote*. Ed. Joseph and John Waldmeir. Westport, CT: Greenwood Press, 1999. 61–67.

Ciancio, Ralph. "Laughing In Pain With Nathanael West." *Literature and the Grotesque*. Ed. Michael J. Meyer. Atlanta, GA: Rodopi Press, 1995. 1–20.

Clarke, Gerald. *Capote: A Biography*. London: Hamish Hamilton, 1988.

Cogdell, Christina. "The Futurama Recontextualized: Norman Bel Geddes's Eugenic 'World of Tomorrow.' " *American Quarterly* 52.2 (June 2000): 193–245.

Cohen, Jeffrey Jerome, ed. *Monster Theory: Reading Culture*. Minneapolis: University of Minnesota Press, 1996.

Coles, Robert. *Dorothea Lange: Photographs of a Lifetime*. New York: An Aperture Monograph, 1982.

Collins, Angus P. "F. Scott Fitzgerald: Homosexuality and the Genesis of *Tender Is the Night*." *Journal of Modern Literature* 13.1 (1986): 167–171.

Cook, Jr., James W. *The Arts of Deception: Playing with Fraud in the Age of Barnum*. Cambridge, MA: Harvard University Press, 2001.

Coontz, Stephanie. *The Way We Never Were: American Families and the Nostalgia Trap*. New York: Basic Books, 1992.

Darrah, William C. *Cartes de Visite in Nineteenth-Century Photography*. Gettysburg, PA: William C. Darrah, 1981.

Davis, Keith F. *The Photographs of Dorothea Lange*. Kansis City, MO: Hallmark Cards, 1995.

Davis, Lennard J. "Constructing Normalcy: The Bell Curve, the Novel, and the Invention of the Disabled Body in the Nineteenth Century." *The Disability Studies Reader*. Ed. Lennard J. Davis. New York: Routledge, 1997. 9–28.

———. *Enforcing Normalcy: Disability, Deafness, and the Body*. New York: Verso, 1995.

Davis, Thadious M. "Erasing the 'We of Me' and Rewriting the Racial Script: Carson McCullers's Two *Member[s] of the Wedding*." *Critical Essays on Carson McCullers*. Ed. Beverly Lyon Clark and Melvin J. Friedman. New York: G. K. Hall, 1996. 206–219.

D' Emilio, John. *Sexual Politics, Sexual Communities: The Making of a Homosexual Minority in the United States, 1940–1970*. Chicago: University of Chicago Press, 1983.

D' Emilio, John and Estelle B. Freedman. *Intimate Matters: A History of Sexuality in America*. New York: Harper & Row, 1998.

Decker, Jeffrey Louis. "Gatsby's Pristine Dream: The Diminishment of the Self-Made Man in the Tribal Twenties. *Novel: A Forum on Fiction* 28.1 (Fall 1994): 52–71.

Dennett, Andrea Stulman. *Weird and Wonderful: The Dime Museum in America*. New York: New York University Press, 1997.

Donaldson, Scott. *Fool For Love: F. Scott Fitzgerald*. New York: Congdon and Weed, 1983.

Donaldson, Susan V. "Making a Spectacle: Welty, Faulkner, and Southern Gothic." *Mississippi Quarterly* 50.4 (Fall 1997): 567–583.

Dos Passos, John. *Three Soldiers*. 1921. New York: Penguin Books, 1997.

Douglas, Ann. *Terrible Honesty: Mongrel Manhattan in the 1920s*. New York: Farrar, Straus, and Giroux, 1996.

Drimmer, Frederick. *Very Special People: The Struggles, Loves and Triumphs of Human Oddities*. New York: Bantam, 1973.

Duberman, Martin Bauml. *Hidden From History: Reclaiming the Gay and Lesbian Past*. New York: New American Library, 1989.

Eliot, T. S. Introduction to *Nightwood* by Djuna Barnes. 1937. New York: New Directions, 1961.

Ellison, Ralph. *Invisible Man*. 1952. New York: Vintage, 1995.

Eugenides, Jeffrey. *Middlesex: A Novel*. New York: Farrar, Straus, and Giroux, 2002.

Fahy, Thomas. *Captive Audience: Prison and Captivity in Contemporary Theater*. Ed. Thomas Fahy and Kimball King. New York: Routledge, 2003.

———. "Enfreaking War-Injured Bodies: Fallen Soldiers in Propaganda and American Literature of the 1920s. *Prospects: An Annual of American Cultural Studies* 25 (2000): 529–563.

———. "Iteration as a Form of Narrative Control in Gertrude Stein's 'The Good Anna.' " *Style* 32.5 (Spring 2000): 25–35.

———. *Peering Behind the Curtain: Disability, Illness, and the Extraordinary Body in Contemporary Theater*. Ed. Thomas Fahy and Kimball King. New York: Routledge, 2002.

———. Rev. of *"The Changing Same": Black Women's Literature, Criticism, and Theory*, by Deborah E. McDowell. *African-American Review* 33.3 (1999): 13–14.

———. "Worn, Damaged Bodies: Literature and Photography of the Great Depression." *Journal of American Culture* 26.1 (March 2003): 1–16.

Faulkner, William. *Light in August*. 1932. New York: Vantage Books, 1972.

———. *Soldiers' Pay*. 1926. New York: Liveright, 1997.

Fearnow, Mark. *The American Stage and the Great Depression: A Cultural History of the Grotesque*. Cambridge: Cambridge University Press, 1997.

Feith, Michel and Genevieve Fabre, eds. *Temples for Tomorrow: Looking Back at the Harlem Renaissance*. Bloomington: Indiana University Press, 2001.

Ferrell, Robert H. *Woodrow Wilson and World War I: 1917–1921*. New York: Harper & Row, 1985.

Fiedler, Leslie. *Freaks: Myths and Images of the Secret Self*. New York: Simon and Schuster, 1978.

———. *Love and Death in the American Novel*. New York: Criterion Books, 1960.

Fischer, Mike. "Pastoralism and its Discontents: Willa Cather and the Burden of Imperialism." *Mosaic* 23.1 (1990): 31–43.

Fitzgerald, F. Scott. The *Great Gatsby*. New York: Scribner's, 1925.

———. *The Letters of F. Scott Fitzgerald*. Ed. Andrew Turnbull. New York: Scribner's, 1963.

———. *Six Tales of the Jazz Age and Other Stories*. New York: Scribner's, 1960.

———. *Tender Is the Night*. New York: Scribner's, 1934.

Forgey, Benjamin. "Wheelchair Dispute Rolls On." *Washington Post.* May 19, 2000: C1.

Foss, Daniel. *Freak Culture: Lifestyle and Politics.* New York: E. P. Dutton, 1972.

Foucault, Michel. *Birth of the Clinic: An Archaeology of Medical Perception.* Trans. Alan M. Sheridan-Smith. New York: Pantheon, 1973.

———. *Discipline and Punish: The Birth of the Prison.* Trans. Alan M. Sheridan-Smith. New York: Vintage Books, 1979.

"Franklin Delano Roosevelt." *The New York World.* June 28, 1928: 12.

Freaks. Dir. Tod Browning. Metro-Goldwyn-Mayer, 1932.

Friedman, John Block. *The Monstrous Races in Medieval Art and Thought.* Cambridge, MA: Harvard University Press, 1981.

Gallagher, Hugh Gregory. *FDR's Splendid Deception.* New York: Dodd, Mead & Company, 1985.

Gamson, Joshua. *Freaks Talk Back: Tabloid Talk Shows and Sexual Nonconformity.* Chicago: University of Chicago Press, 1998.

Gary, Brett. *The Nervous Liberals: Propaganda Anxieties from World War I to the Cold War.* New York: Columbia University Press, 1999.

Gerber, David A. "In Search of Al Schmid: War Hero, Blinded Veteran, Everyman." *The Body and Physical Difference: Discourses of Disability.* Ed. David T. Mitchell and Sharon L. Snyder. Ann Arbor: University of Michigan Press, 1997. 111–133.

———. "Volition and Valorization: The 'Careers' of People Exhibited in Freak Shows." *Freakery: Cultural Spectacles of the Extraordinary Body.* Ed. Rosemarie Garland Thomson. New York: New York University Press, 1996. 38–54.

Gidley, M. "Notes on F. Scott Fitzgerald and the Passing of the Great Race." *American Studies* 7.2 (1963): 171–181.

Gilman, Sander L. *Difference and Pathology: Stereotypes of Sexuality, Race, and Madness.* Ithaca: Cornell University Press, 1985.

Gilman, Susan. *Dark Twins: Imposture and Identity in Mark Twain's America.* Chicago: University of Chicago Press, 1989.

Gleason, William A. *The Leisure Ethic: Work and Play in American Literature, 1840–1940.* Stanford, CA: Stanford University Press, 1999.

Goddard, Henry Herbert. *The Kallikak Family: A Study in the Heredity of Feeble-Mindedness.* New York: Macmillan, 1912.

Gordon, David. "A Common Design: Propaganda and World War." *The Costs of War: America's Pyrrhic Victories.* Ed. John V. Denson. New Brunswick, NJ: Transaction Publishers, 1999. 301–320.

Gould, George M. and Walter Pyle. *Anomalies and Curiosities of Medicine.* 1896. New York: Julian Press, 1956.

Gould, Tony. *A Summer Plague: Polio and its Survivors.* New Haven: Yale University Press, 1995.

Grady, Sandy. "Let's Not Put FDR's heroism in a wheelchair just to be PC." *Milwaukee Journal Sentinel* April 27, 1997: 3.

Grant, Madison. *The Passing of the Great Race.* New York: Scribner's, 1921.

Greer, Andrew Sean. *The Confessions of Max Tivoli*. New York: Farrar, Straus, and Giroux, 2004.

Griffiths, Frederick T. "The Woman Warrior: Willa Cather and *One of Ours.*" *Women's Studies* 11 (1984): 261–285.

Grosz, Elizabeth. "Intolerable Ambiguity: Freaks as/at the Limit." *Freakery: Cultural Spectacles of the Extraordinary Body*. Ed. Rosemarie Garland Thomson. New York: New York University Press, 1996. 55–68.

Guimond, James. *American Photography and the American Dream*. Chapel Hill: The University of North Carolina Press, 1991.

Gunther, John. *Roosevelt in Retrospect: A Profile in History*. New York: Harper & Row, 1950.

Harpham, Geoffrey Galt. *On the Grotesque: Strategies of Contradiction in Art and Literature*. Princeton, NJ: Princeton University Press, 1982.

Harris, Neil. *Humbug: The Art of P. T. Barnum*. Boston: Little, Brown, 1973.

Harris, Trudier. *Exorcising Blackness: Historical and Literary Lynching and Burning Rituals*. Bloomington: Indiana University Press, 1984.

Hartman, Saidiya. *Scenes of Subjection: Terror, Slavery, and Self-Making in Nineteenth Century America*. New York: Oxford University Press, 1997.

Hawkins, Joan. " 'One of Us': Tod Browning's *Freaks.*" *Freakery: Cultural Spectacles of the Extraordinary Body*. Ed. Rosemarie Garland Thomson. New York: New York University Press, 1996. 265–276.

Hays, Peter L. *The Limping Hero: Grotesque in Literature*. New York: New York University Press, 1971.

Hemingway, Ernest. "In Another Country." 1927. *The Complete Short Stories of Ernest Hemingway*. New York: Scribner's, 1987. 206–210.

———. "Soldier's Home." 1925. *The Complete Short Stories of Ernest Hemingway*. New York: Scribner's, 1987. 111–116.

———. *The Sun also Rises*. New York: Scribner's, 1926.

———. "A Way You'll Never Be." 1938. *The Complete Short Stories of Ernest Hemingway*. New York: Scribner's, 1987. 306–315.

Herndl, Diane Price. *Invalid Women: Figuring Illness in American Fiction and Culture, 1840–1940*. Chapel Hill: University of North Carolina Press, 1993.

Hevey, David. *The Creatures Time Forgot: Photography and Disability Imagery*. New York: Routledge, 1992.

Higham, John. *Strangers in the Land: Patterns of American Nativism 1860–1925*. New York: Atheneum, 1975.

Huet, Marie-Hélène. *Monstrous Imagination*. Cambridge, MA: Harvard University Press, 1993.

Hutchinson, George. *The Harlem Renaissance in Black and White*. Cambridge, MA: Belknap Press of Harvard University Press, 1995.

Johnson, Randy, Jim Secreto, and Teddy Varndell. *Freaks, Geeks & Strange Girls: Sideshow Banners of the Great American Midway*. Honolulu: Hardy Marks Publications, 1996.

Kaplan, Amy. " 'Left Alone With America': The Absence of Empire in the Study of American Culture." *Culture of United States Imperialism*. Durham, NC: Duke University Press, 1993. 3–21.

Karl, Ferderick R. "Introduction." *Soldiers' Pay*. By William Faulkner. New York: Liveright, 1997.

Kartiganer, Donald M. " 'So I, Who Never Had a War . . .': William Faulkner, War, and the Modern Imagination." *Modern Fiction Studies* 44.3 (Fall 1998): 619–645.

Kasson, John F. *Amusing the Million: Coney Island at the Turn of the Century*. New York: Hill and Wang, 1978.

———. *Houdini, Tarzan, and the Perfect Man: The White Male Body and the Challenge of Modernity in America*. New York: Hill and Wang, 2002.

Kasson, Joy S. *Buffalo Bill's Wild West: Celebrity, Memory, and Popular History*. New York: Hill and Wang, 2000.

Katz, Jonathan Ned. *Gay American History: Lesbians and Gay Men in the U.S.A.* New York: Meridian, 1976.

Kenschaft, Lori J. "Homoerotics and Human Connections: Reading Carson McCullers 'As a Lesbian.' " *Critical Essays on Carson McCullers*. Ed. Beverly Lyon Clark and Melvin J. Friedman. New York: G. K. Hall & Co., 1996. 220–233.

Kettle, Martin. "Roosevelt's wheelchair comes out of the closet." *The Guardian (London)* July 3, 1998: 24.

Kevles, Daniel J. *In the Name of Eugenics: Genetics and the Uses of Human Heredity*. New York: Knopf, 1985.

Kunhardt, Philip B., Jr., Philip B. Kunhardt III, and Peter W. Kunhardt. *P. T. Barnum: America's Greatest Showman*. New York: Knopf, 1995.

LaFeber, Walter. *The New Empire: Interpretations of American Imperialism 1860–1898*. Ithaca: Cornell University Press, 1963.

Lange, Dorothea and Paul Schuster Taylor. *An American Exodus: A Record of Human Erosion*. New York: Reynal & Hitchcock, 1939.

Larsen, Nella. *Passing*. 1929. Reprint. New Brunswick, NJ: Rutgers University Press, 1986.

Leff, Leonard J. *The Dame in the Kimono: Hollywood, Censorship, and the Production Code*. Lexington: University Press of Kentucky, 2001.

Levine, Lawrence W. *Highbrow/Lowbrow: The Emergence of Cultural Hierarchy in America*. Cambridge, MA: Harvard University Press, 1988.

Leuchtenburg, William E. *The Perils of Prosperity 1914–1932*. Chicago: University of Chicago Press, 1958.

Lhamon W. T., Jr. *Raising Cain: Blackface Performance from Jim Crow to Hip Hop*. Cambridge, MA: Harvard University Press, 1998.

Lindberg, Gary. *The Confidence Man in American Literature*. New York: Oxford University Press, 1982.

Longmore, Paul K. "Of Mice and Men." Online posting. February 24, 2005. Disability Studies LISTSERV. <DS-HUM@LISTSERV.UMD.EDU>

Lott, Eric. *Love and Theft: Blackface Minstrelsy and the American Working Class*. New York: Oxford University Press, 1993.

Ludington, Townsend. *The Fourteenth Chronicle: Letters and Diaries of John Dos Passos*. Cambridge, MA: Harvard Common Press, 1973.

———. *John Dos Passos: A Twentieth Century Odyssey*. New York: Carroll and Graf, 1998.

Mackenthun, Gesa. "State of the Art: Adding Empire to the Study of American Culture." *Journal of American Studies* 30 (1996): 263–269.

MacMillan, Duane J. "Fictional Facts and Factual Fiction: William Faulkner and World War I." *The Faulkner Journal* (Spring 1987): 47–54.

Mannix, Daniel P. *Freaks: We Who Are Not As Others.* 1976. New York: Juno Books, 1999.

Marshall, David P. *Celebrity and Power: Fame in Contemporary Culture.* Minneapolis: University of Minnesota Press, 1997.

May, Elaine Tyler. *Homeward Bound: American Families in the Cold War Era.* New York: Basic Books, 1998.

McCracken, Elizabeth. *The Giant's House: A Romance.* New York: Avon, 1996.

McCullers, Carson. *The Ballade of the Sad Café.* 1943. *Carson McCullers Collected Stories.* Boston: Houghton Mifflin Company, 1987.

———. *The Member of the Wedding.* Boston: Houghton Mifflin, 1946.

———. *The Member of the Wedding: A Play by Carson McCullers.* New York: New Directions, 1950.

———. *The Square Root of Wonderful: A Play by Carson McCullers.* New York: Houghton Mifflin, 1958.

McDowell, Deborah E. *"The Changing Same": Black Women's Literature, Criticism, and Theory.* Bloomington: Indiana University Press, 1995.

Mellow, James R. *Hemingway: A Life Without Consequences.* Boston, MA: Houghton Mifflin, 1992.

Meltzer, Milton. *Dorothea Lange: A Photographer's Life.* New York: Farrar, Straus, and Giroux, 1978.

Michaels, Michael Benn. *Our America: Nativism, Modernism, and Pluralism.* Durham, NC: Duke University Press, 1995.

Mitchell, David T. and Sharon L. Snyder. "Modernist Freaks and Postmodern Geeks." *The Disability Studies Reader.* Ed. Lennard J. Davis. New York: Routledge, 1997. 348–365.

———. *Narrative Prosthesis: Disability and the Dependencies of Discourse.* Ann Arbor: University of Michigan Press, 2000.

Mitchell, Michael. *Monsters of the Gilded Age: The Photographs of Charles Eisenmann.* Agincart, Ontario: Gage, 1979.

Montaigne, Michel de. "Of a Monstrous Child." *The Complete Works of Montaigne.* Trans. Donald M. Frame. Stanford, CA: Stanford University Press, 1967.

Morrison, Toni. *Beloved.* New York: Plume Contemporary Fiction, 1988.

Muller, Gilbert H. *Nightmares and Visions: Flannery O'Connor and the Catholic Grotesque.* Athens: University of Georgia Press, 1972.

Nasaw, David. *Going Out: The Rise and Fall of Public Amusements.* New York: Basic Books, 1993.

Norden, Martin. *The Cinema of Isolation: A History of Physical Disability in the Movies.* New Brunswick, NJ: Rutgers University Press, 1994.

Nye, Russel. *The Unembarrassed Muse: The Popular Arts in America.* New York: The Dial Press, 1970.

O' Connor, Flannery. "A Temple of the Holy Ghost." *A Good Man Is Hard to Find and Other Stories*. New York: Harcourt Brace & Company, 1955. 80–97.

Olsen, Tillie. *Yonnondio: From the Thirties*. New York: Delta/Seymour Lawrence, 1974.

Orvell, Miles. *The Real Thing: Imitation and Authenticity in American Culture, 1880–1940*. Chapel Hill: University of North Carolina Press, 1989.

Ostman, Ronald E. "Photography and Persuasion: Farm Security Administration Photographs of Circus and Carnival Sideshows, 1935–1942." *Freakery: Cultural Spectacles of the Extraordinary Body*. Ed. Rosemarie Garland Thomson. New York: New York University Press, 1996. 121–136.

Pare, Ambroise. *On Monsters and Marvels*. 1573. Trans. Janis Pallister. Reprint. Chicago: University of Chicago Press, 1982.

Paret, Peter, Paul Paret, and Beth Lewis. *Persuasive Images: Posters of War and Revolution from the Hoover Institution Archives*. Princeton, NJ: Princeton University Press, 1992.

Parrish, Michael E. *Anxious Decades: America in Prosperity and Depression 1920–1941*. New York: W. W. Norton & Co., 1992.

Pugh, William White Tison. "Boundless Hearts in a Nightmare World: Queer Sentimentalism and Southern Gothicism in Truman Capote's *Other Voices, Other Rooms*." *Mississippi Quarterly* 51.4 (Fall 1998): 663–682.

Raico, Ralph. "World War I: The Turning Point." *The Costs of War: America's Pyrrhic Victories*. Ed. John V. Denson. New Brunswick, NJ: Transaction Publishers, 1999. 203–248.

Reiss, Benjamin. "P. T. Barnum, Joice Heth, and Antebellum Spectacles of Race." *American Quarterly* 51.1 (March 1999): 78–107.

———. *The Showman and the Slave: Race, Death, and Memory in Barnum's America*. Cambridge, MA: Harvard University Press, 2001.

Reynolds, Guy. *Willa Cather in Context: Progress, Race, Empire*. New York: St. Martin's Press, 1996.

Reynolds, Michael. *Hemingway: The 1930s*. New York: W. W. Norton and Co., 1997.

Rhodes, Chip. *Structures of the Jazz Age: Mass Culture, Progressive Education, and Racial Discourse in American Modernism*. London: Verso, 1998.

Ricard, Serge. "World War One and the Rooseveltian Gospel of Undiluted Americanism." *Hyphenated Diplomacy: European Immigration and U.S. Foreign Policy, 1914–1984*. Ed. Helene Christol and Serge Ricard. Provence: University of Provence, 1985.

Riis, Thomas L. "The Legacy of a Prodigy Lost in Mystery." *New York Times* March 5, 2000, Art and Leisure, Part 2: 35–36.

Ringelberg, Kirstin. "His Girl Friday (and Every Day): Brilliant Women Put to Poor Use." *Considering Aaron Sorkin: Essays on the Politics, Poetics, and Sleight of Hand in the Films and Television Series*. Ed. Thomas Fahy. Jefferson, North Carolina: McFarland and Company, 2005. 91–100.

Ross, Stewart Halsey. *Propaganda for War: How the United States Was Conditioned to Fight the Great War of 1914–1918.* Jefferson, NC: McFarland and Company, 1996.

Russo, Mary. *The Female Grotesque: Risk, Excess, and Modernity.* New York: Routledge, 1994.

———. "Female Grotesques: Carnival and Theory." Reprint. *Writing on the Body: Female Embodiment and Feminist Theory.* Ed. Katie Conboy, Nadia Medina, and Sarah Stanbury. New York: Columbia University Press, 1997. 318–336.

Ryan, Maureen. "No Woman's Land: Gender in Willa Cather's *One of Ours.*" *Studies in American Fiction* 18.1 (Spring 1990): 65–75.

Rydell, Robert. *All the World's a Fair: Visions of Empire at American International Expositions, 1876–1916.* Chicago: University of Chicago Press, 1984.

Said, Edward. *Culture and Imperialism.* New York: Knopf, 1993.

Saxon, A. H. *P. T. Barnum: The Legend and the Man.* New York: Columbia University Press, 1989.

———. ed. *Selected Letters of P. T. Barnum.* New York: Columbia University Press, 1983.

Scarry, Elaine. *The Body in Pain: The Making and Unmaking of the World.* New York: Oxford University Press, 1985.

Schickel, Richard. *Intimate Strangers: The Culture of Celebrity.* Garden City, NY: Doubleday, 1985.

Sedgwick, Eve Kosofsky. *Epistemology of the Closet.* Berkeley: University of California Press, 1990.

Skal, David J. and Elias Savada. *Dark Carnival: The Secret World of Tod Browning, Hollywood's Master of the Macabre.* New York: Anchor Books, 1995.

Smith, Felipe. "Figure on the Bed: Difference and American Destiny in *Tender Is the Night.*" *French Connections: Hemingway and Fitzgerald Abroad.* Ed. J. Gerald Kennedy and Jackson R. Bryer. New York: St. Martin's Press, 1998. 187–213.

Sollors, Werner. *Beyond Ethnicity: Consent and Descent in American Culture.* New York: Oxford University Press, 1986.

———. "Immigrants and Other Americans." *Columbia Literary History of the United States.* Ed. Emory Elliott. New York: Columbia University Press, 1988. 568–588.

———. *Neither Black Nor White Yet Both: Thematic Explorations of Interracial Literature.* Cambridge, MA: Harvard University Press, 1997.

Sontag, Susan. *On Photography.* 1977. New York: Anchor Books, 1990.

Stein, Sally. "Peculiar Grace: Dorothea Lange and the Testimony of the Body." *Dorothea Lange: A Visual Life.* Ed. Elizabeth Partridge. Washington: Smithsonian Institution Press, 1994.

Steinbeck, John. *The Grapes of Wrath.* 1939. New York: Penguin Books, 1992.

———. *In Dubious Battle*. 1936. New York: Penguin Books,1992.

———. *Of Mice and Men*. 1937. New York: Bantam Books, 1955.

———. *"Their Blood Is Strong": A Factual Story of the Migratory Agricultural Workers in California*. San Francisco: Simon J. Lubin Society of California, 1938.

Stern, Milton. *Tender Is the Night: The Broken Universe*. New York: Twayne Publishers, 1994.

———. *The Golden Moment: The Novels of F. Scott Fitzgerald*. Urbana: University of Illinois Press, 1970.

Steward, Susan. *On Longing: Narratives of the Miniature, the Gigantic, the Souvenir, the Collection*. Durham, NC: Duke University Press, 1993.

Stoddard, Lothrup. *The Rising Tide of Color Against White World-Supremacy*. New York: Scribner's, 1922.

Strandberg, Victor. "In a Farther Country: The Goyen-McCullers Freak Show." *Appreciations of a Writer's Writer*. Ed. Brooke Horvath, Irving Malin, and Paul Ruffin. Austin: University of Texas Press, 1997.

Strauss, Darin. *Chang and Eng*. New York: Plume, 2000.

Sundquist, Eric. *To Wake the Nations: Race in the Making of American Literature*. Cambridge, MA: Belknap Press, 1993.

Thompson, C. J. S. *The Mystery and Lore of Monsters: With Accounts of Some Giants, Dwarfs and Prodigies*. London: Williams & Norgate, 1930.

Thomson, Rosemarie Garland *Extraordinary Bodies: Figuring Physical Disability in American Culture and Literature*. New York: Columbia University Press, 1997.

———. "Imaging FDR: Separate Still." *Ragged Edge Online* 2 (2001). <http://www.ragged-edge-mag.com/0301/0301ft3.htm>

———. "Introduction: From Wonder to Error—A Genealogy of Freak Discourse in Modernity." *Freakery: Cultural Spectacles of the Extraordinary Body*. Ed. Rosemarie Garland Thomson. New York: New York University Press, 1996. 1–19.

Toomer, Jean. *Cane*. 1923. Ed. Darwin T. Turner. New York: Liveright, 1975.

Trachtenberg, Alan. *The Incorporation of America: Culture and Society in the Gilded Age*. New York: Hill and Wang, 1982.

———. "The Journey Back: Myth and History in *Tender Is the Night*." *F. Scott Fitzgerald Critical Assessments*. Ed. Henry Claridge. Vol. 3. London: Helm Information, 1991.

———. *Reading American Photographs: Images as History Matthew Brady to Walker Evans*. New York: Hill and Wang, 1989.

Tremain, Shelley. "DSQ: Disability Studies Queered." *Disability Studies Quarterly* 18.3 (March 1999): 166–168.

Trumbo, Dalton, dir. *Johnny Got His Gun*. Perf. Timothy Bottoms. 1971.

Turnbull, Andrew, ed. *The Letters of F. Scott Fitzgerald*. New York: Scribner's, 1963.

Tuttle, William M. *Race Riot: Chicago in the Red Summer of 1919*. Chicago: Holiday House, 1972.

Twain, Mark. *The Adventures of Huckleberry Finn.* 1884. New York: Bantam Books, 1981.

Twitchell, James B. *Carnival Culture: The Trashing of Taste in America.* New York: Columbia University Press, 1992.

Vaughan, Christopher A. "Ogling Igorots: The Politics and Commerce of Exhibiting Cultural Otherness, 1898–1913." *Freakery: Cultural Spectacles of the Extraordinary Body.* Ed. Rosemarie Garland Thomson. New York: New York University Press, 1996. 219–233.

Wagner-Martin, Linda. *Ernest Hemingway: Seven Decades of Criticism.* Ed. Linda Wagner-Martin. East Lansing, MI: Michigan State University Press, 1998.

———. *"Favored Strangers": Gertrude Stein and Her Family.* New Brunswick, NJ: Rutgers University Press, 1995.

———. *Zelda Sayre Fitzgerald: An American Woman's Life.* New York: Palgrave Macmillan, 2004.

Washington, Byran R. *The Politics of Exile: Ideology in Henry James, F. Scott Fitzgerald, and James Baldwin.* Boston: Northeastern University Press, 1995.

Watkins, T. H. *The Great Depression: America in the 1930s.* Boston: Little, Brown, 1993.

Weiss, M. Lynn. *Gertrude Stein and Richard Wright: The Poetics and Politics of Modernism.* Mississippi: University Press of Mississippi, 1998.

Welling, William. *Photography in America: The Formative Years 1839–1900.* New York: Crowell, 1978.

Welty, Eudora. *A Curtain of Green And Other Stories.* 1941. New York: Harcourt Brace Jovanovich, 1991.

West, Nathanael. *The Day of the Locust.* 1939. New York: New Directions Paperback, 1962.

———. *Miss Lonelyhearts.* 1933. New York: New Directions Paperback, 1962.

Weston, Elizabeth. *The International Theme in F. Scott Fitzgerald's Literature.* New York: Peter Lang, 1995.

Wilson, Dudley. *Signs and Portents: Monstrous Births from the Middle Ages to the Enlightenment.* New York: Routledge, 1993.

Wilson, Woodrow. *The Papers of Woodrow Wilson, January 24-April 6, 1917.* Ed. Arthur S. Link. Princeton, NJ: Princeton University Press, 1983.

Wonham, Henry B. " 'I Want a Real Cool': Mark Twain and Late-Nineteenth-Century Ethnic Caricature." *American Literature.* 72.1 (March 2000): 117–152.

Woodress, James. *Willa Cather: A Literary Life.* Lincoln: University of Nebraska Press, 1987.

Wright, Richard. *Black Boy: A Record of Childhood and Youth by Richard Wright.* New York: Harper, 1945.

Wright, Richardson. *Hawkers and Walkers in Early America: Strolling, Peddlers, Preachers, Lawyers, Doctors, Players, and Others, from the Beginning to the Civil War.* Philadelphia: J. B. Lippencott, 1927.

Wulfman, Clifford E. "Sighting/Siting/Citing the Scar: Trauma and Homecoming in Faulkner's *Soldiers' Pay*. *Studies in American Fiction* 31.1 (Spring 2003): 29–43.

Yaeger, Patricia. *Dirt and Desire: Reconstructing Southern Women's Writing, 1930–1990.* Chicago: University of Chicago Press, 2000.

Zeman, Zbynec. *Selling the War: Art and Propaganda in World War II.* London: Orbis Publishing, 1978.

INDEX

Abrahamson, James, 52
Adams, Bluford, 139 n.8, 142 n.19
Adams, Rachel, 13, 17, 135 n.1,
    162 n.1, 163 n.11
Admiral Dot (Leopold Kahn), 8
African Americans
    and culture, 14, 19–20, 21, 23–24,
        28, 32–33, 54, 57, 89–90, 115,
        142 n.20, 145 n.30, 149 n.10
    and racial freaks, 14, 19–20, 22,
        27–28, 32–33, 34–35, 41,
        44–46, 53–54, 114,
        128–129, 139 n.7
    and stereotypes, 21, 28, 33–34,
        35–37, 44–45, 54–55, 57,
        138 n.2, 139 n.7, 141 n.16,
        142 n.17, 142 n.19,
        150–151 n.12, 163 n.12
Alexander, Eben, 136–137 n.7
Allen, James, 20–22, 138–139 n.6
Allen, Robert, 136 n.3
Altick, Richard, 6
Ammons, Elizabeth, 152 n.16
Arbus, Diane, 149 n.7
Armstrong, Louis, 28
Augustine, Saint, City of God, 4

Baker, Josephine, 28
Bakhtin, Mikhail, 155–156 n.8
Barnes, Djuna, Nightwood,
    167–168 n.19
Barnum, P. T., 4, 7, 9, 22–23,
    28–29, 37–38, 42, 44, 53, 54,
    60, 92, 128–129, 136 n.4, 136
    n.6, 136 n.7, 139 n.8, 141

n.16, 142 n.18, 142 n.19, 143
    n.22, 157 n.10, 159–160 n.21
bearded lady, 2–3, 8, 13, 16, 22,
    107–108, 111, 119, 132
Bedlam, 6
Bellows, George, Both Members
    of This Club, 31, 37; Club Night,
    31
bisexuality, 109, 116, 162 n.1, 163
    n.14, 166–167 n.18, 167–168
    n.19,
Blotner, Joseph, 153–154 n.18
Blyn, Robin, 167–168 n.19
body, 2, 3, 4, 7, 8, 11, 13–17, 19,
    20–25, 53–58, 59–76, 79–81,
    83–103, 107–109, 111–124,
    128–133, 143 n.23
Bogdan, Robert, 7, 12, 17, 53,
    135 n.1, 136 n.5, 136 n.7,
    138 n.5, 139 n.7, 142 n.18,
    143 n.21
Bourke-White, Margaret, You Have
    Seen Their Faces, 81, 94,
    97–100, 132
boxing (staged fights), 28–37, 130,
    165 n.15
Brady, Mathew, 9, 23
British Museum, 6
Britten, Thomas, 52, 149 n.10
Browning, Tod, Freaks, 12
Bubbles, John, 28
Butler, Judith, 146 n.32

Cain, 5, 135 n.2
Caldwell, Erskine, 97–98

immigrants, immigration, 14, 16,
19, 22–26, 27, 41, 52, 130,
131, 139 n.9, 139 n.11,
140–141 n.14, 142 n.19, 143
n.25
imperialism, 5, 15, 52–53, 142
n.17, 144–145 n.29, 145–146
n.31, 148 n.6, 151–152 n.13,
152–153 n.16

James, Will, 21, 138–139 n.6
Joice Heth, 9, 137 n.8, 139 n.8,
143 n.22, 159–160 n.21

Kafka, Franz, "The
Metamorphosis," 80–81
Kaplan, Amy, 148 n.6
Kartiganer, Donald M., 153–154
n.8
Kasson, John, 12, 137 n.12
Katz, Jonathan Ned, 162 n.4
Kenschaft, Lori, 165 n.14
Kettle, Martin, 154 n.4, 155 n.6
Kevles, Daniel J, 139 n.10, 141
n.15
Kinsey, Alfred, 110–111

Lange, Dorothea, 15–16, 81,
94–100, 102, 132, 158
n.13–n.18
An American Exodus: A Record
of Human Erosion, 95–96,
158 n.16
Larsen, Nella, 14, 20, 28, 40, 41
Passing, 47–48, 130, 131, 146
n.32, 163 n.13
Leff, Leonard J., 162–163 n.6
Leuchtenburg, William, 53, 153
n.17
Levine, Lawrence, 136 n.3
Lind, Jenny, 92, 157 n.10, 157
n.11, 159 n.21
Longmore, Paul K., 156–157
n.9
Lott, Eric, 21, 144 n.28

lynching, 19, 20–22, 40, 52, 130,
138 n.4, 149 n.10

Mackenthun, Gesa, 148 n.6
MacMillan, Duane J., 153–154 n.8
Mannix, Daniel, 135 n.1
marriage, 8, 42, 72, 109–124,
145–146 n.31, 162–163 n.6
masculinity, 60, 73, 111, 118–121,
133, 166–167 n.18
May, Elaine Tyler, 162 n.5
McCracken, Elizabeth, The Giant's
House, 8
McCullers, Carson, 16, 107, 109,
111–112, 122–123, 162 n.1,
163 n.7, 163 n.8, 165 n.14
The Ballad of the Sad Caf8E, 165
n.15
The Member of the Wedding,
109, 111–117, 133, 162 n.1,
163 n.9, 163 n.10, 163 n.11
The Square Root of Wonderful,
115–116
McDowell, Deborah, 146 n.32
Meltzer, Milton, 158 n.14, 158
n.15
microcephaly, 22
Minehan, Thomas, 83
minstrelsy, 19, 20, 21, 33, 41–42,
44, 141 n.16, 144 n.27, 144
n.28
miscegenation, 14, 20, 25, 41, 42,
45–49, 54–55, 71, 131, 139
n.12, 139–140 n.13, 143 n.25,
144 n.28, 150–151 n.12
modernism, 32, 48
monsters, 4–5, 7, 11, 15, 56, 57,
81, 147–148 n.5
Montaigne, Michel de, "Of a
Monstrous Child," 5
Morrison, Toni, Beloved, 26–27, 46
mulatto, 41–42, 54
museums, 2–10, 44, 53, 136 n.6,
141–142 n.16, 142 n.19; See
also specific museums

CPSIA information can be obtained at www.ICGtesting.com
Printed in the USA
269888BV00003B/2/P